Petals from a Rose

Dedicated to the
Holy Spirit, and to
my mother and father,
Rose and Tony Pagna

Petals from a Rose

Tom Pagna

Introduction by Ara Parseghian

HARDWOOD PRESS
South Bend, Indiana
1998

Contents

Acknowledgments

To all my former coaches and teachers, Marv Levy, Les Olson, Harold Nichols, Roy Engler, Steve Sitko, Russ Pastuck, Lajoie Daum, Paul Shoults for helping to form my philosophy. A special acknowledgment to Ara Parseghian and Katie, for their lifetime of help, friendship, and caring.

To Joe Martori, a lifetime friend and an employer, who encouraged me to write, by providing time, space, and salary to stop talking about it and get it done!

To Tim Truesdell for his keen eyes, ears, and wit in perusing the manuscript and his help in critiquing it. Also, thanks to Karen Anderson for her timely typing and patience. A special thanks to Susan Danner for her hard efforts in typing, organizing, and laying out the chapters.

To Jim and Jill Langford for their vision and direction. To Bruce Fingerhut, whose vast intellect could see far beyond the written words, enough so that he was willing to edit and publish *Petals* into this book.

To Tony Roberts, Art and Pat Decio, Donna Potter, Elaine Landick, Lorraine, Bill and Joe Cochran, Ellie Knight, and Sam Girardi for reading the drafts and giving me positive feedback to continue on.

To my sister Terry and brothers Sam and Joe, for having lived this story to a far higher measure of quality than I could write it.

To the dozen daughters I refer to as the petals: Toni Ewing, Keri Riggs, Kristi Conlon, Michelle Susanj, Sherri Pagna, Lisa Farringer, Judy Brant, Sandy Major, Susan Staszewski, Tony Gardiner, Vicki Srail, and Lori Scaduto.

Lastly, to my wife Shirley, whose critical eye kept me from being too maudlin or self-serving in telling the story. She also did many of my household chores, freeing me to concentrate enough to write this. Her constant love and support, her work ethic, her level head, have made me cherish and love her not just for the forty-five years of marriage, but forever.

Foreword

As I read through the manuscript of *Petals from a Rose*, it evoked a multitude of memories and emotions from me. I've known Tom Pagna as a close friend for nearly half a century. That Tom has written about the lives of his family and in particular, his mother, seems very natural. If you etch out anyone's life and describe the poignant peaks and valleys, each life really does contain a book. As apparently true as that statement may be, it is rare actually to set it down on paper. It takes devotion, time, and effort to achieve this.

I recall Tom exclaiming on more than one occasion, with a lilt of humor in his voice, "I'm going to write the great Italian novel someday, and it's going to be about the good Italians!" He has certainly done this through his true family epic, spanning four generations and focusing primarily on his mother, Rose. Her life and what she makes of it seem remarkable. A mother of four by choice, a young widow by fate, she defies huge odds, admirably raising and educating her children. Through it all, the family maintains a loyalty to one another, exceeding even what she and her late husband had hoped.

My association with Tom has allowed me to know him quite thoroughly, but the book gave me even greater insight into his past, his motivational drive, and multifaceted personality.

Our meeting in 1949 has proven both providential and fortunate for both of us. At the age of 27, I was at a personal crossroad in my own life. In only my second year as a professional halfback for the Cleveland Browns, a career-ending injury forced a decision upon me. I got the opportunity to return to my alma mater, Miami of Ohio, to pursue a master's in business. It had not been my plan to coach, and Head Coach Woody Hayes offer me the job of freshman football coach. I accepted the position and returned to my hometown of Akron, Ohio to do some prospecting for freshmen football recruits.

I recall vividly attending an industrial league basketball game, where several of the possible recruits were going to play. This was the first time I would meet Tom, introducing myself after the game. Since I was not that far removed from my own playing days, I was pleasantly startled by the similarities in size and resemblance between Tom and myself. I didn't view him as a prospective college basketball recruit (I was also the freshman basketball coach), but from his stocky frame and muscular torso, he had halfback written all over him.

He was a competitor with quick reflexes, alertness, and aggressive savvy. His high-school football career had just ended with an undefeated, untied season. The system the high school ran on offense was the T formation and sometimes a shift from the T into single wing. He would be either the quarterback in the T or the single wing in the shift, but I thought he was too short to be a quarterback in college.

After the game, I invited three of the young men out for an ice-cream treat and some conversation. I found Tom responsive, and I think we both felt a mutual rapport and respect after this short meeting. That very evening, we set a date for Tom to visit Miami of Ohio's campus.

When I learned that Tom had graduated at mid-year, January 1950, I sought to get him enrolled immediately, well aware that he had other offers. I believe I cemented the deal when he said, "I've got to help out the family and get a job till fall."

I replied, "Maybe I can help."

When he reported to Oxford, Ohio, in September of 1950, the freshman recruit class elected him their captain. It was my very first team to coach. We went undefeated that year.

That first year of coaching, for me, was invigorating and taxing. Whatever I felt, that year outlined my future. Miami's varsity football team had a highly successful year also and Woody Hayes was hired as the Ohio State football head coach. By virtue of several friendly alumni, the athletic director, John Brickles, the undefeated freshman schedule, and fate, I became Miami's head football coach.

It has been said about many first-year head coaches, that "he doesn't know what he doesn't know." I did know, however, that I had a pretty good nucleus of players returning. Among them were two really gifted athletes in the backfield. At fullback was Jim "Boxcar" Bailey. At 212 pounds and 9.6 in the 100-yard dash, he was one of the mainstays during the previous season. The other player was one of the great halfbacks in Miami history, Johnny Pont. At 5' 7" and 175 lbs., John was leader of the 1950 Salad Bowl Champions in Tempe, Arizona.

The right halfback position was open, and Tom won the position primarily as a blocker in 1951. Though he fought several injuries that first varsity year, he garnered much game experience as a sophomore. In 1952, with Bailey and Pont now gone, Tom became a full-fledged running back, breaking several Miami records and recording his best season while at Miami. His senior year, he was again voted the captain but was plagued by injury, missing the first game completely and three-quarters of the last.

It was that year (1953) that the NCAA made rule changes regulating players must play both offense and defense. Even with two games missed and playing both ways, Tom accumulated 750 yards in seven games. He was not exceptionally fast but had wonderful balance, gave great effort, and was extremely elusive.

In retrospect, like many successful athletes, he was an overachiever who sometimes, through sheer will power and effort, inspired his teammates. When he graduated he insured his place among the many Miami standouts.

I've outlined briefly, the first few years of Tom's association with me, to better focus the reader on what you will find on the following pages. It is apparent to me that you can know a person very well . . . their strengths, weaknesses, hot buttons, etc. . . . and not really know what drives and motivates them unless you examine their background.

I guess I knew fragments of Tom's life and the names of his mom, his brothers, and sister, but the book filled in some marvelous gaps about life in general and his life specifically. The book, however, is not Tom's story, though he is a major part. The story is of his mother! I met Rose Pagna and other family members through the years, but these were those fleeting moments before or after a game and under crowded circumstances.

Tom spoke of his family often, with humor, with sadness, with love and respect. In the book they all became much more real to me and that includes Tom himself.

Tom left Miami of Ohio for the pros and then the Air Force. Years later at an awards banquet where Tom was one of the recipients and I was asked to make the presentation, I said simply, "Fate decreed Tom work under me; it could just as easily have been the other way around."

In 1959, in response to Tom's inquiry about an opening on our staff, I hired him as the freshman coach at Northwestern University. Those were tough years, and I was not really certain whether or not I was helping or hurting his career, nor did I know how stable our jobs were. Fortunately our success there propelled us to Notre Dame. The rest, as they say, is "history."

During Tom's playing days, the coaching years, and the past coaching ones, we have had many, many talks. We have discussed the most humorous things along with life's trials and tribulations. Tom and I will always be friends forever. We are not blood relatives, but we are close enough to be related through the thousands of threads woven into our lives' fabric.

One thing he credits me with often is that I urged him to always be himself. If you ever hear him speak or entertain, you can see that his style is solely his own. Whether or not my influence helped, I am proud he has fulfilled that advice. I am always amazed and constantly reminded of the power and influence a coach or mentor has on associates. In many ways it is a humbling realization because whatever a coach is, he or she nurtures the same attributes in the student.

I think that this book will capture the heart of anyone who has deep family ties. I believe people who really have a grasp of what life is all about will appreciate the humility and sincerity found in this story. I found myself nostalgically reflecting on my own past and family. Both of my parents knew sacrifice and hard work. It made me really think about their lives, ambitions, and hardships Such reflection caused some wonderful moments of appreciation for what transpired before me. My father was from Armenia but left that country of persecution to be free. My mother, who was French, immigrated to the U.S. where she met my father. Together, they would pursue the American dream.

Reflection of one's heritage forces one to consider the raw courage our ancestors had. Not only does this history foster an awe along with reverence, for what they had accomplished, a sense of gratefulness pours over me at their bravery.

Passages in the book, merging the old world with the new, caused laughter on one page and gave me a lump in my throat on others. There is an old quote that says, "Examine a thing that is humorous, for therein lies a grain of the truth."

There is a personal realization that comes through strongly. It made me aware that even though each one of our paths are different, our pursuits are varied, our circumstances shuffled by the winds of fate, we eventually are exposed to all the same lessons.

Immigrants coming to America dreamed dreams and I feel certain they were much the same. They wanted honest work, a decent wage, freedom in their lives to carve a niche for themselves and their children. A certain old-world mentality and honor prevented many of these seekers from ever being a burden on society.

Most of my world, until I resigned from coaching football at Notre Dame, was tied to athletic endeavor. I thought it a worthwhile pursuit and one that formulated many of my own values in life. Much the same as a military group or a family, tough rules and disciplines became a way of life. Without belaboring the point, that last statement is a mere hint of the intrinsic values one learns when trying to compete to be the best.

One of the most powerful carryover values from sports to life that I can think of is the ability to sustain hope and effort when all seems lost. There is an indescribable greatness in players and in people, perhaps even in countries, that triggers resiliency. The heart to "bounce back," to "keep on keeping on," to have unwavering faith in the face of great adversity, is indeed the heart of a champion. Such fortitude is paid for with a price and must be practiced; athletics teaches that.

None of us are immune to the hardships of life. Whether it is from lack of talent or fortune, or lack of health, we are all creased by the bullets of hardship, sorrow, and tragedy. Our reaction in meeting these dreaded enemies defines our lives.

One success or one flawed moment, one hundred gains or one hundred losses, none of these constitutes the sum total of a person's life. The sum includes everything.

In the story of Rose's life, the reader is exposed to daily lives almost in a humdrum tempo. It was exactly that, the push and grind from days to weeks and from weeks to months and years, that gives the total story beauty for me. It is the totality of one life lived well with perseverance that gives it meaning. It is easy to identify, relate, and appreciate what this family achieves. Most of us experience many of life's same quandaries and dilemmas. As they say, "only the names are changed."

I found myself exhilarated by the story because I knew the

characters and I also knew that plots of drugs, violence, or sensationalism did not exist. A much more rare and exotic stimulant is observed: the truth. I believe the story is a tribute to the human will of all people. Tom says that his mother was his h``ero. I knew her primarily through her son and his actions. He is energetic, nervous, impressionable, always pursuing, climbing, clawing. I often kidded him, "A nervous mother makes a nervous child." Undaunted, he will accept such a legacy and always have more mountains to climb.

In our early years together, witnessing great mood swings in Tom, I labeled him "Otis" after the elevator company. The staff shared in the dubbing because it fit him so well. He has, in middle age, found middle ground. Bravo!

There is an old anonymous quote I recall, and it seems highly appropriate in the context of the point I have tried to make. It goes like this: "When you lose it isn't over. When you quit. it's over." Tom came from a family where it will never be over! It explains to me why some do in life, and why some do not.

Tom says in the introduction that this book was written to glorify God and to honor his mother and father. I believe he's done that with both style and grace.

May each reader enjoy the story as much as I have. May it cause him or her time to reflect and rejoice in his or her own life, observing that a certain heroism is present in the lives of all people who give their very best. Whether or not the world recognizes personal heroism does not subtract from the majesty of such a life, well lived.

Preface

It is said that all truth passes through three stages: It first appears false and ridiculous, then it is obviously held up to ridicule, and finally it is accepted as self-evident. These three phrases describe me as I regard aging. Though I do not feel old, and my memory of youth is fresh, sixty-five years have shot by me in a proverbial "twinkling of an eye." For the past twenty years, I've carried a loosely sketched story in my heart and in my head.

Part of my personal income for the past thirty years was made from speaking engagements. Being a professional speaker gives rise to much self-doubt. Will the crowd be interested? Will they enjoy, laugh, applaud? Is what I'm saying candid, appealing, clear? Most important, is it true? Since I have never risen to a position of easy name recognition, people, when informed who their after-dinner speaking would be, usually respond with: Who is he?

The answer was always the same for me. Nobody. The question of why they listened or enjoyed became paramount. I finally determined that it had to do with *what* I was saying. Oh, I had timing and a vast repertoire of humorous phrases and stories, but there was a larger essence that warmed the audience. They identified with the things I said about *life* and *lives*.

About life, I relied on my daily observance and personal experiences. About lives. I realized most of what I said had to do with my splendid mother or my incredible father, who died young. Enough experience gives one style and forges delivery, but content seems to be everything. Since no renowned agent wanted to handle a virtual unknown or as they referred to it, "not a marquee name," all my engagements were from referrals of people who had previously heard me.

Often people greeted me after the speeches and begged me for a tape or at least a copy of the speech. When I analyzed what they were requesting, it was apparent that the love of my parents, and more specifically that of my mother, was the most vital and interesting.

Her name in Italian was Rosalia (pronounced Rosa-lee). My father merely called her Rose. In 1982 my mother, Rose, died. I've carried her story around with me since before 1982. It was with me since I was a boy and has never left. Not being a writer, I never felt capable of doing the story justice. As I grew older, had the time to devote to it, and the intellect to put it all in perspective, I took the plunge.

For me, it is the autumn of my life, perhaps even late autumn. It is the time when most people can easily reflect on their lives and consider that they have been failures. I do that daily. All the dreams and mighty aspirations, my fantasized achievements seem to have fallen through the cracks of the retirement porch. I know now that I'll never own the company, be president of the United States, or even be a state senator. It is the time in life when you're not sure you've done anything that is lasting. In weaker moments, that would depress me. In the bright ones, I am inspired.

I knew that if this story were written, it would be lasting. Most of what I am is a positive result of my mother Rose's influence. My two brothers and my sister feel the same about their own lives. In the following pages you'll see unfold a relative complex life. Rose's life is not much different from millions of others. The difference you will see is the ability she had to teach herself, to evaluate life, to depend upon the truest treasure each of us possesses, but few know how to identify – intuition and faith in God.

Indomitable in spirit, effort, courage, never subdued, never beaten, never giving up, never despairing, and always, but always having hope, Rose's faith and the practice of it marks her as the quintessential mother and wife. I am sure God had to have laughed and cried at Rose's antics. That God could even create the versatility and the creativity in one so tiny had to be a point of Godly pride. My mother's philosophy, having been totally self-taught, was uniquely her own. Whether they were angels or demons who spoke to her, she somehow always used it for good.

At first I thought to change names and identify myself in the third person. I could not do that as it becomes less than true. Forgive the times I use "I" because though I appear through the story as I saw it, I am not the focus. The focus is Rose and glorifying God through her life and sacrifice.

In Ecclesiastes 7: 3, there is a line probably too lightly taken. It says simply, "WHAT God has bent, who can straighten?" That line describes our lives. Somehow in my life that line has become paraphrased to "God writes straight with crooked lines!" It is through those crooked lines, the ups and downs, and, yes, even sideways moves that our lives are made worthy. When all becomes revealed to us, Rose won't be surprised. She never doubted that God's purpose would be served, that He would truly write straight. Other than the smallest of details to link the story together, everything written about Rose and her family is true.

Chapter 1
La Femmina (The Lady)

The crust of cement mix was splattered upon his large hands and across his work pants when Joe Crimaldi heard the lunch time whistle blow. He rubbed his hands lightly and wiped his brow. After he ran his hands under the hose extending from the work area, he sought his lunch bag.

Joe's powerful frame stood nearly six foot. His dark hair was wetted down with sweat and hugged his head in tight curls. Across the street were park benches where many of the cement-block-factory workers liked to have their lunch. He too strolled to an empty bench under the shade of a maple tree. It was as though he were living a dream because only six short months ago he had entered New York's harbor for the first time.

He opened the brown bag and viewed each item wrapped separately in neat waxed-paper bundles. Joe's wife Josephine had packed a small loaf of her homemade bread, olives, provolone cheese, and a stick of pepperoni. There were also two hard-boiled eggs, some salt, a cucumber, and a tomato. Because Josephine had baked biscotti the night before, she added this treat also. Left in the bag was a pint of Joe's favorite red wine. He was hungry and broke the loaf of bread into bite-sized pieces.

Mr. Billello, the concrete-block-factory's owner, liked to stroll the area at noon. He insisted that the men have a full hour for lunch. When he himself had been a laborer with the dream of ownership, it was a vow he had made. Men work better well fed and rested. Joe welcomed the routine.

He was alone on his own bench but easily within sight of the other men. Most of them he had known from the old country. There were Paulo and Joe Lombardo, Dominic Barbuzzo, Tony Conti, and a few others, resting nearby.

Tearing off a bite of the pepperoni and following that with a swig of wine and a bite of cheese, Joe felt pride. He surveyed the sky and the park area. He was elated. At 26 not only was he employed in a trade he knew and loved, but he was in America. Just the word "America" played on his tongue and in his mind. He practiced it; his *compadres* gave it an H sound like "HUMERICA." That bothered Joe just as the American supervisor did when he would say, "Damned EYE-TALIANS, they're good workers!" Joe reasoned to himself that if they were EYE-TALIANS why didn't they call his country EYE-TALY?

Musing about Italy and America, his memory faded to that last morning of their long voyage to this great country. He had not slept the night before and was on deck long before the dawn, long before the harbor was in sight. The weather had been fore-casted as cloudy, and heavy fog settled low on the water.

Though one could not see very far off the side of the main deck, the captain had spread word that they would arrive in the New York harbor at 6:30 AM. It was only 5:30 AM and still dark when Joe pulled his gold watch out of his pocket and checked it for the third time. Seeing several of the men and women passengers beginning to assemble, he hurried to awaken Josephine, his young wife. She was up and feeding their new-born baby, Rosalia. Rosalia was this very day six months old.

Presto, presto! ("quickly, quickly!") Joe hurried his wife. *Tuta vida la femmina*. ("All want to view the lady.") The Statue of Liberty would be the symbol that told them emphatically . . . they were now in America.

It was October 20, 1909, a day he would always recall. He guided Josephine, who carried Rosalia in a thick blanket as protection against the brisk wind. They were along the port side of the ship now, searching the horizon for the occasional light that broke through from one of the tall buildings. The sunrise burst through for a short time, and the fog was beginning to scatter.

There was an air of great excitement among the passengers on deck. They were talking in passionate and warm tones. They radiated their anxiety, and their anticipation grew ever stronger. All were aware of the steady waves slapping the side of the vessel with rhythmic consistency. It was Josephine who first caught a glimpse of the immense outline of the statue's head.

She pointed to what she saw and said excitedly, "*Veda, veda, veda.*" ("Look.") She said it louder each time as she pointed almost skyward. It was then that the murmurs from the crowd united into happy shouts and laughter. Everyone aboard seemed to have spotted it at the same moment. There went up a unified cheer, "*La Femmina, la Femmina. . . . Viva La Femmina!*" There was backslapping and handshaking, hugs and kisses.

By now the sun had burnt away most of the fog, and the head

and right arm of the statue were plainly visible. The lower body was still engulfed, but with a studied gaze, one could make out the silhouette. It was a delicious, ecstatic moment.

Josephine's eyes were wide open and full of awe and respect. People were electric with emotion, holding their toddlers high to see the symbol of America. Joe Crimaldi was an emotional man. His eyes streamed tears as he lifted his baby daughter from his mother's arms, sunlight now bright on all their faces, and stared at *"La Femmina."*

"See . . . see, Rosalia, your new home!" His voice choked with emotion, Joe squeezed the waistline of his wife closer to him, and he uttered to her and his daughter, "America, the land of opportunity and freedom. . . . *Dio Grazia.*"

They cruised into the harbor for the processing, through Ellis Island. The processing lines were very long and crowded. People's luggage, their bedrolls, their children all cluttered together. Many could not speak any English. The few interpreters who spoke a little Italian could not comprehend the dialect of the Sicilians. Because Joe Crimaldi could speak a little English, was Sicilian, and was very fluent in the Italian of the mainland, he offered his assistance. In return for this gesture of help, one of the administrators, seeing Joe had a wife carrying a new baby, expedited his registration.

When the threesome walked down the steps from the Ellis Island registration building, they faced a huge crowd of people, relatives expecting the arrival of their own kin.

"How will I find my brothers?" Joe was startled at the masses in the roped-off area marked for waiting relatives. The administrator had written "CRIMALDI" in big letters on a white cardboard placard and hung it around Joe's neck.

In the crowd of waiting people, many of them held up similar cardboard signs with names. Some Joe recognized as countrymen of his – "Paolello," "Gentile," "Ferranti," "Conti." Somewhere in the mix were his brothers. The oldest of the brothers, and the one Joe most expected to see, was "Sal." In order, they were Sal, himself, Charles, and Jim.

The noise and commotion and the sporadic cheers when one family found members were very rewarding but distracting. For a brief instant Joe Crimaldi, wife and child in hand, was dismayed and felt quite alone and lost. But no sooner had this fearful thought gripped him than it instantly disappeared. Out of the crowd emerged the tall strong image of his brother Sal. His one arm was linked to Charles, who in turn was linked to Jim. They had found each other and, when they met, formed a circle of hugs – the brothers, Josephine, and Rosalia.

It was Sal, or as he was known to them in Sicily "Salvatore," who said a brief prayer while they were huddled. "Thank you, dear God, thank you for this family and their safety. Welcome, *fratre mia,* to America! Welcome Josephine and Rosalia."

The younger brothers managed Joe's and Josephine's luggage, and Sal carried Rosalia as they worked their way through the crowd toward the line to board the ferry to the mainland. Once there, Sal ordered a carriage to transport them to the train depot. With luck, they could make the 2:15 train to Cleveland. They made one stop on their way, where Sal bought bread, olives, cheese, and wine for their trip. This done, he ordered the driver to hurry.

In Sicily, the four brothers were known tradesmen. They were stonemasons, layers of brick and concrete blocks, and cement finishers. In a thriving America, Sal had taken the gamble and brought his wife and two single brothers with him. Once they were established, they would send for Joe, his wife, and – by then – family. The fact that they had trades meant work. When one works, one could eat! In Sicily people were starving.

Sal and Joe made Josephine and baby Rosalia comfortable on the leather train seats, then arranged the luggage and lined the area left with their coats. In this way the seat formed a cradle for Rosalia. Opposite this seat sat Josephine. She was very tired and, after seeing the baby fall asleep, gathered herself into a blanket and relaxed.

The four brothers occupied the seats across the aisle. The older two faced the other two, and their conversation flowed easily. They had two years of catching up to do. The waiting and dreaming for their reunion was over.

When the train gradually picked up speed and the passengers were settled, Sal broke open the food basket he had purchased at the open-air market. They were very hungry. Once they had eaten their fill, the brothers were again in animated

The Crimaldis in America: Mary, Joe, Flora, Rose, Ann, and Josephine, holding Dixie.

conversation about their plans. Josephine watched the scenery change from her window view. The train had passed huge buildings, more buildings than she had ever dreamed of. She saw people in throngs, walking the streets. She spotted several more horseless carriages and many open-air markets not unlike those near her home in Messina. The slow gentle lurch of the train picked up a little more speed as the crowds of people seem to thin out. Never in her lifetime had Josephine seen so many people all at once. Soon there were open fields of grain to explore and huge barns and windmills to view. Her eyes measured the patchwork of evenly plowed furrows and the occasional wave of a farmhand as he rested a moment to view the passing train. "So big, so grand," she thought. They were nearly a day's journey from Sal's home in Cleveland. At long last, Josephine closed her eyes and slept.

Joe Crimaldi gazed at his young wife's face. He saw the high cheekbones of his young wife, the premature graying of her hair, the tired lines that were the product of stress and the long hard voyage. To make her life better was his dream.

Joe Crimaldi was too exhilarated to sleep. His stocky frame

nestled into the seat as his gaze turned outward through the sun-faded train window. He fingered his mustache as he thought of what fate would deal him in the new country. His trade would allow him to seek immediate employment.

Slowly, his eyes fell upon tiny Rosalia. The cherub was asleep on the seat opposite his wife. "What," Joe thought, "will her world be like?" Will she be educated and speak fluent English? Will she someday be the beauty that her alabaster skin promised? His hands felt through his thick curly hair as he pondered how to make all that happen.

America was surely in the building stage, and Joe Crimaldi easily caught on with the Billello Construction Company. He hired in to produce cement blocks. His work afforded him a small apartment near his brother's home, and he was pleased that his dream had begun. Joe worked from 6:00 AM until 6:00 PM. His enthusiasm and keen mind easily picked up the routine of molding the blocks. An industrious man, he instantly caught the eye and respect of the owner, Joe Billello.

The whistle blew, awakening Joe from his reminiscences, and Joe cleaned up the remains of his lunch and resumed his work.

In the five years that followed, Joe went from apprentice to supervisor, and from supervisor to plant manager. The company grew considerably, and with it, so too had Joe and his family. Within the first year he had rented a small house in the city. Within two more he had bought his own home. The births of two more daughters, Mary and Ann, required more space. In the next three years, Josephine bore three more children – Theresa, Michael, and Francesca. Shortly thereafter would come Bessalia and Augustine, but Augustine would succumb to pneumonia in just her second year.

All told, from Rosalia down to Bessalia, his six daughters and one son would be his legacy. But Josephine, his wife, was very ill, and there would be no more children.

Rosalia, the eldest, was eleven years older than Bessalia. It fell to Rose, in the custom of the Italians, to be a second mother to the smaller children. That her mother was weakened by the move and the bearing of eight children within an eleven-year span were strong reasons for a rapid maturing of Rose.

Rose kneaded dough for their daily bread. She laundered clothes for the family almost nightly and prepared breakfast and dinner for her father and family daily. Josephine's stamina was depleted. She hated to see her first-born so burdened with household chores. It was not uncommon for Rose to fall asleep across a study book, too tired to do her school work.

At 14, Rose was near full blossom. She was at her maximum height of 5' 2". Her penetrating hazel-green eyes and fair skin fairly illuminated her face. She had boundless energy through the day. Beyond household chores she also dressed her sisters and brother, fed them, and sometimes disciplined them.

She never really thought of her life as a terrible trial in these early years. These things needed to be done, and no one could do them better or faster than she. She loved her mother, and everything she did was to help this saintly woman. To think beyond what she was presently having in her life was not her way. She truly worked each day out as it came. She enjoyed school when she attended and felt a certain pride in her ability to read, write, and speak well. Though she could speak the Sicilian dialect with ease, she never would know how to write or read Italian.

Rose's beauty – her fair complexion, and raven-black hair – was clear to all but herself. She had no time for vanity and never wore makeup. The boys who tried to carry her books or walk her home gave Rose no special thrill. "I haven't got time," she would tell Annie Alleo, her neighbor, in a "don't bother me" tone.

In the few free moments afforded her, Rose loved to sit on their front porch with Annie and, with gentle pushes, swing back and forth on the oak porch swing her father had crafted. They would talk about school and what life would be like when they grew up. Sometimes Rose's sisters would join them. In rare times of leisure, Joe would bring his guitar out onto the porch, and they would sing current melodies. Annie Alleo's brother, Tommy, had a crush on Rose. She never spoke of it, though Annie had approached the subject often at Tommy's urging.

"What do you want to be when you're older, Rose?"

"I am already what I want to be," Rose stated matter of factly.

"I am me, and me is all I'll ever be . . . maybe you mean to ask what will I want to do?"

"Yes," Annie replied somewhat thrilled, for it was the first time Rose ever responded to this specific question.

"Well," Rose spoke slowly and weighed her words carefully. "I would love to have a beautiful home someday." She thought awhile and then added, "with carpeting like in your house."

"Well, Rosie, that's not wanting very much."

"Everything is very much when you don't have it, Annie!"

The Alleos had many creature comforts and took them for granted; the Crimaldis did not. Rose was very self-conscious of her clothes and those that her sisters and brother wore. She also was aware of what the insides of other homes held. Whenever one of her girlfriends would invite her in, Rose's eyes measured and recorded all she saw. It had never crossed her mind to be jealous or envious of these things or of other people. It was just that these were to be added to her dreams of "someday." She never doubted that she could make it all happen . . . someday. But the someday list was getting long.

My grandfather Joe Crimaldi

Joe was now a minor partner in the Billello cement block factory. The plan was to buy out Mr. Billello over the next five years, and then the Crimaldi brothers would be the sole owners. Joe managed to save little money over the years – the provisions for his large family and his wife's illness took their toll on his progress. He began to drink a little too much wine and frequently came home long after Rose had put the children to bed. Too frequently after she herself was in bed, his voice called from the kitchen to her upstairs bedroom. "Rosalia, come down and fix your father's supper!"

On those occasions where drink was involved, Rose never knew what this otherwise kind man would do. He demanded to be served a hot meal, and he also demanded Rose's presence in place of bed-ridden Josephine. While he was eating, he slurred out orders to Rose, some in Italian, others in English. "Go getta my guitar." Rose could do this easily, but dreaded it when he ordered, "Sing . . . sing in Italian." Even worse . . . "Go getta my gun!"

Rose was afraid to handle the .45 automatic her father kept in the top drawer of the hallway cabinet. He would clean it in front of her, while her eyes would be wide with fear. One night, after ordering the gun, he said, "Sing, Rose," but she pleaded that she was too tired. He picked up the gun and pointed it at her in general, mumbling his words and said again, "I said, 'Sing!'"

Sober, he was a warm wonderful father. He was compassionate, smart, and a hard worker, but the years of pressure and stress, the concerns for his children, his very sick Josephine, and, finally, the wine sometimes spilled over into these frantic outcries. Rose, not gifted with the musical abilities of her younger sisters and brother, sang as best she could. Her father sensed her fear and relented, "Come here, Rose, gimme a hug and a kiss and go to bed."

Coming from a Sicilian village, Joe Crimaldi, like most of his countrymen, had been steeped in Catholicism. Every Sunday he ordered Rose to get the children ready for church. In many ways, Rose looked forward to it. It was a chance to get out. In church, the high soprano voices soothed her troubled heart. Here she could view tapestry, architecture, painting, delicately stained glass windows, and gorgeously expensive chandeliers. There was a grandeur about it that eased her burdens.

When they took the collection, Rose's father pressed a nickel into her palm to light a candle to the Blessed Mother. Rose knelt reverently, knowing full well that *this* Mother could cure her own. Rose also knew that the Blessed Mother somehow knew of Rose's longings and her innermost thoughts.

"Please, Blessed Mother," she prayed fervently, "make my mother well and bless my life and all that is in it, now and forever." Though it was not every Sunday Rose could go to church, her simple faith never doubted the existence of a hierarchy that watched over their lives.

Returning home Rose always questioned Josephine in hopes that her mother would reveal to her, the eldest daughter, secrets that the others would not appreciate. Josephine told Rose of occasions when she spoke to the Blessed Mother and was spoken to in return. In one of those conversations Josephine was told she would not be on earth very long and that she would not see her children fully grown.

Rose's eyes became tear-filled, and her heart ached with sorrow. Josephine said, "We cannot know what God has in store for us, but I do know that your life will be long and full. Our lady has told me this."

"You mean," almost in disbelief, "she talks out loud to you?"

"No," her mother spoke, hushed and tenderly. "It is as though your ears cannot hear sounds, but your mind expresses the words that come into your heart. They are not my own thoughts . . . I cannot explain it, but if she speaks to you, you'll surely know it!"

"Will she speak to me, Momma?"

"I cannot say, dear Rose. only Our Lady decides that."

"What will I do? What will we do if you die, Momma?"

"Shush, Rose, only you are aware of what the Lady has told me. You must keep the secret."

"I will . . . I will, but what are we to do?"

"Do? Do?" Josephine asked almost incredulously. "You do what you already do. You do whatever it takes! Our Lady will not leave you alone, child. She'll watch over you every day of your life!"

Rose branded that sentence in her mind. She would recall it whenever her life needed strength.

Responsibilities of the home burdened Rose's progress in school. Her last grade card was full of C's in work she could have easily done if given the time. Fourteen, in those days, was young womanhood. She was still shy around boys and participated in none of the school's social functions. Her younger sisters, Mary and Ann, spoke of boyfriends often. They mentioned "love," and Rose wanted to vomit. She could never have entertained the thought for very long that she could love a man and accept his love in return. These things were too far away, too hazy. She, frankly, was too busy.

Rose's teacher, Mrs. Hambra, came to her home and spoke to her father. "She's bright, very bright, but doesn't do homework. She's like a thirty-five year old, and yet she's only fourteen!"

"Can you bake bread?" asked Joe.

"No," the startled Mrs. Hambra looked puzzled.

"Can you raise six children?"

"Maybe," she replied cautiously, "I have only one."

"Aha," Joe seized on this. "Mrs. Hambra, I don't mean to offend you. You are a good woman and an adult. To raise a child, care for a husband, teach school . . . you are busy?"

"Very."

"Well, that'sa what my Rose does. She fixes all the meals, she does the laundry, she fix all the clothes and iron for the kids. And . . ." he paused. "She goes to school like you!"

"I see," Mrs. Hambra's eyebrows peaked. Indeed, Rose was thirty-five at fourteen.

"I will try, Mr. Crimaldi, to keep what you have said in mind."

When Mrs. Hambra left his home that evening, Joe lit his pipe and sat in his big chair. He was sober, indeed he had not tasted wine for several weeks. Josephine was growing weaker – this he knew. He also knew that Rose did not ever have a childhood. She was that very moment preparing their evening meal. The other little ones were reading or playing. He had not meant to cheat his oldest. He knew she had within her a greatness, and Joe hated to see it sacrificed.

Josephine's pneumonia was now critical. Not only was it impossible for her to care for the house and children, but someone needed to care for her.

That evening, after supper and after speaking with his wife, Joe sent everyone to bed early, then said to Rose, "Sit, sweetheart, we musta talk. Rosalia, I never," his voice choked a bit, and he paused, "wanted to see you work so hard."

"Pappa," she said softly. "Pappa, don't cry."

"I don't cry for me, Rose, I cry for you."

"Why?. . . Why Pappa? What's so wrong that you cry for me?"

"Rose, for now we needa you home for Momma and the rest of the kids. The school, she don't need you so much."

For a moment there was utter silence. Rose remembered what her mother proclaimed about "Our Lady" watching over her all her life. She looked at her father softly and said simply, "It's okay Pappa. We will do whatever needs to be done and don't worry about me. I'll have plenty of time for me."

With this, Joe could no longer hold back his sobs. He hugged his lovely daughter in his arms and told her, "Whenever there is something to be done, you always seem to do it. I love you, Rosalia, and your mother loves you too. Don't ever forget that."

For a long moment, Rose hugged her father. Though saddened that she must drop out of school, she felt pride that her father and mother could depend on her. They always said, "Rose did whatever needed to be done." She liked the sound of it, and strangely it would become her distinction throughout her lifetime. With her apron she blotted the tears of her father's face and brought him new tobacco for his pipe.

"It will be all right, Pappa. It'll be all right."

Little changed from day to day for Rose. The urgency and sameness of events trudged on. She noticed the passage of time only by the growth of her younger sisters and brother Mike. On the rare occasions when Josephine was well enough, she taught Rose how to mend clothing. Working with her hands held a fascination for Rose. She especially was thrilled when Josephine would allow her to try the sewing machine. She loved the whir and hum of the mechanism and the results she could produce. There was a magic in cutting and fitting material, placing it in matching patterns, and then stitching both by hand and machine into a finished product. The work exhilarated Rose and, more than anything she had ever done, fulfilled her.

When her mother was able to sit in a chair, the both of them hand-stitched together. At such times, they shared conversations that would mold Rose's thoughts well into the future. They spoke of many things: the children, homes, furniture, Rose's father, and life in general. But it was death that filled Rose's thoughts – not her own death, but her mother's.

During one such day, Rose and her mother were talking about prayer. It was a large part of Josephine's day.

"The Rosary seems so repetitious," said Rose, her voice rising at the end, leaving the unasked question, "doesn't it?"

"When I was a girl, Rose, and entertained thoughts of becoming a nun, I felt the same."

"What happened that you didn't?"

Josephine smiled, "I met your father."

"I know that," Rose said impatiently, "but go on."

"Well, I was taught that each prayer was a thin thread, and the repetition was the binding together of many threads for the strengthening of the prayer, and the concentration and effort it took to hold one's attention gave the prayer beauty."

"There are words I say in prayer, I don't even know what they mean," said Rose.

"What words?"

"Well, Momma, when they say the Our Father, they say hallowed be thy name. I don't know what *hallowed* means, and I'm ashamed to ask."

"Don't be ashamed, Rose . . . find out, ask. It means," Josephine searched her mind for the right word. "*Holy*. Yes, that's what it means very holy."

"Why don't people just say it that way then . . . *holy*?"

"Because, Rose, the prayer is the one given to us by Jesus Christ. Why would we want to change the words?"

"Do you believe everything written in the Bible is true, Momma?"

"Men have re-written the words and done it in many languages. The words may change, but the truth of what God has said, I believe, finds its way to a faithful heart."

"What an expression," thought Rose, "a faithful heart." She repeated it under her breath, more impressed than ever at the knowledge her mother held.

"God did not instruct men to make up what He has written using their own meaning. It is for us to study the words so that the Holy Spirit gives us the true meaning."

"Do you have doubts sometimes . . . like sometimes don't you think men have twisted meanings and printed things that are not true?" Rose asked.

"Yes, I have doubts, Rose, but when you pray and believe in God and his Son, with a little time, these doubts are erased. He lets us see things a little at a time. Over a long time all the pieces fall into place."

"Molly Goldstein told us one day that her family believed Christ never rose again and that men only said it so people would think it was true. She said Christ was in a coma and then just woke up again."

"Maybe Molly and her family believe that, but they are Jewish and believe the Messiah is yet to come."

"What do you believe, Momma? Did he really die and come back to life?"

Josephine was silent for a moment. She was measuring cloth for a shirt she was forming for Michael. It gave her a moment to ponder. Once she had finished the cut, she sat down again and did not fidget with the material.

"I always thought, Rose, that if Jesus Christ did not truly die and become alive once again, that the whole thing would be a lie."

"My mind thinks that way sometimes. Does that make me a bad person, Momma?"

"No . . . no, Rose. Those are the pieces you're trying to fit together. For me they all fit. They fit differently for each person at different times in her life. When I was younger, I thought like you do now."

"What changed for you?"

"What changed? Well, as the years went on and I prayed and observed my life – the births, the deaths, weddings, funerals . . . everything, I realized there was proof, and it was there for all to see. Some never will, but one day I saw it very clearly."

"You mean you saw Christ?"

"No, not Christ, but the proof I needed."

"What was it . . . tell me!"

"I'll tell you, Rose, but don't expect it to take hold of you as it did for me. Someday it may he there for you. Right now, I'm not sure."

"Oh, please, Momma, tell me before I bust. I've already sewn an extra button on this blouse!"

Josephine laughed a bit at her daughter's interest and attention. She thought it good that they could share in this quiet and private way. Josephine's faith would be the one inheritance she could leave to Rose.

"In the New Testament," she began, "I read each of the four Gospels several times. They all tell nearly the same story, only the details differ as the writers put into their own words, how they saw the story of Christ. My reason told me that if the story were a lie it would have been dropped after his death. What reason would there be for those same disciples to trudge another sixty or eighty years of their lives preaching the gospel, being punished, whipped, stoned, persecuted, and some killed. Why? I would ask myself over and over. Why would they bother if all of this was for a lie? And then, dear daughter, it came to me in a flash as I prayed. Why? Because it was not a lie!"

Rose's mother stopped with that. Rose could only look upon her with awe. She had no idea how thoroughly her mother had thought this through. This day and moment would always be special to Rose.

Rose had no regrets about leaving school because she knew how important it was to be her mother's helper. In those two years Rose learned how to paint, wallpaper, sew, cook, launder, shop for groceries, write checks, and prepare their monthly budget for bills. She kept abreast of the sisters and occasionally read their books. Mary, two years younger than Rose, was becoming quite grown up. Annie was next in age, and Mary did Ann's hair with the new styles of the day. Mary was finicky about her nails, her hair, and even sneaked on lipstick and powder once away from the house. She spoke of cosmetic school, owning her own beauty shop, and then maybe she could help pay some bills.

Behind Mary and Ann were Francesca (Flora, for short) and Theresa (or Dixie).

While Flora was bringing home good grades, Theresa was only average. It became obvious to Rose that Flora and Theresa had musical ability. They were in the school chorus and sang perfect harmony. They brought home their lyrics and melodies where all the sisters would join in. Joe Crimaldi purchased a worn and torn high-back piano. Everyone of the kids except Rose could play it. The two young ones, Mike and Bessalia

(Betty), were extremely gifted, with good ears for music. Mike could strum his father's guitar and, at ten, knew enough chords to sing some of the old favorites. Noting his son's talent, Joe started him with violin lessons.

Except for the dwindling health of Josephine, these were good years for the Crimaldis, and the time was growing near for Joe to buy out Mr. Billello. With his three brothers, they would own the company outright.

Joe purchased a large Packard car that could easily sit Josephine and his seven children. His drinking now behind him, business prospects looked better every day. Joe bought furniture for the house and better clothes for his kids.

Rose asked her father whether they could have carpeting.

"Rose, Rose . . . carpeting? What is so important about a rug?"

Throughout the house was linoleum. Rose hated linoleum. "It was so damned old fashioned, Italian," she complained to herself. Once she had been with Annie Alleo in their kitchen. It was the only room where they had linoleum. Mrs. Alleo was cooking them breakfast and sliding along the floor bare-footed.

"I'm never gonna do that," Rose promised herself. The expression popped into her head from school days, "barefoot and pregnant." Mrs. Alleo was pregnant. "Damned old dagos," Rose thought, with no disrespect toward her father. "Their taste is in their mouths."

"Someday," she kept it to herself, "I'll have carpet in every room, big rooms where everyone has his own closet, several bathrooms, bedspreads, draperies, linens and linen napkins on a real dining room set." She mentally filed it with her list of "somedays." First was her own home, luxuriously furnished, her own children to fill it, and of course eventually a man she could love and be loved by in return. Then she added travel, driving a car, weddings, and music. So many, many things accumulated on Rose's someday list.

Chapter 2
Nino

In 1909 when Joe and Josephine had sailed with their baby daughter Rosalia to America, they left behind a Sicily that had not recovered from the pillage of its former governors. Eleven different countries had ruled Sicily during the preceding 150 years. Sicilian land, resources, and most of her wealth had been scattered to other European governments. Portugal, Spain, and France had all been guilty of the theft. Sicily was rubble, trying to recover. Those that remained on the tiny island eked out livings through service, meager olive and fruit crops, fishing, and the trades.

Not fifteen miles from the Crimaldi's home in Messina, and unknown to the Crimaldi's, lived a widow, Donna Theresa. Theresa's own mother was born out of wedlock. Until Theresa married, she bore the family name Geoffre. When Theresa married at sixteen, her new name thrilled her. It was Pagna . . . and legitimate. Her husband, Salvatore, was a respected man and known throughout the village as a hard worker. He had acquired several small commercial fishing vessels, and plied his trade daily.

Salvatore and Theresa Pagna had four children in the following order: Charles, Gaetano, Mary, and Antonino. Antonino, nicknamed "Nino" was born in 1900.

A tragic circumstance fell upon the Pagna family in 1905, when the eldest son, Charles, drowned. There had been a terrible storm and though Charles, at 18, was a strong swimmer, a few survivors reported his being caught in a whirling undertow, never to be found. It had such a stunning effect on Salvatore, he lost his desire to work the sea any further. His thoughts turned to America.

"Theresa," he said to his young wife, who also bore the death of Charles heavily, "we need a new start. Let me sail to America. There are many jobs there. There is opportunity there. A man can become rich in a few short years, I have heard. My cousins have told me this is true. Within the year I'll bring all of you there!" With much displeasure and apprehension, Theresa agreed.

Leaving behind him his wife Theresa, his son Gaetano, now

16, his daughter Mary, 14, and young Nino at 5, Salvatore sailed for America.

Only one letter came back to Theresa from New York. Salvatore had walked the streets, not knowing the language or customs, and fell upon hard times. In the dead of winter 1905, just before the new year, word had reached Theresa from the Italian consulate that Salvatore had been found frozen in the park. Not having any relatives who claimed the body, the city had buried him in a potter's field. His only identification or possession was a passport, listing his home town.

Years later, when Gaetano and his wife emigrated to America, he would search furtively and with futility to locate his father's grave. Until his dying day Gaetano anguished over his inability to do so.

Theresa bore the news and grieved long and hard for her broken family. She supported them the only way she knew how and became a laundry woman for the few rich of Sicily.

Donna Theresa arose every morning in her small village of San Marco. Holding the hand of five-year-old Nino, they climbed the rocky path up the mountain to the convent and school of the parish. Her oldest son, Gaetano, was working in Messina, and her daughter, Mary, was soon to wed.

Nino was a bright boy – obedient, shy, and quiet. He wore an expression of alertness but also of haunting sorrow. The nuns took over his education willingly. Because Donna Theresa could not walk the boy home until her long hours were over, Nino had many hours to fill after school. It was here that the gracious priest took Nino under his wing. He took the boy into the parish garden and showed him the wonders of nature as they cultivated tomatoes and weeded the melon patch. Always, Fr. Trivassano was a kind teacher. Born in San Marco but educated in America, the good Father was, in his own mind, Nino's surrogate father. In the years that followed, they shared many hours together.

Fr. Trivassano taught Nino the masterful art of chords on the priest's mandolin and guitar. By the time Nino was eleven, he could handle the instrument with ease. His young voice matured, he sang duets with Fr. Trivassano, and they sang both in Italian and English. The breadth of Nino's knowledge was rapidly becoming whatever the good priest could offer. Speaking of

America often and using the English language to communicate, Fr. Trivassano anglicized Nino's name to "Tony." He explained that in America "Antonino" was "Anthony" and the abbreviated form of Anthony was of course, "Tony."

Since the convent taught only four levels (the equivalent to America's eighth grade), Fr. Trivassano asked Donna Theresa to allow Tony to stay within the school and retake the math, science, and English courses. It could not hurt him, and he was too young to work the manual-labor jobs available. He assured Donna Theresa that he would see to it that Tony be taught a trade. Theresa agreed, since it seemed a welcome opportunity for her son.

In the years that Tony spent in school at San Marco, he had become deeply religious, and Fr. Trivassano taught him to become an altar boy, and he became familiar with Latin and English. When Tony reached his fourteenth year, Fr. Trivassano entered him as an apprentice in the trades school governed by the church.

Tony's brother Gaetano and his sister Mary both married during these years. They sailed for America and, from their letters, seemed fairly settled. It was their dream to send for Donna Theresa and Tony when money and time allowed, but times had been tough in America also. World War I was a financial drain on the American economy. Whereas Gaetano had settled in Cleveland and found employment as a tool maker, Mary had become a "Conti" and settled in Akron, thirty-five miles away. Having their own families to raise, money for their mother and youngest brother was a luxury they could not afford.

Because Tony displayed great manual dexterity with the mandolin and guitar, Fr. Trivassano thought he might make a good shoemaker. From the age of five, Tony's schooling was under the influence of the widow, the nuns, and Fr. Trivassano. Here he learned music, Italian, English, math, science, and shoemaking. He was exposed to the Deity, to Jesus and the Apostles. He grew broad and strong as a bull, but he was very gentle, humble, and quietly self-directed. By the time he was sixteen, Tony developed a beautiful baritone voice and played his mandolin with his *compadres* at weddings and feasts.

Young Tony saved his earnings as an apprentice shoemaker,

and, with mandolin and guitar outings, he dreamed of America for himself and his mother. "Someday," he thought, hopefully, as he lit a candle to the blessed Mother.

At this time, fascism permeated Italy and all the surrounding area. Though Sicily was apart, fascism was creeping there also. The Mafioso families were the last to be governed by the soon-to-be-dictator, Mussolini. King Victor Emmanuel was on his way out, and the black shirts of fascism were a real threat. The call for all young men went out to bring them into Mussolini's military.

Fr. Trivassano, violently opposed to the efforts to overthrow King Victor Emmanuel, went to the widow Theresa Pagna.

"Donna Theresa," he said, in soft respectful tones that were hushed, since the walls had ears. "If you do not remove Tony from this area, most surely '*Il Duce*' will recruit him for the Army. He will be sheep for slaughter." It was obvious the priest had grown to love Tony, who was fast approaching manhood. "It will be either the Army or the Mafia!"

"How," she said concerned, "and with what?"

With this, Fr. Trivassano opened a packet. From it he withdrew several large bills of Italian currency. "Here," he said, "is enough money for yours and Tony's passage to America. Go to your son who already lives there."

Concerned with owing anyone, Donna Theresa took the money in her hands. "How will I ever pay you back?" Then she spoke firmly, "It must be paid back!"

Fr. Trivassano countered, "That is less important than that you leave here!" As an afterthought, he added, "Tony has a trade. Someday he will have a good job in America, and you can pay me back then."

Donna Theresa agreed, and the preparations were made. The sailing time would take nearly two months and the voyage a long and hard one, but Theresa knew it was for the best. She had missed her son, Gaetano, and her daughter, Mary. The trip was a sacrifice she was willing to make if only to see them again. When Fr. Trivassano saw them off to board the ship, he embraced the muscular Tony with both arms, gave him a hearty hug, and said, "Tony, never forget your mother or the Blessed Mother." He continued after a pause, "And never forget me!"

Tony thanked him deeply and managed to say to him,

"Never, Father . . . you are the only father I've really known. *Arrivederla.*"

Once out of the harbor the long voyage settled into a routine. Tony's skill as a musician was discovered by the captain, and he was asked to play the mandolin in the dining hall during the evenings, joining several other musicians. When the ocean was calm, they entertained and played dance music. The young musicians divided a "passed hat," and Tony relished the opportunity for income. Each night he would turn a fist full of change and a few bills over to Donna Theresa. She folded the bills carefully and put the change into a long black sock she knotted at the top. The sock was buried in her suitcase.

"For a rainy day," she exclaimed to Tony and slipped him a sly wink.

The ingenuity and general good humor of the passengers invented many games of skill, chance, and strength. Tony, at 19, was incredibly strong and entered the competition. A man would place a coin in his hand. It would be in the amount of how much he wanted to wager. Women on the ship would try to open the hand for the prize within a time limit. Again, Tony saved the winnings for the sock. His hands were strong and his body powerful. Though short at 5' 6", he was a very mature man.

When the men arm wrestled, few of the young ones were matches for the men in their thirties and forties, where mature strength really lies. It was on such an occasion, when the hot sun shone brightly on the main deck, that the men pitted their wits and strength into arm wrestling for money. A man they called "Cavallo" was the recognized champion. He was about twenty-four years old, a tall wiry brute of a man with thin slits for eyes and a thread-like scar down the left side of his cheek. It had been rumored that he left Sicily because he had strangled a jealous husband.

His real name was Giovanni Carpentieri, but almost everyone called him "John" or "Cavallo," meaning "horse." Cavallo's mean look was made yet worse when he smiled, for his teeth were jagged, tobacco-stained, and decaying. Dental care had not yet come to Sicily. Teeth were a gift from God, and only Divine protection insured them into adulthood.

Tony had known John Carpentieri, or John Carpenter as he would be known in America, from their days together at the convent. They had been friends and classmates. Tony also knew that John's passage to America was being paid for by an uncle in Boston who was a *capo* in the Mafia. The uncle had sent for his nephew, knowing "El Cavallo" would be loyal and strong as a member of his chiefdom.

"Only one man can beat Cavallo," John Carpenter shouted to all who could hear. "He is the best, *'El Champione,'*" and he pointed his finger at Tony. They had pitted their strength against one another many times before. Tony smiled at the recognition but took no part in the major gambling; his earnings were too scarce to risk. A voice crackled through the crowd as the ship's captain yelled down to Cavallo, "I have a man that might give you a tussle, Cavallo! Would you wager a sum on yourself?"

The captain was smiling a knowing smile, and Cavallo yelled back, "Captain, I will wrestle any man but my *compadre* Tony, and wager all I have won!"

It was exactly what the captain had been waiting to hear. He hurried down the railed steps leading from his deck to the main one. The crowd, sensing the competition, stirred itself into excited conversation and made a path for the captain.

"How much have you got there, Cavallo?" said the captain, pointing to Cavallo's stocking cap full of coins and bills, his winnings on that day alone. Cavallo set about quickly to count it. He straightened all the bills and separated the Italian lira from the American coins neatly on the floor of the deck. After a quick calculation he stared up at the captain almost gleefully and responded, "About $250 American." The crowd let out a roar. It was more money than most of them could realize in six months' time while in Sicily.

"Send for Ramon," the captain yelled up to his aide. Word was sent through the ships whistle system to the boiler room. After a short wait, the crowd almost announced Ramon with its ooohs and aaahs. A splendidly built man of 40 exited the staircase from the boiler room. His huge torso fairly rippled, and the sweat and grease of his trade covered him. Not an exceptionally tall man, but with hands of steel, he strode to the captain and said earnestly, "My captain, you called?"

"Ramon," the captain said with a wry and knowing smile as they had played their game for several years, "If you can pin 'El Cavallo' or John Carpenter or Giovanni or whoever he is, you are entitled to one-half of my winnings!"

Before their arrival in America, the Pagna family: Tony Conti (husband of Mary, my father's sister), Mary, my father Tony, and his mother Donna Theresa.

A circle was cleared on the deck, and members of the crowd

began making their side bets. Some were giving two to one on Cavallo. Others were doing the same on Ramon. The captain brought $250 American cash from his wallet as the two men approached the barrel. He threw the money almost flippantly into Cavallo's hat. He then said so all could hear, "No man wins if it is a tie or after thirty minutes. No man wins if either foot leaves the floor! Agreed?"

"Yes," said Cavallo, as he stripped away his undershirt. "Let's begin!"

"Tony," he said in a low voice. "Watch the hat."

The two men straddled opposing stools with a barrel drum between them. They interlocked hands. Cavallo's squinty and menacing eyes glared at Ramon, hoping to discourage the effort of the Spaniard, but Ramon appeared placid, confident, and eager. The crowd was soon a throbbing, cheering mob. Crew members, who had witnessed the same spectacle many times, made their own bets. No one in their collective memory had ever beaten Ramon. Ramon reached up a hamhock of a hand marked with grease from the boiler room. John Carpenter put up his own sinewy arm, resting his elbow on the barrel and spreading his broad and very large fingers one last time before the clasp.

When all was ready, the Captain counted, "One . . . two . . . three." A tension of muscle and sinew bonded itself in struggle. Ramon leaned hard to one side, knowing that if John Carpenter were the least off-balance, one foot might leave the deck. John Carpenter stretched wide his long spider-like legs and grounded them with a firm base. They stared eyeball-to-eyeball for nearly five minutes. They had offset each other's pressure, and their strained arms remained upright. John, perceiving that his youth might be the advantage, thought the odds in his favor the longer the contest went. Ramon kept unflinchingly steady pressure as their hands writhed in convulsive squeezes.

During a period of prepared and mutually acknowledged rest, each was content to remain tense in an upright position. John then made his move. He had squeezed hard on Ramon's huge hand, pulling it slightly away from Ramon's torso and toward his own. It was a subtle trick and could not be made too obvious. The slight change of angle from the side-to-side pull was changed to one toward John. He gained some ground and held Ramon about a quarter of the way down.

For a moment it appeared Ramon would be beaten, but as John thrust hardest for the kill, the greasy hand of Ramon slipped out of his own. It was a save for Ramon, and they had to reclasp into the original upright position. John's eyes seethed in anger and hatred for the placid Ramon as they began again. Slowly, inch by inch, Ramon wore John down and the crowd that had bet for Ramon went wild . . . when he pinned John.

The captain grabbed John's hat and tipped it into a big handkerchief. He patted Ramon on the shoulder as he said, "Good man, Ramon, and still champion."

"No! No!" John Carpenter was excited and yelling in the Captain's face. "Ramon is not champion until he has beaten Tony."

"And who is this Tony?" the captain asked with his perpetual half-smile. John pulled Tony from the crowd in front of the captain. Tony didn't want this and was shy of gambling or any show of physical strength.

"John," Tony pleaded humbly, "I have not the money to gamble."

"My money . . . my money," John said loudly. "We will bet my money!"

"No, John."

Sternly, in Italian, John whispered passionately to Tony, "*Compadre mia, por favore*. Only this time no grease on Ramon's hands." Tony nodded a reluctant acceptance.

"All right," John yelled. "Everything, $500 American!" It was everything John owned in the world. Tony was startled with this announcement.

"Tomorrow," the captain said for all to hear. "My man needs rest now, but tomorrow at noon."

That evening Tony spoke with John. "John," he confessed, "maybe I cannot win over this man, and then you lose everything."

"*Senta*" ("say no more."), John interrupted Tony, "No man has beaten me, except you, and I knew the strength of Ramon as soon as we grappled. I also know that if his hand had not slipped from mine from the grease, I would have beaten him! Do this for me, Antonino, and I promise you half of the earnings."

"And if I lose? Then what?"

"If you lose, I go to America broke, but my uncle gives me a job in his family business. A temporary loss, don't worry. You can lose nothing!"

Tony spoke with Donna Theresa. She looked deep into the innocence of Tony's soul. She knew of her son's great strength, a strength Tony himself could not know or measure.

"*Figlio mia*, I have prayed daily since the loss of your father and oldest brother. I pray to the Blessed Mother, who is real and watches over us daily. So long as what you do is not evil, She blesses you. This is not an evil thing. The captain has set this all up. It is his living!"

It was a sleepless night for Tony. He knew in his heart that $250 could repair his mother's decaying teeth and feed them for several months in America. He was afraid to pray for victory because money was involved. He fell asleep shortly, but just before he did spoke openly to the Blessed Mother.

"Dear Lady," Tony spoke in a whisper, "let all that I do be blessed by you and your Son."

Throughout the night John Carpenter had spoken to two crew members who told him that Ramon really wasn't a sailor, that the captain had lured him from a bar off the coast of Spain for just this kind of wagering. Through it, the captain had won handsomely and Ramon would have the run of the ship once a voyage ended. It was all a scam to loot the passengers of their hard-earned savings before entering America.

Everyone carried some cash or merchandise of value. One crew member confessed to John that the captain had once shown his treasure chest to him when they shared a bottle. It was full of wedding rings and gold crucifixes, pearl rosaries, diamond stickpins, and ruby cufflinks. This was the last of many voyages, and Ramon was nothing but a shill.

The ship hands and all the passengers were excited about the noon match. The main deck was the gathering spot, and all but a few passengers jostled for a viewing point. Bets were being taken up to the eleventh hour.

Tony had arisen early. He washed briskly and looked in on

his mother. She was still asleep. Tony left to bring her coffee and bread. It was his daily routine that he see that his mother ate and got a full ration of drinking water.

Shortly before noon, John Carpenter knocked on his cabin door. No words were spoken as both men wore grim looks of determination and concern. The captain was awaiting them, and the barrel and stools were set in place. Glancing at his watch, he yelled out to the top deck, "Whistle up, Ramon." In a few minutes Ramon appeared. He had the same look as the day before, but this time the crowd had adopted him, and the betting made him an easy favorite.

"Ramon! Ramon!" The chant seemed endless as Ramon straddled his stool. Tony also assumed the position. Just before they clasped hands for the starting count a deep voice bellowed out, "*Aspetto! Aspetto!*" ("Wait! Wait!")

It was John Carpenter, appearing with a huge towel wet on one side. He took hold of Ramon's big hands and washed them and rubbed off the grease. With the dry end, he wiped them thoroughly.

"What are you doing?" The angered captain yelled.

"It is not fair that Ramon should have slippery hands," John fired back so that all might hear.

"Yes, yes," the crowd agreed. "It should be fair!"

Once the grease was wiped clean from Ramon's hands, the two men again prepared for battle. John Carpenter belied his earlier concern as he displayed his unsightly and jagged decaying teeth in a broad and rare smile.

Ramon and Tony clasped hands, and the captain counted out loudly, "One . . . two . . . three!" Again, the two arms of the men strained upright into a vice-like tie. No one could gain advantage over the other. Ramon's eye's were no longer placid, but intent. Tony focused only on the duel. His head showed beads of heavy perspiration as it slid from his hair line down his face and across his eyes. The salt water burned his eyes until John wiped his brow. He remained focused. Again the first five minutes saw no advantage to either combatant, and then Ramon slowly, subtly, angled Tony's shorter and stouter forearm toward himself. Tony knew well the trick and reinforced his hold by hunching his lead shoulder closer to his own arm. His short stocky legs hugged the barrel with both feet firmly planted upon the deck, so that no false move would allow Ramon a victory by forfeit. Both men, bare-waisted, bristled in the sunlight from their own perspiration. Their torsos straining, the sculptured mass of muscle from the backs of both men spoke of reserve and power.

Ramon was the taller of the two men and nearly twenty-one years Tony's senior. Though taller by five or six inches, and given the distinct advantage of leverage by virtue of longer arms, Ramon was outweighed. Tony's thirty or so extra pounds were deceivingly disguised into his compact and thick chest and legs. To view Tony as a small man would be a mistake, for he weighed 200-plus pounds and had labored long and hard with physical work.

The one ingredient Tony felt was his own advantage was the discipline of mind Fr. Trivassano had so often spoken of and cultivated. Tony knew how to focus his mind.

"The strength of my entire mind and body goes into this one arm, for this one moment, with one purpose," Tony formed the thought and summoned all his strength.

Ramon weakened a few inches from the upright position. With it, his leverage changed. Ramon, now on the defensive, would play his old trick to regain position. He attempted to allow his hand to slip from the grasp. With no grease, he could not. Fully expecting this lapse in Ramon's concentration, Tony seized the moment to his advantage and won a few more precious inches. Sensing that it was time for the kill, Tony shifted the angle of Ramon's arm. Now he bent it slightly toward himself. Just a slight margin, and his short arms allowed his powerful shoulder to act in unison with his arm. Ramon, with his arm extended slightly, could not withstand the weight of Tony's shoulder and the pressure of its weight. Ramon succumbed to it in near exhaustion. He had been pinned. The crew seemed in disbelief. Tony thought it had been too easy. He felt Ramon could easily have gone another five minutes, but he was glad he had not. The throng of voices screamed praise or disappointment. A scowl came over the captain and, reluctantly, he paid John Carpenter $500. With anger and disbelief in his eyes, he had retreated to his quarters. Ramon was sent back to the boiler room, and John Carpenter brought a cup of cold wine for Tony.

"You beat his ass, Tony, I knew you could!"

John Carpenter knew many people among the passengers. Most were boyhood acquaintances, such as Tony. Those who were not friends knew of his reputation and were silently afraid of him.

Back in his bunk Ramon was looking at the note he had received the night before. He stared at it blankly, feeling nothing.

If you win, you lose!
Your throat will be slit from ear to ear and your body
shipped to your family in Madrid, piece by piece. Capisco?

John Carpenter wrote the note, left it unsigned, and Ramon not only knew who had written it but also knew that that person could make it stand.

Tony was never aware of the threat. He accepted John's $250 with graciousness and added it to Donna Theresa's savings.

John Carpenter had been an orphan waif and roamed the streets of Sicily to exist. He had stolen often, eaten from garbage cans, and known only a hand-to-mouth existence. Those who knew him were afraid of him and called him *"animale"* because he was much like a wild animal who would do whatever it took to survive. Only Tony, at the convent, had become his friend. Donna Theresa often allowed John to sleep at her home and fed the boy solid meals. Sometimes, when he allowed, she washed his clothes. It had been the only kindness he had ever known.

In America John's uncle knew exactly what he had in mind for this nephew. He would become muscle for the Mafia. Before he had been in America two months, John was told by his uncle to "teach a violent lesson" to a man who had beaten his wife. She was the daughter of a friend. She had done the unthinkable and married a non-Italian. He had done the unthinkable and beaten her physically. With his payment from the "violent lesson," John had replaced his own decaying and jagged teeth. He had preferred gold, and his smile reflected a wide menacing metallic grin. In those years they were not called "hit men," only enforcers. It would be years before Tony would ever meet with John again, but when they parted at Ellis Island, neither knew this.

"Donna Theresa," John spoke to the widow and her son respectfully, "you and Tony . . . you are the only family I have ever known. If ever you need me, you must write my uncle in Boston." Then he handed them a piece of folded paper with a name and an address.

"Tony," he spoke, a little unsure. "You could come with me, and I'm sure my uncle would give you work."

Donna Theresa, knowing well of the uncle's profession and what would become of John, stepped between them.

"John, we go to Cleveland. Tony has a trade. He knows nothing of your uncle's world. We will be safe and we wish you *Bueno fortuna.*

John understood and bent down to embrace the tiny Theresa and kiss her on the cheek. He then wrapped his arms around Tony and said in his ear, "goodbye, *el champione!*"

"Goodbye, John, *bueno fortuna.*" They parted and soon were lost among the placards and people outside of Ellis Island's Administration Building.

The new year of 1920 was to be ushered in shortly, and Gaetano Pagna had found a place for his brother Tony and his mother to live. Gaetano's wife, Mary, and Donna Theresa together ran a small produce shop he was able to procure. Gaetano spent most of his time in the tool-and-die shop but managed a few hours each day in the store.

Tony was hired by the Jaffe Leather Company, since he was unable to break into the shoe factories. It was while he delivered goods from Jaffe to the surrounding shoe-repair shops that he became familiar with Akron. He noticed that Akron, with the Goodyear, Firestone, General, U.S. Hardrubber, and other factories, would be a nice place to live, a place where maybe someday he could have his own shop.

Donna Theresa, through her work in the produce shop, met a widower, Joe Fazio, from her own village. In the old country he was a chicken farmer, producing poultry and eggs for the major stores and restaurants of Messina. All of his children had grown up and departed for America. When his own wife died, Joe took his few belongings and joined his children in the farmland between Akron and Cleveland. Not only had he known Donna Theresa from their Sicilian home, but also his wife and Donna

Theresa had been good friends. Every day he delivered fresh eggs to the store and would spend a little time with Theresa, since he enjoyed speaking in his native dialect. As the years passed, and the lonely Joe Fazio tired of the few minutes of coffee and conversation, an idea crept into his mind.

"Donna Theresa, you are alone, your children are grown. The same is true of me. We have much in common. Come live with me and be my wife. We can have a good life." Theresa had weighed this option long before Joe had formed it in thought or word. She accepted, and they moved to the outskirts of Akron. Tony moved into his own apartment and managed to meet with some of his *paisans* who had a musical group. They played for weddings, parties, and baptisms. It was the Italian way to have food and music for the slightest reason. Tony joined a quintet of musicians and played evenings and weekends to supplement his income.

Ever mindful of their mother, the two sons drove Gaetano's automobile to Akron on weekends. They brought fresh produce, fruit, and wine. It was as Tony had learned, *respetto* ("respect"). Fr. Trivassano had urged: "One must never forget the love, sacrifice, and work a mother gives. Return, always, love, and respect. That is the only payment or payback there can be!"

The brothers and Mary Conti held this as an irrevocable law of their lives and would teach it to their own children.

When Jaffe Leather laid Tony off during tough economic times, he sought employment nearer to his mother and applied at the Goodyear Tire and Rubber Company. He appeared there in his only suit, a white shirt, a cravat with a tiny ruby stick pin, and a pair of patent-leather dress shoes. It was the latest of men's dress styles and the best he owned. They hired him and sent him to the mill rooms to work. Working in a flooded area, where the main sewers could not run off the drain water from the mill fast enough, Tony was knee deep in water. He swore under his breath *dishonorada* ("dishonorable"). "This was work for pack mules or water oxen."

The next day he applied again under an assumed name. He re-applied a total of five times under five different names. Each time he was brought to a job dirtier than the one before and at the lowest possible pay. It was here he had spoken of the promise and resolved it in his heart: "For a man to prosper, he must be his own boss." He returned to Cleveland.

There were things about living in Cleveland he liked, such as the open-air markets, where the farmers would back their produce trucks in a row after row of spaces. They laid out makeshift tables and displayed every type of vegetable and fruit he had ever seen.

On his break from apprentice school he walked through the open market and watched the variety of people it attracted. Tony loved to stop and observe the groups of strolling musicians and listen to their renditions of popular songs. He tried diligently to use only English, and, though he read the dictionary and news pieces, a small accent would never leave him.

My father as he was dressed when he applied for factory jobs.

It was a spring morning in April of 1923 when Tony sat upon a park bench and unfolded his lunch. The park was adjacent to the open-air market and only a two-lane side road separated the two. At right angles to the ends of the park and the adjacent market were two main drags of traffic always busy with pedestrians and autos.

Rose Fazio, Tony's new step-sister, lived with Gaetano's family and also worked at the produce store. She happened by with her lunch, as she often did, and shared a carton of milk with Tony. They spoke of many things and laughed about the things they saw people do and the words they spoke.

From their view of the market they could see all the bargaining and bickering and still maintain the quiet of the park bench, its shade trees, and cool repose. Tony caught a glimpse of a large automobile with many children, parking alongside the road, dividing them from the market. The driver, obviously the father of the children, exited the car first. He was a dapper, stout man, graying at the temples against his original shiny black hair, thick with curls. He had a dark, trim mustache and was dressed in a beautiful dark suit with a white shirt and red tie. Tony noticed his patent-leather shoes and the tidy felt gray spats. The man obviously was somebody. He went to the curb side of the car and opened first the front door and then the back. From the front climbed out what appeared to be his eldest child, a daughter. Tony was struck with the beauty of the girl. So much had he been caught up in the tiny-waisted girl with her light pink gingham dress, he barely noticed the four more daughters and son who exited the back door.

In the short time it took for the girl to straighten her dress and await the orderly assemblage of the rest of the brood, Tony had indelibly etched the face of the girl in his mind. Her hair was shoulder length, raven black. Her skin was unlike any that Tony had ever seen . . . flawless, red-cheeked but fairly pale. The girl's eyes, for a fleeting moment, glanced at Rose Fazio and then to Tony. He saw at once the gray-green tint of her hazel eyes. They were soft, innocent. Fr. Trivassano's thought flitted through his mind instantly.

"The eyes," he had told Tony, "are truly a mirror of the soul."

Tony could not forget this delicate, almost tiny beauty, who could not have been more than fifteen. As the family held each other's hands, the girl on one end of the line, her father on the other, and each of the little ones in between, they crossed the street into the market place.

Rose Fazio saw the gaping mouth of Tony.

"Aha," she laughed at Tony kiddingly, "the thunderbolt . . . did it hit?"

Sheepishly Tony turned to Rose and smiled a half-smile, saying, "She is beautiful. I wonder who she is?"

"Don't you know the man?" asked Rose.

"No, I've never seen him before."

"He comes in the store every week," Rose offered. That is his family. They are the Crimaldis. Joe Crimaldi owns the cement block factory."

"Where is his wife?" Tony asked.

"I have heard she is very ill and rarely goes out," Rose answered him quickly, and before he could ask another question said, "I gotta run, Tony. I gotta get back to the store."

Many times thereafter, Tony sought to get a glimpse again of the petite beauty that stirred his heart. Alas, he did not. He had seen Joe Crimaldi pull up to the curb on two occasions, but on each occasion he was alone.

"Ah," he thought, "she is too young for me. It will be several years before she is a woman."

At the Italian Club, a hangout for the *paisanos*, one could get a good meal, play cards, meet young girls and dance, or just meet good friends. It was a short walk for Tony, and he went there often for his supper, now that Donna Theresa was married.

Tony's apartment was the downstairs in a six-apartment complex. With what he earned from his guitar and mandolin, he could easily make the rent, and soon his apprenticeship from repair school would end, and he would earn a full salary. A friend of Tony's and the accordion player in their small band approached him while at the club.

"*Bueno serra*, Nino," he spoke in Italian.

"*Bueno serra*, Roland," Tony answered politely, "but I prefer we learn to speak good English, Roland."

"*Si* . . . I mean, 'yes,'" Roland corrected himself. "Tony," he said. "We have a big wedding at the end of this month. It will be the biggest we've played for."

In many ways, it was.

Chapter 3
An Italian Wedding

The years 1909 to 1922 were good years for Joe Crimaldi, and, except for his wife's illness, life in the new country had treated him well. Though he carried a huge loan at the bank, he was the sole proprietor of his own business, the Quality Brick and Block Company. His oldest brother, Sal, had gone to work in nearby Canton as a brick-kiln supervisor. Sal was raising a large family and sought the countryside to raise his children. His company offered him a free home to live in, with several acres. His pay and supervisory capacity presented too great an opportunity to pass up. So Joe Crimaldi took part of the bank loan to buy out his brother's share. Charles and Jim, the younger brothers, also struck out on their own as private contractors in the cement-finishing business.

The Joe Crimaldi family remained in Cleveland in the same home. Rose had had the full responsibility of the household for nearly two years. She had nursed her mother through the tough times but always found time to do laundry, bake bread, clean house, and prepare meals for the entire family.

Rose, on the ancient sewing machine, made simple blouses and dresses for her sisters and even shirts for Michael. Just before the children returned from school were the quiet moments alone with her mother. They spoke of many things, but most often they spoke of Rose's "somedays." Josephine told her that she was already a little mother and "someday" she would meet a man with whom she could fall in love and marry. Rose thought this a far-off time. Also it became hard to see herself as married. "Who would want me? I'm so plain," she thought to herself.

Surely her sisters Mary, Ann, Theresa, Francesca, and Bessalia were much prettier.

"You have a beauty, Rose," her mother once counseled her, "that does not grow old or wrinkled or get fat. Your beauty is inside!"

Whatever she was, Rose was most of all a realist. Even her conversation was blunt and direct. She didn't mince words. Though Ann Alleo and her sister, Mary, were her closest friends, Rose thought them vain and boy-crazy. Both of them took hours primping their hair, doing their nails, and trying on different clothes.

Then, at one Sunday dinner, Joe Crimaldi had an announcement to make. He removed his large white napkin tucked into the top of his vest and laid it on the table. Rose poured her father a glass of wine, as he was accustomed to after his dinner, and the family awaited his decree.

"One month from yesterday," he said carefully, not wanting to give up the information too quickly, "we are all invited to . . . ," he paused.

"Where? Where?" the girls asked. They loved events.

"Do we all get to go?" one asked.

"Yes," Joe said simply. He resumed, "We all get to go to Frankie Alleo's wedding!"

There was an outburst of laughter and chatter. The Crimaldis rarely got to see or do much, and these wedding outings were a chance to see and be seen. Even Josephine would muster strength to attend. Rose was secretly elated, for she rarely ventured into public and, though she loved music and dancing, rarely had the opportunity. Only in their home, when Joe Crimaldi played his guitar, had the girls sung and danced. Every Crimaldi child became a self-taught piano player. Their musical ears allowed early interest and one sister taught the next. They loved to harmonize when they sang the love songs of the 1920s. Their only outings as a family were trips to the market in the one luxury item Joe Crimaldi allowed himself, a large Packard Sedan.

The wedding hall was decorated with crepe paper adorning the side walls and draped into great splashes of red and white. In the center of the large hall, hanging from the ceiling, was a mirrored ball that rotated slowly, throwing its reflections throughout the room. At the furthest end was a small stage where the musicians in tuxedos were setting up their instruments. At the bottom of the stage were several long tables piled high with pastries of every sort. There were plates of small cream puffs and delicious chocolate wedding cookies filled with almonds and several heaping plates of mixed nuts placed equidistantly across the span of the tables. There were several large plates of multicolored candy-coated almonds. In the center of the tables, and also fronting the center of the stage, rested an enormous six-layer cake, trimmed to perfection. Each tier of the cake descended to a larger size layer, the base being quite large. Crowning the tip was a small set of candy dolls, exact replicas of the bride and groom. To the right and left of the centered table, along the side walls, were two long and mirrored bars. Here were stocked every wine and liquor one could envision. Behind the bars were huge washtubs full of iced beer. At the end of each bar, there were two huge barrels of draft beer, ready to be tapped.

Flowers adorned each table that surrounded the dance floor, and several large spreads of flowers and wreaths hung from the curtains drawn back from the stage. At the entrance to the hall, there were small concession stands. Behind these booth-like areas, workers were preparing hundreds of ham and cheese sandwiches in small Italian buns. They were neatly wrapped and stacked into huge wicker baskets that appeared to be what any laundry woman might have used. Nearly twenty of the wicker baskets, two feet wide and at least that high, were lining the back of the booths. Older Italian-looking women, their hair in neat buns, wearing their best social dresses, were supervising every preparation and service.

Behind the hall were neatly trimmed lanes for bocce ball, where mustachioed older gentlemen with twinkling eyes and stiff joints swore, cajoled, and coaxed the little balls to their targets. Still others were content to sit in the shade with a cold drink and watch the contests. They smoked their DeNapoli cigars and stunk up the area. Others inhaled their pipes of aromatic tobacco, the good and bad smell intermingling. The younger men, their dark hair slicked back, all seemed to carry cigarettes.

The very young, though dressed to the teeth before they had left home, would soon have shirts pulled out, grass stains on their pants, or bruised shins, knees, or elbows from playing the pure little boy games of shove, kick, run, and punch. All of this was done with a Coca Cola in one hand and a half of ham sandwich or cookie in the other. Wedding feasts were great fun.

As the age of these young male ruffians approached puberty, their behavior took a sudden turn. Still impeccably dressed in their best suit of clothes, the teenagers and young men aligned in front of the building to observe a view of the parking lot. It was here where the families drove in, dropped off visitors, and parked. It was also here where the young men eyed the sweet young things. Without looking directly, they tried to appear to be seen, while not looking. There were constant discussions, the small talk from some who were slightly related to the others.

"Whaddya mean she's a cousin?"

"How close a cousin if I never seen her?"

"Can you screw cousins?"

The young ladies, the objects of their interest, exited the family cars and entered with their chaperone aunts and mothers.

"God, how beautiful!" was more often quoted than the occasional "she's a dog . . . a real bow-wow!"

Always, the game was played. One must look cool, reserved, alluring, never perspiring, even though the warm June evening saturated everyone with high humidity, and the huge ceiling fans helped little.

The music began. It brought a warmth and fullness to the hall. A large cheer from outside the hall alerted those inside that Frankie Alleo and his tender bride of 17 had arrived. Her name was Gina, and, until that morning, her last name had been Allegro. She was the daughter of Eugene Allegro, city councilman. He was a powerful politician, influential, and, when it came to city politics, a good friend or bad enemy depending on what side you were on. Frankie Alleo, at 22, had been assigned as Councilman Allegro's personal detective and bodyguard. It was on a visit to the councilman's home where he first set eyes on the stunning Gina.

Gina entered the foyer to the great hall and was met with applause. Someone took her wrap, revealing her beautiful imported white silk wedding gown. She pulled her veil back over her tiara, and her face fairly glowed. She was indeed beautiful and ready to enjoy her wedding reception. Soon, Frankie was at her side, and they entered the music hall to the view and cheering of all.

As the music switched from polkas to waltzes, fox trots to an occasional ballad, the orchestra would squeeze in one of the old Italian favorites. On occasion, one of the more gifted guests led them all in song. Such was the case when the orchestra played "Oui, Marie," a long-time favorite. "Hurry back to Sorrento" was another much-requested ballad. The variety of music allowed fathers to dance with daughters, mothers with sons, little girls with sisters or aunts. The smaller boys just took the floor on their own and would sway to the music alone, with each move an original innovation.

The Crimaldis were sitting at a round table near the right side of the stage not twenty feet removed from the drums, bass, and guitarist. It was a gala evening for young Rose. She began dancing with her sister, Mary, but before long, Tommy Alleo, the groom's brother, and Ralph Comito had cut in on

The Crimaldi sisters: Ann, Flora, Mary, and Rose.

them. Tommy had always been sweet on Rose, and Ralph had an eye for Mary.

Josephine and Joe sat observing their daughters dance, and they listened to the pleasing music.

When Tony Pagna began strumming his guitar that evening, he had not expected to see the lovely *signorina*. She was wearing the same pink gingham dress she had worn the day he first saw her at the market. It was trimmed in white lace with a lace belt tied in a bow behind. He had no way of knowing that Rose had sewn the dress herself and that it was her only "good dress." Tony thought the Crimaldis to be wealthy people. He saw the Packard they drove and the dapper Joe Crimaldi. What else was there to think?

Tony did not know Tommy Alleo, but he made up his mind that he didn't like him. He danced too often with Rose and laughed too much. Tony also thought he hugged her too tightly. He was examining his jealous feelings and had to admit that Tommy Alleo was a handsome guy.

For Rose, Tony felt almost possessive. She was his, he thought. Though he didn't even know her name, he had burned her radiant face and smile into his memory. He watched her slight, lithe body gracefully perform the intricate dance steps. He could hear her laughter when she glided by in front of him. Her eyes had a sparkle of maturity and knowing, and yet he knew at a glance that she was innocent and childlike. No one had ever captured his heart so easily. It bothered him that she was not aware of who he was.

Rose, however, did know who Tony was. Annie Alleo had spotted Tony when first she saw the band. Annie told Rose, "He keeps looking at you."

"Why me?" Rose could not understand.

"Maybe he'll ask you to dance, Rose."

"Can orchestra players dance when they are playing for a wedding?" Rose asked, naively.

"Everyone can dance at a wedding, dummy." With this Annie nudged Rose, and they both laughed. Rose looked at the guitarist.

"How old is he?" she asked herself.

The evening was half over now, and most of the young children had either reached the point of exhaustion or indigestion. The floor now naturally appeared reserved for the adults. It was time now for the older couples to remember when they were young and for the young ones who wanted to grow old together. The music matched that timing. Soon the father of the bride, Eugene Allegro, took his daughter into center floor. The approving crowd acknowledged. Then the groom and his own mother, then the fathers-in-law and mothers-in-law, and then they switched partners, only soon to return, each to his own mate. Much applause, and an orchestra break announced . . . intermission.

At the intermission, the young men at the bar began to show wear. They seemed not as pin neat; some were glassy-eyed from wine, liquor, and beer. All seemed too loud. The game played was *mora,* where two men squared off throwing the fingers of one hand to compare with the fingers of the opponent. It was an anticipatory game, as old as Italy. The idea was to anticipate how many fingers of one hand your opponent would throw. This could be as few as none by throwing a fist or any number up to all five. The opponent would throw fingers at the same time. Both would shout simultaneously, a number from one to ten in hopes that both hands equaled the total they shouted. The number-shouting part was always in Italian. This added the touch of ethnic ownership the game enjoyed. To win three times, or three points, was a game. The loser had to down a drink. Losing frequently, one could easily become drunk.

As several groups of young men were shouting and laughing, Tony and Rolando, the orchestra's accordion player, strolled to the bar for a glass of draft beer. Rolando had followed Tony's gaze, for Tony could not keep from looking at Rose. Rolando Gentile spoke to his friend, "Would you like me to introduce you to her, Tony?"

"Do you know her, Rolando?"

"We're related."

"You're related? How is this?"

"She's a distant cousin," Rolando said easily.

"That's the Crimaldi family," he said, as he half-pointed with his glass of beer in the direction of their table. "My mother was a Crimaldi before she married my father. The Crimaldis and the Gentiles go way back, and there are a lot of Crimaldis. They were a big family. Each brother from the original family made his way to America separately. If I remember right, several of the Crimaldis married Gentiles. It's all mixed up that way, but legit."

The two men strode to the Crimaldi table. Rolando shook hands with his uncle, Joe Crimaldi, and said "Hi" to all the cousins and Aunt Josephine. Then he stepped back a step and announced in a relaxing manner, "May I introduce my *compadre*, our mandolin player, Tony Pagna?" Joe Crimaldi stood up and shook Tony's hand. Tony nodded to the Mrs. Crimaldi and also to each daughter and Michael, who was nearly asleep, with his head upon the table. When Tony was introduced to Rose, he felt his face flush. She was more beautiful up close than he had realized.

After the introduction, Tony asked Joe Crimaldi if he could ask the *signorina* Rose to dance.

"Ma, sure . . . but, of course," was Joe's answer. "She loves to dance!"

Annie Alleo caught Rose's eye. She was only a table away. She winked at Rose.

Tony excused himself, found his good friend Paul Lombardo, and asked him to fill in on the guitar. Freed of his duty, he returned to Rose. As the music began, Tony spoke in his mildly broken accent, "*Signorina* Rose, you lika to dance with me?"

Rose nodded acceptance and, somewhat self-consciously, took Tony's hand and walked to the edge of the dance floor. Tony's skill as a dancer was in direct proportion to his musical ability. He was smooth and light on his feet.

Rose, by her size alone, was light as a breeze. Tony at 5' 6" and Rose at 5' 2" seemed a matched couple. Joe Crimaldi noticed their smoothness as they had waltzed, did the polka, and then a slower tune. He also realized that Tony was several years older than his Rose. "These things don't matter," he said to himself. "If he is a good man, that matters!" Tony was only seven and one-half years older than Rose.

Rose was enjoying herself and was thrilled to be dancing with a man other than her father or Tommy Alleo. It was true Tommy was very handsome, but he was very immature. Here was a man . . . polite, gentle, but still Rose could feel the power packed within his arms and back. She had decided she liked Tony Pagna.

While the two were near the finish of their last dance, a commotion broke out from the bar on the right side of the hall quite close to Rose and Tony. Tommy Alleo and a large young dark-haired man in his twenties had been playing *mora* at the bar. The large man was probably one of the uninvited guests, since passersby loved the music and sought out the free wine and food.

The sponging was allowed and acceptable if one behaved, but this stranger was not even dressed as a wedding guest.

The argument began when money had been wagered. Someone accused another of cheating by folding his thumb under. They exchanged insults, and Tommy Alleo had thrown a drink in the stranger's face. The much-larger fellow and Tommy grappled with each other and crowded onto the floor. In a flash, the area cleared, and the orchestra halted. The two men were glaring and ready to attack. It was at this point where the councilman came to hold off the groom's brother, but the large opponent closed in. Tony darted to him from the side and wrapped his powerful arms around the man and restrained him. When the man started to swear, Tony squeezed yet harder. The man was red-faced and struggled slightly, his feet not touching the floor. All the while Tony tightened his vice-like grip around the man's chest. He said sternly, "This is not the place . . . watch your mouth . . . this is not the place."

Tony dragged him slowly toward the exit and made the man promise to cool off before he would release his grip. Slightly numb from the squeeze hold and short of breath, the man nodded. Tony released him and returned. Eugene Allegro thanked Tony and shook his hand. "I'm glad you grabbed that one," he said, grinning at Tony.

"They get a little too much vino," Tony winked. Both understood. All weddings seemed to have these explosions, some worse than others.

Joe Crimaldi had seen it all in a flash. The small bullish dart of speed by Tony and the vice grip meant not to hurt but to hold. Joe liked the way young Tony had handled it all. When it was over, Tony had made no display other than to Eugene Allegro's offered hand of thanks. From there he walked over to Rose, said something, and politely excused himself with a nod to the family. He walked unassumedly to the bandstand and picked up his mandolin.

As the evening wore on, the dance of the bride and groom took place. Applause greeted them. Soon the maid of honor and the best man . . . there was more applause, and in this way the entire bridal party. Again, another bridal dance started by the groom only to be cut in by anyone who would pin a one-, five-, ten-, or twenty-dollar bill onto her bridal train. It was tradition. It said, "I'm glad to pay for this great privilege . . . and besides it helps them get started." These pinned dollars were merely a tip, a token. Behind the Allegro family's table was another table piled halfway up the wall with presents and a large decorated box with a slit in it for those who gave cash in an envelope. It was here the councilman's prestige and influence would create a small dowry for Gina. "What the hell," he had reasoned. "It's old-fashioned and tacky, yes, but it's tradition!"

It began to wind down. The young romantics, with the hungry eyes, were making sure it wasn't a distant relative they were planning to drive home. A family was known to kill for such an offense. That was a sacred trust, and no man dared breach it.

An announcement was being made by one of the dozens of neatly combed females who seem to come out of the woodwork and assert their authority. "It's time . . . It's time," she announced, "for the Grand March." With this, she pranced to the marching music over to the bride and groom. She would lead, and they would follow. Everyone else had to join hand-in-hand with his or her partner and fall in behind. The entire hall of people would eventually join the line. The "little dictator" would shout out orders. "Make a line here! You go there! This way! That's it, make a tunnel!" It was an intricate design of parade and dance that would make proud a drill sergeant. All the while she was having them turn and spin and form arches and tunnels.

The baker, truly the "king" of the party and probably the husband of the "little dictator," appeared majestically behind the cake. Piled before him on the tables a thousand little cardboard plates and another thousand little plastic forks. The "king" wore his two-foot-high white chef's hat and another twelve women, in neat little hairnets, were ready to administer "the cake."

With a flair that would make Blackstone envious, he deftly removed and preserved the candy bride and groom on top of the cake. Gently and artistically, he lifted the top layer and set it before him. It was at this precise moment that the dictator wife had her troops form abreast, marching directly for the cake. When the bride and groom, maid of honor and best man appeared immediately in front of the baker, he lifted a thin veneer that held the top layer steady. As he did this, two white doves flew out of the cake. With not so much as a pause, only a smile of accomplishment, he acknowledged the oohs and aaahs of the crowd. With a long narrow, pearl-handled knife, he made about twenty-four quick two-handed presses against the first layer. Quickly he did the same crosswise. Before he could prepare another layer, the dozen ladies had lifted each piece with their own personal spatulas and placed them just as deftly onto the cardboard plates. If a man took a slide rule and measured, they would be very close in size. The next layer was removed, and two more doves took flight. In all, a dozen white doves had been cleverly inserted into the hollow areas of the cake design. Each release was greeted with admiration and applause. The doves were symbols of peace and happiness, a hope for the future of the bride and groom.

As each foursome in the Grand March received their cake, they broke ranks and found a table to sample the many layers separated by a moist pudding cream. It was delicious.

Joe Crimaldi spoke to his daughter, "Rose, this Tony seems to be a very fine gentleman." It was almost a question.

"Yes, Papa," Rose stated simply, "I like him." She went on as the opportunity had presented itself. "He asked if he could call upon me some evening."

"What did you tell him?"

"I told him I would ask my father and let him know."

"Do you want to see more of him, Rose?"

She thought a moment, not quite sure whether to seem anxious or indifferent. At last she looked squarely in her father's eyes, "I would like it if he visited."

Secretly, Joe Crimaldi was pleased. Rose was nearly 16 now. She had been a wonderful daughter, and it was time she had a life outside of her homemaking duties.

"Tell him so then."

As the Crimaldis rose to leave for home, Rose walked to the bandstand where the musicians were finishing the evening with "Goodnight, Ladies."

When it ended, Rose whispered something in Tony's ear.

A smile crept upon his face and he said, "Good. See you soon."

In the weeks and months that followed, Tony was a frequent visitor to the Crimaldi home. Each time he appeared, he always brought with him a fresh basket of fruit for the family. When he drove his Ford into the driveway, Rose's sisters became more excited then Rose herself. When Rose examined how she felt, she sensed a warm glow whenever in Tony's presence. He was so polite, so neatly dressed, and ever so thoughtful. Always he greeted "Mr. Crimaldi" and "*Signora* Crimaldi." He would then present whatever little gift he brought for the family.

"This is not necessary, Tony," Joe Crimaldi always advised.

"Yes," was his sure answer, "but it gives me pleasure to bring something for the children."

Joe Crimaldi was impressed and said to himself, "He has old country respect, this man, but fits well into the new world."

On one of these visits, Tony asked Rose whether she would like to take a walk. The two of them walked to the park leisurely. Here he offered to buy Rose an ice cream bar. She enjoyed these walks and looked forward to the time they could spend alone. One of the most striking things about Tony's appearance, Rose thought, were his black and piercing eyes. It was as though he had lived through much, but it had not embittered him or in any way allowed him to lose hope for the future. He was optimistic, sure of his ability to earn a good living. He spoke often about how anxious he was to complete his apprenticeship.

They spoke of many things, and Rose, not given to speaking in many long paragraphs, found Tony a good listener. She revealed her innermost thoughts. She wanted a home, her own children, some of the finery of life, and, if she could, travel. They grew in understanding. Rose knew instinctively that Tony, though he was slow to anger, could reach a high degree of emotion. She thought of it as a gentle fierceness.

Rose learned that he was a deeply religious man and that his mother was a sacred person in his life, one he dearly loved and respected. Rose was convinced Tony was a good man; her instinct had told her so. As for love, Rose was not sure what that was. She only knew she loved to be around him and listen to his wisdom in many things. She also knew that when several days passed without being with him, she was miserable.

On Sunday afternoons, Tony brought along his guitar or mandolin. He and Mr. Crimaldi played duets on the porch while Rose, her mother, and her sisters sang lyrics. Tony played rhythm, and Mr. Crimaldi picked up the melody. Mike Crimaldi, if he knew the tune they were playing, picked up the melody on his violin. These were wonderful moments for all, and each seemed to know it.

On a particular Sunday, Joe Crimaldi asked Tony to invite his mother, Donna Theresa, to come for dinner. It was a time when Josephine and Theresa spoke of Sicily, and it went well.

As Tony was driving his mother home, she said in Italian, as her English was limited to merely a few correct words and the rest swear words, "This girl, Tony, No," she corrected herself, "this woman . . . don't let her get away. She is a jewel!"

Tony told her then that he planned to ask her to marry as soon as he had a steady job and his apprenticeship was over.

"Good," she said, proud of his choice.

Tony had revised his first impressions of the Crimaldis. They were far from rich. He saw that Rose had very few clothes. He had also observed that their furniture in the home was badly worn. Mr. Crimaldi was struggling. The automobile was for business. It was important never to let on that things are not going well, he thought correctly.

Rose accepted Tony's proposal for marriage, and they planned the wedding for the spring of 1924. Alas, Josephine's bronchial condition worsened, and they postponed the date. That winter, before the Christmas of 1923, Josephine died.

Chapter 4
A Land of Milk and Honey

The death of Josephine Crimaldi brought long-lasting and drastic change in the Crimaldi family. Joe Crimaldi drank far more than his normal glass or two of wine. His grief over the loss of his wife and the responsibilities of seven children, plus the downturn of his small factory's production, thrust him into bouts of depression.

Tony finished his apprenticeship and was now realizing a full salary as a shoemaker and repairman in a Cleveland shop that featured eight cobblers who did "while you wait" business.

The Crimaldi children began to scatter, their lives in disarray. Tony, viewing the instability of their lives, spoke to Rose and her father.

"Let Rose and me marry, *Sa* Joe. (it was the abbreviation in conversation for *Signor* Joe). We will make a home and make room for the girls to have a place to live."

Joe Crimaldi, although despondent and weary, knew that it made sense. Rose would see to the care of the girls. Michael would stay with his father, and the baby, Bessalia, would be schooled and housed at the nearby convent. Before Joe Crimaldi would claim bankruptcy, he would try to provide his eldest daughter with a decent wedding.

Rose and Tony had just a small wedding. Tony invited his brother and his family, his sister Mary and the Conti family, and his mother Donna Theresa and her second husband's family, the Fazios. On the Crimaldi side were the families of four brothers, Sam, Joe, Charles, and their youngest brother, Jim.

Tony arranged for one week off to get married and search out a home to rent. For his honeymoon, he and Rose returned to his small apartment. Before they entered, Tony lifted his bride in ceremonial tradition. She was as light as a feather, her eyes wide as saucers. This new chapter of her life was a total mystery. Tony sensed her apprehension. He knew her innocence and carefully assured her with his gentleness.

Rose was full of love but had never discovered how one should display it. She had received hardly any attention from anyone in her lifetime except Josephine. The attention of Tony, his caring and thoughtfulness, erased her doubts.

In the next five years, Rose saw her sisters struggling to make their own lives. Her sister Mary married Ralph Comito and was training as a hair dresser. None of the older girls had graduated from high school because the demands of everyday living would not allow it. Their names changed accordingly as they entered into adulthood. Antonio became "Ann," and married at eighteen; Francesca became "Flora"; and Theresa took the name "Dixie." The two of them became waitresses. Bessalia or "Bessie" hated her name and

Uncle Mike at age 13.

dubbed herself, while in the convent, "Betty." Only Betty would complete high school and arm herself with the knowledge of typing, shorthand, and other secretarial skills.

Mike, only ten at the time of his mother's death, had stayed with his father. He grew tall and alarmingly handsome. His musical skill at the violin and the piano progressed though he had long ago quit the lessons. Girls flocked to Mike, and he learned at a very early age that he could manipulate them for whatever the reason.

Joe Crimaldi kept life and limb together through his own skill as a block layer. Gone were his business, his home, and the Packard. Mike was constantly in and out of trouble. He was arrested for shooting pigeons, peeing off the curb in broad daylight, and for stealing a pack of cigarettes from a grocery shelf. The judge knew him too well. The young toughs Mike ran the streets of Cleveland with were a bad lot, and, once started, they became strong influences that would govern Mike's habits all of his life. He was held by the draw that many young men are overcome with – excitement, drink, women, money, and cars. The only outside love that seemed legitimate, ironically, became the tool that provided the rest – music.

Within five years, Rose and Tony were able to purchase a small home in Parma, Ohio. Rose gave birth to her oldest son, Sam. In the Italian tradition, the first-born child would be named after the father's mother or father. Since all the names would be taken from the saints'

My parents' wedding picture.

names, and in turn from ancestors, it was easy to see the repetition of the same names often. Tony was vowed to the American customs, and though officially it was "Salvatore" after his own father, it would forever be "Sam."

It was 1925, and the country's economy was in a turmoil. It had not been planned, but in 1927, Rose gave birth to their second son, named for her father Giuseppe, called "Joe." In the hard winter of 1928 little Joe caught pneumonia and died. She grieved the loss by doubling her efforts in the household. Their little home had been painted throughout. Rose had wallpapered each room and sewed bedspreads and draperies for the bedrooms.

When the stock-market crashed in 1929, Tony was laid off. Yet another mouth came to be fed that year, another son. Rose insisted that this boy be again called Joe. If not in name, this Joe would be in every other way an original. In an effort to provide food for his family, Tony piled his shoe-repair tools, a portable last, several sets of rubber heels, and some leather materials into a basket. In the cold of winter, he went afoot seeking work. The snow was constant and stayed long as he walked neighborhoods from door to door. Many were on relief, many stood in bread lines, but Tony's pride would not permit him to do so. He worked for a can of pears, a dozen eggs, a chicken, or whatever the people could offer.

The papers were full of bad news, hard times, and hard luck. People who had risen to financial heights were jumping off bridges and buildings at the news of the market crash. Hunger became a way of life. Tony was determined this would not touch his family, and prayed about it often.

On a Friday morning in 1930 he had gathered his peck basket of tools and materials and headed for southeast Cleveland, nearly nine miles away. To preserve what little money he had, he forsook the streetcar and walked through the snow with no boots or cover. His soft patent-leather shoes became saturated, and the high snow pounded against his shins. He wore a heavy dark overcoat, gloves, and a brimmed felt hat, tucked hard down to allow the visor to keep the wind and snow from his eyes as it came directly at him. All day he had trudged through the snow. Upon each respective door, he knocked. Most people needed repair for their shoes. New shoes seemed out of the question. His destination had been the city, where more affluent people lived.

To get warm, have a chance to rest, and grab a bite of bread, olives, and cheese Rose wrapped as a lunch, he entered into the foyer of a Catholic Church. There were several women praying as Tony entered the foyer. His feet were nearly frozen, and he removed his shoes and put them over the register, walking in his stocking feet inside the neighborhood church. He felt no appetite and kneeled in one of the back pews, placed his hat on the bench, and unbuttoned his overcoat. Leaning forward, he stared hard at the crucifix at the back of the altar. His thoughts went back to Sicily for a moment, when he had been an altar boy. He followed the two young boys dressed in their red gowns, topped with white lace shirts. They were just dousing the candles, since the last Mass of the day had just ended. To the left of the altar was a carved image of the Blessed Mary. Many candles for special intentions had been lit for the Holy Mother to intercede prayers. Somewhat ashamed that he could not pay for a candle, Tony walked to the little altar, knelt, and prayed.

"Blessed Mother," he began, "I have never wavered in my faith for you and your son, Jesus Christ."

Tears began to fill his eyes, and a shiver started at his lower back and ran upwards to the base of his head. "I believe," he continued, "that it was you and your son who directed me to this country. It was you who gave me the strong body and will to overcome scarlet fever as a boy and bring me and my own mother to America. I wish to work. I wish to support my wife and my children, but where do I turn, O Blessed Mother?"

It had been a long hard pull since his arrival to America. He had struggled hard to learn the new ways and language. Often at night, he would pick up a dictionary of English and just study the meanings and pronunciations of words. It was disheartening to hear his own parish priest lash out at the use of birth control. It had made Tony question what was really right. He saw the death of his second son and only a year later the birth of another. "Could a man make his own decision about the size of his own family? Did God truly make this law or were these again, the man-made laws of clergymen?"

Tony loved his young wife and his two sons, but the responsibility of their support and sometimes Rose's family weighed on him heavily.

"Blessed Mother," he was near a conclusion with his prayer to her, "Grant me strength and show me the right direction."

When he left the church and ventured again into the snow, it was late afternoon. It was his intention to work his way back home, trying the few homes on the opposite side from those he had canvassed that morning. At only his second stop, Tony was met at the door by a large man with a large family. It was obvious that this family had means. The man of the house asked him in, and Tony repaired the shoes of each of the man's five children. As payment, he was given several pounds of sausage, two pounds of spaghetti, and a can of peaches, put up by the woman of the house last summer. It was simple payment, but Tony was lifted in spirit.

After the job, he began trudging home. As darkness came fully upon him, the wind swirling and the temperature decreasing steadily, Tony began to feel again the chill of fatigue. The walking distance was nothing to him, but as the snow mounted and he had to fight every step, balancing a basket of tools in one hand and the groceries in his other, his thoughts turned to his own father. "Frozen," he thought wistfully as he tramped through the drifts of snow. "Frozen in America and buried in potter's field in an unmarked grave." The thought troubled him deeply.

Nearly three hours from the time he had left the church, Tony made the last turn in his approach to home. The streets were devoid of traffic or any pedestrians. An occasional light from a distant house was all that showed signs of life. His shin bones were stinging now from the exposure to the wet and snow and cold wind. He thought he was within a half mile now and felt sure he could make it. He thought about Rose, Sam, and Joe, his own son, and pressed on with his dwindling reserve.

When Tony had reached the small home and saw the glow of light in Rose's kitchen, he was grateful. He sighed deeply as he knocked, and Rose answered the door quickly.

"My God," she said in dread when she saw him. He was pale now, nearly frozen, and his overcoat and hat were loaded with wet snow. Rose undressed him hurriedly, rubbing him down with dry towels. She found Tony his robe and poured a shot of brandy into a cup of coffee.

"Drink, drink, Tony," she said, forcefully, "It'll warm you." Tony was near exhaustion. He mumbled that he needed to be in bed, and Rose helped him there. By now Tony had gone into a case of chills and shivers. He could not get warm. Rose fixed two hot-water bottles and placed them wrapped in towels on Tony's frozen lower legs. She got extra blankets out and, in time, came to bed with him, hugging her body to his to provide warmth. "Tony, Tony," she kept saying to him. "You stayed too long . . . too long."

Tony slept pretty well through the night. Rose never left his side until she heard the cry of her baby Joe and the stir of Sam. She quickly fixed their breakfast and got them dressed, telling them to "be quiet," as their father was asleep. While Tony slept, Rose examined the grocery basket he had brought in. She baked her bread for the day and prepared a broth for when Tony would awaken. Then she heard a startling groan from the kitchen. It was Tony. She hurried to the bedroom. He was awake now and examining his lower legs. The frozen flesh had actually been burned by the hot-water bottles. He had not been able to feel it and was shaken as he peeled away dead skin.

"My God, my God," Rose cried in distress. "What did I do?"

"It's okay, Rose," he reassured her, "I'll be all right." She brought him broth and some toast with honey and strong coffee. He would bear those leg scars all of his life.

Tony recovered in a few days, and Rose had learned that hot against cold was the wrong treatment. It had been a good thought, but Tony's thrashing legs, in the throws of his chills, had uncovered the hot-water bottle from their towel wrappings. He had been unable to feel their burning.

The winter had been a long hard one, but the Pagnas had survived it well. Rose learned how to stretch pasta and beans into many meals. Her homemade bread was a staple. When spring came, Tony planted a rather large vegetable garden. Rose, resolved not to weather another such meager winter, read articles on how to can vegetables and fruits. It was during the heat of summer, but she canned quart jars of peaches and pears. Rose also put up quarts of tomatoes, pickles, and several dozen quarts of preserves. With bread, milk, and pasta, they would not go hungry.

One day that summer, while she was wiping her hands on a towel, her face marked with flour and her tiny apron full of dough, Rose heard a knock on the screen door. She was surprised and happy to see "Sa Joe" and welcomed him in. Her father embraced her and kissed her softly on both cheeks. He had taken the streetcar to see his oldest daughter and carried a basket of fresh fruit for her and her family.

"Pa, Pa," Rose was excited. "It's so good to see you."

Rose had freshly baked raisin tarts she had set upon the tablecloth to cool. She quickly got a plate, put one on it, poured hot

Joe and Sam Pagna.

coffee in a cup, and bade her father to sit down. The boys were playing in the yard, and Tony was working at the small grocery store his brother Gaetano still managed to hang onto in Cleveland.

"You are well?" her father asked.

"Yes," Rose assured him, "we are all quite well, Pa . . . *Eh tuo?*" ("and you?"), she spoke in Sicilian.

He drank from his cup slowly and tasted the tart. He gave a small smile and an "umm," assuring Rose the tart was tasty.

It was evident her father had much on his mind. He had aged considerably these past few years. His top, once full of thick and curly hair, was now quite thin and pure white, as was his mustache. His face was somber, and he appeared to Rose not as tall as she had remembered him to be.

"What is it, Pa? What's troubling you?" His daughter's intuition had recognized the symptoms.

"It shows?" he asked.

"It shows," she said softly.

"Your brother, Mike," he began. "Maybe, it's my fault, I don't know, but he is too free, too wild. He is in trouble, Rose. Judge Cabrizzi has asked us to come to his chambers."

"Where is Mike?" Rose asked.

"In the reform school, awaiting trial," was the reply. "He was caught selling bootleg liquor."

Rose threw both hands in the air, "What the hell is wrong with him that he does these things?"

"*Danaro*," her father used the Italian word for money as he rubbed his thumb and forefinger together. "These young ruffians would do anything for money but play the piano inna beer joint," he said in disgust. "Such a talent he has . . . wasted, wasted!" With this he feigned a spit . . . pulling his tongue quickly through his pursed lips.

They sat in silence a moment, and then Rose spoke.

"*Vene Antonino*," she began and quickly changed to English, "When Tony comes home, he will drive us. He now has a car."

It was the third time Rose appeared before Judge Cabrizzi, pleading for her brother. The other charges had not been this serious.

"Please, Judge Cabrizzi," Rose pleaded once more, "sending Mike to reform school will not help him!"

The judge had faced Mike before. He asked Rose and Mike to his chambers and withdrew a dusty violin case from under his desk.

"Play *Gianina Mia*, Mike, miss one note and your ass is in reform school."

Mike knew the song by heart. The judge had requested it twice previously. He would always sit in his swivel leather chair, tilt back his head, and close his eyes. At the end of the romance tune, the judge's eyes would be streaming tears . . . a longing for another time and another day. Judge Cabrizzi's gray head shook slowly.

"Your mother, God rest her soul, Mike, was a saint. You're

breaking her heart wherever she is. . . . Now go . . . and this is your last chance."

If Mike Crimaldi had been less talented or good-looking or intelligent, he would not have been the problem he would become.

He tried. He found work at the local gas station. A fellow worker, jealous of Mike's popularity with women, held up the gas station one night. With five men in the car, one got out and held a sawed-off shotgun at the back of Mike's neck. It was after the gun exploded into his neck and head that Mike swung a powerful right-handed haymaker. It knocked the robber unconscious.

"Please, God . . . please . . . help him. He really is so young and has good in him. Please let him live," Rose pleaded for her misguided brother as he lay between life and death.

Mike did live, and as he matured into his early twenties he would marry twice and divorce twice. Women flocked to him. To hear him play piano and see his style and rhythm all were inclined to like and admire him. But Mike did all the things one hopes one's sons will never do. He gambled, drank, caroused, and did nothing in moderation. In his lifetime he would amass a fortune, only to dissipate it away with foolish actions and rotten luck. It would leave him penniless, crippled from a car accident while in a drunken stupor, and bitter through life's lack of justice. Through it all, though he abused and misused many, he would be long remembered and much loved. He was, after all, Mike, with talent, looks, and charm. The next forty to fifty years would take many different turns for him.

Rose, though she tried to give direction to Mike and each of her sisters, had her own family to worry about. Early in 1932 in the midst of winter, January 28th, Rose bore another son. The tradition of the third child's name fell back to Tony's brother. Again Tony strove for simplicity. So they called me Tom, short for *Gaetano*.

The three sons – Sam, Joe, and I – were the pride of our parents. Seven years spanned us, with four years between Sam and Joe, and three between Joe and me. Sam and Joe strongly resembled our father. All possessed the olive complexion, the coal-black hair, and the piercing black eyes. I favored my mother, was fair, with light-colored hair more brown than black. I had my mother's hazel eyes and her high cheek bones. There was no mistaking the three boys in body build, however. Each son had inherited the big shoulders and barrel chest of their father. Each had a powerful set of arms and legs. We were like peas in a pod to watch run or walk. Tony and Rose delighted in their sons.

When I was only two, Mom found employment in a shirt factory in the city of Cleveland. Here she learned how to form the yokes and shoulders of blouses and shirts. She skillfully formed collars and pockets, cuffs and seams. It was a refinement of an innate skill she would only improve throughout her lifetime. When the family could afford it, Dad bought Mom a second-hand Singer sewing machine. The model had the broad foot pedal where the placement of both feet tipped forward and back, generating the sewing mechanism. Later, when Mom quit the shirt factory, Dad still could find her at work. Her tiny feet on the treadle, making the whirring sound, had become so familiar around our home.

Mom's sisters, different ones at different times in their lives, came to live with us in Parma. It allowed her some freedom from home, and her sisters filled in well as sitters. In this way, Sam, Joe, and I became almost brothers to our not-much-older aunts.

Since Sam had already begun grade school, Mom made shirts and corduroy pants and jackets for all the boys. She took a special pleasure in seeing her threesome well groomed and fitted perfectly in our tailored clothes. It filled her evenings, while Dad and we boys listened to the radio programs and studied.

One evening, Dad had news for Mom. He himself was excited at the prospect, but he didn't know how she would take to the idea he wanted to present. Moving to another town thirty-five miles away could upset her. Sam was reading a book, Joe was listening to a radio program, and I was on the floor next to Joe. Mom was occupied in the kitchen at the sewing machine. From his chair in the living room, Dad could peer easily through the open doorway at the intent Mom. He studied her as he often did, when she was unaware. He surveyed the mighty mite with her boundless energy and her thirst for doing things. He noticed a thin white line of hair that began from her forehead through the middle of the complete head. He watched her nimble fingers manipulate the cloth she held and form flawless seams on whatever she was sewing. He dearly loved her face, untouched by rouge or powder. It was radiant, a slight hue of pink on her cheeks. When she was happiest, he could hear a light guttural sound coming from her. She actually hummed music to the hum of her machine. After a while she finished the garment she had been working on and put away her sewing things. It was time for the boys to get ready for bed. She and Dad would have their evening coffee now and either talk or listen to the radio news before retiring themselves.

Now was the time to approach the subject, he thought.

"Rose," he began, "would it be possible that one of your sisters would move in if I were gone for awhile?"

"You leaving me?" she asked teasingly.

"No . . . no." He was embarrassed at such a thought.

"What's on your mind, Tony?" Words were never minced by the Sicilians. They just said whatever was on their minds, whether it be in anger, humor, or normal conversation.

"There is a place in Akron, Rose," he began again. "It is a small shoe-repair shop, and a man could make a good living there."

"How far is Akron?" she asked.

"It is about thirty-five miles away," he responded. "It takes about an hour and a half to drive it."

"Would we still live in Parma?"

"For a while," he answered, "until we see how it goes."

"Will you be your own boss?" she asked. She well knew the importance of all this to her husband.

"Yes."

"Do you want that?"

"Yes."

"Then do it, Tony," she said much to his relief. He loved her sense of adventure. She hesitated at nothing. "Do what needs to be done," she finished.

Dad closed the deal by pouring all of his cash into the first month's rent and the last month held in escrow. He would live with Donna Theresa during the week and drive to Parma on the weekends.

The day he opened the shop as his own was a day of mixed emotions. He sensed a fear of failure, for all he owned went into it, but his spirits soared knowing it was his own. After all of the negotiations had been made – a new sign, leather and rubber heels for inventory – he invested his last seven dollars into change for his cash register. He did not even hold back lunch money or gas money. He reasoned that he would sleep in the shop if need be.

When time had come for the new sign for his shop to be painted, he had already given it much thought. It was his own special code. In America 'A' and the number '1' were significant letters and numbers. An A-1 job was meant to be first class. The A stood for Anthony and the #1 would represent God to watch over him.

He had not meant to put his own initial before the symbol of God, but 1-A didn't sound as classy, and he knew God would understand. A-1 Shoe Repair became a fixture in East Akron.

Though Dad had several tough months when work had been slow, he had shrewdly calculated the turn of the economy with the new president Franklin Delano Roosevelt. When he first heard the shop was for sale, he noticed its location. It was not in the heart of the city but in a newer development. Across the street and up the hill from him were giant buildings that spanned a dozen city blocks. It was the Goodyear Tire and Rubber Company. Automobiles were more and more in demand. The economy would turn, the factory workers would need shoes. There must be tires for cars. He had been right and fought through three months of shaky income and began to prosper.

At the end of one year, Dad had saved enough for a small down payment on a house. He brought Mom to Akron with him for one week, and after closing his shop in the evening, they would drive to look at neighborhoods.

Mom was very excited at the prospect. She loved everything new. It was a forward step toward all she desired. To the east of Akron, up beyond the Goodyear factory, were several developments where Goodyear had financed homes for their executives.

It was labeled, simply, Goodyear Heights. These homes were modest but better than most, and it was one of these they found, one not too far from my Dad's shop and near a grade school called Seiberling. It was a simple two-story frame house with a small front porch that was roofed. It rested halfway up the side of a mile-long hill that led to the grade school. It was to this school that she sent her boys, and it was here where she began redoing her first.

Chapter 5
The Steady Drop Fills the Bucket

Neither Cleveland nor Parma held any special charm for Tony Pagna, other than it had been the birthplace of his sons and where he had met his wife. If it had not been for Judge Cabrizzi, he could easily have been jailed there.

It was early 1932, the year of my birth. I was still being breast fed, but Mom's milk soured. The only food acceptable was a prescription formula sold at the pharmacy. Without money, Dad was at a loss where to turn. The story owner had refused him credit. Adopting what both he and my mother had sworn as an unspoken motto . . . Dad did what he felt he had to do. He reached into his bureau drawer, withdrew his .45, and went into the pharmacy.

"This is not a robbery," he said calmly. "I only want a week's ration of that formula, and I'll pay you at the end of the week." The druggist denied him, and Dad pointed the .45 at the man's head.

When Judge Cabrizzi heard about the incident, he dismissed the two attorneys and brought the owner into his chambers with my Dad. The judge heard the druggist's story, and then he allowed my father to speak. The stories were the same. Inflamed, Judge Cabrizzi said to the druggist, "This man is not a thief! Can't you see that? Did he rob you of any money or any other things? Did he not ask you first for credit? If it were your baby crying for food, would you have done the same?"

The druggist whimpered a "yes" to the last question.

"If the money is that important," the judge said, "I'll pay you."

"No," the man refused. "I was foolish and angry," he said with shame. "YOU are right, Judge. This man is not a thief." It never came to trial. There was no record, and Dad did pay the pharmacy owner back.

Cleveland and Parma were behind them now, and a new job and home gave our parents hope in Goodyear Heights. Not long after they moved what little furniture they had into the home, Mom began her plan of attack.

Working systematically, one room at a time, she first painted and wallpapered. Where there was natural wood, she would refinish. After painting and wallpapering each room, she set about to make curtains and matching drapes and bedspreads.

Visiting sisters, nieces, and neighbors marveled at her taste and ability. They liked her simplicity of pattern and the light modern colors she chose. Many of the older aunts and relatives seemed secretly envious. One by one, each room would be carpeted as they could afford it. For the kitchen, she bought linoleum and installed it meticulously by herself.

With each improvement our parents enhanced the value of this home. In the warm summer air Dad painted the outside and trimmed a neat lawn. In the summer evenings they sat on their porch swing proud of their achievements.

During their third year in this first home, Mom's sister Ann called her from Cleveland. Mary had been struck several times by Ralph Comito, her husband. Hearing the report, Mike beat Ralph within an inch of his life.

"No one," his hot anger vented itself on Ralph, "lays one hand on my sister while I'm alive!" It was the best of Mike, and he meant it thoroughly. Mike then took Mary to her home and helped her pack.

"I'll never live with that bastard again!" she said. Mike then took her to the only place he knew to go, to his sister Rose's.

The family made room for Mary, and when the divorce was final, she opened a beauty shop with an attached apart-

Here I am as a ring bearer in 1938, aged 6.

ment in Cuyahoga Falls, about eleven miles from the house. Shortly thereafter, Dixie came to Cuyahoga Falls, found a job in a nice restaurant as a waitress, and the two sisters shared an apartment. Dixie was four months' pregnant at the time; her fiance had been killed in a motorcycle accident.

Mom's father and her brother Mike stayed in Cleveland. Also remaining in Cleveland were her sister Ann (now Ann Greer), Flora (now Flora Weiss), and Betty, working and single.

When sister Dixie had her baby, it was Mom who cared for the child, named Donna Marie. Dixie had assumed her dead fiance's name for the sake of her daughter. It was always to be Dixie and Donna Cramer. Donna lived with our family for much of her youth and was known and treated as a sister by my brothers and me.

Eventually, Dixie became more established, working for an Italian restaurant that thrived off of its location near the Goodrich and General factories. Later she was promoted to the night manager. Dixie, Donna, and Mary had standing invitations to our home on weekends and holidays.

Flora too had become enmeshed with a man she had planned to marry. But at the news of her pregnancy, he had abandoned her. Flora too made the move to her sister Rose's home. Flora's son Carl became a brother to Sam, Joe, and me. Flora worked at the same restaurant as Dixie but maintained the Crimaldi name. When she was able to realize life on her own terms, Flora met a man who dearly loved her, and they married. His name was Weiss. Nathan Weiss was Jewish, a good man, and he adopted Carl and gave him his surname.

In their own time and for their own personal reasons, each sister had her turn at being a member of the Pagna family. Dad never raised an objection. He had watched them grow from tiny children. They were as much his family as they were hers. The sisters always remained close, and they were never judgmental or critical over what one or the other had done with their lives. They were always there for one another. Mom loved Dad for many reasons, but she loved him most of all for his love and care for her brother and sisters.

Mom knew while they were all growing up that there was too

little supervision outside the home. Each of her sisters were attractive people. She also knew the world would attack each one.

In her whirlwind way, my mother busied herself with family and home. She had little patience with the squabbling between five-year-old Joe and two-year-old me. We were pretty good kids, but she knew well we would not, or could not, be expected to be saints. Only her sense of humor saved her from much irritation when we argued with one another. When she had time, and before she made us take naps, she would tell us a story or maybe rock us in her rocker while singing an old ballad.

One particular day, she was especially tired of the whining and crying. Joe teased me, and I cried. Mom yelled out a warning. "I'll get the broom," she said to Joe threateningly. In defiance, Joe whacked me across the back and made a run from the kitchen, through the living room, and up the staircase. He was headed for the safety he felt under his bed. When whacked, I let out a scream. It was enough for Mom, and she scurried for her broom. When I saw Joe running, I followed him only a few steps behind. Our little butts scrambled up the staircase as fast as possible. We were sure Mom was in hot pursuit. When we reached the top step, she appeared with the broom in front of us. She smiled at our obvious surprise.

"She's a witch," Joe screamed out. "She can fly." Neither of us saw or heard her pass us on the staircase.

Laughing, Joe ran by her and under his bed. Mom followed with the broom. If she poked the handle at Joe, his favorite trick was to grab it. He felt safe. This day, Mom had the patience and the time. She winked at me, then made pronounced false steps downward to the kitchen and then silently crept back up and hid outside of Joe's room. I stood in the hallway giggling at the scene.

About two or three minutes had passed since Joe had heard Mom descending the staircase. He emerged from the room, entering the hallway. In an instant he felt a solid smack on his behind. Mom yelled at him in a kindly way.

"The wicked witch strikes again!" We all began to laugh. Mom stopped her household work and grabbed us to savor the fleeting moment. She sat on the top step and hugged us, one under each arm.

"Mom," Joe said seriously. "How'd you get ahead of us upstairs?"

"Magic," she laughed easily as she said it, "I can fly!"

Until my father had come along, my mother had never known and been shown much affection or attention. She was trying to show it to her boys because she knew well the importance of those early years . . . plus it was one of the big things on her someday list. She dearly loved all of us and making our home comfortable, clean, and orderly was a way she could show her love best.

"The family," both Mom and Dad said often, "is everything."

Both Sam and Joe played in the Seiberling grade school band. Sam played the accordion and Joe the drums. Aware that Seiberling grade school was a tough neighborhood for us, Dad worried about our ability to take care of ourselves. At Christmas one year he had bought us boxing gloves. He would spar with Sam, Sam would spar with Joe, and Joe would punch the hell out of me.

"There's a pecking order," Joe explained.

"And some are bigger peckers than others!" I thought to myself.

"Be careful, my friend," Dad spoke to Joe. "One day he's going to grow up, and you'll want to make friends." Dad could tell that I, as the youngest, would probably grow up to be the biggest of them all.

My father delighted in games of physical skill with his sons. Evenings he wrestled with us on the floor, and sometimes he would let us have tiny victories. Our favorite games were Indian arm wrestling, and he would show us "his subtle trick." Also, we would Indian leg wrestle. With our feet pointing in opposite directions, we would lie on our backs side-by-side on the floor. Three times we lifted our inside legs. On the third, we would interlock legs and try to topple the other without letting one's back leave the floor.

Dad knew many games of strength and balance, reflex and poise. He taught us all he knew. The favorite game of all, because size did not control who actually won, was the reflex game. Two contenders stood face-to-face about two feet apart, their open palms facing outward, chest high. The object was to thrust your hands in the other's palms and jar him off balance. One slip or movement of the feet and you lost. The great equalizer was this: Should you thrust and the opponent move his palms to avoid you, and you touch him, you lost again. We became experts. Our hand dexterity, eye and hand coordination, balance, and reflex were tested constantly.

One last game we played was very simple. Two contenders faced one another, one with palms up at the waist, the other with palms down resting on those of the other. The bottom player was the "striker." The object was to move quickly from the bottom position and strike the back of the hand of the contender on top. So long as you made contact, you continued as the "striker." It easily could sting the backs of your hands, and quickness became all important. We became very good at these games.

Mom asked Dad one evening, "Where did you learn all those games?"

"As a boy growing up," he responded. "We didn't have toys, so we would invent games of skill and balance to have contests."

"Is that also where you learned to box?" She was against the boxing-gloves idea.

"Rose," he said patiently. "The priest that raised me, Father Trivassano, used to say to me as a child, 'Don't be a tough, Tony, just be tough! Otherwise, the whole damned world beats up on you.'"

"Do you think our kids will be tough but not toughs?" she asked.

Dad laughed, "After Father Trivassano became the boxing champion at Yale, he never had to fight again. When he taught me to box, he said it was to know always, but to use only when forced. Our boys will never be bullies, Rose, but there are many bullies they will meet in life."

Dad could not have known how prophetic he would be, nor did he consider that many of the bullies in life were not necessarily physical ones. Always there would be politics and power figures. Always there would be the petty prejudices of others.

Each of us grew strong, and each had his own separate personality. Mom admired these separate qualities. Sam would

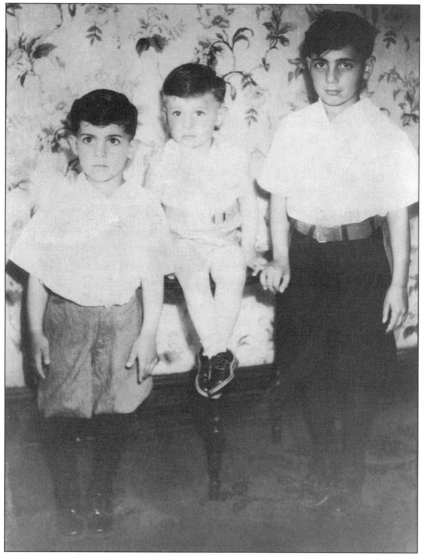

The three Pagna boys in 1936: Joe, Tom, and Sam.

never be trouble throughout his life. As the eldest, he was held in high esteem. His judgment and actions at school, at home, or in Dad's shop, were without flaw. Sam seemed to sense his position of leadership for Joe and me and reacted accordingly. He was very gifted musically but was far from being a "sissy." His grades were honor-roll status, and his behavior excellent. Everyone thought well of "Sammy."

Joe, on the other hand, had rebellion in his eyes and his actions. Joe was not afraid to step off the beaten path. In many ways, he was like his mother – full of adventure and daring, hard to tame. Whatever Joe set out to do, he did well.

When Mom thought about me, I caused her to chuckle. I was still in the clumsy stage. My little thighs and barrel chest toppled over furniture and tripped up steps (and sometimes myself) pretty easily. Mom could readily see, however, that I laughed easily and that one day her chubby chunk would take on his own personality. At this stage, I could only emulate the two older brothers I adored.

The three brothers always walked back and forth to school together. After school Joe and I would wait for Sam. It was not an order, but Dad had told Sam, "They're your brothers . . . the best friends you'll ever have! Watch over them and they in turn, will watch over you."

Within the next four years, our family moved at least six more times. We always sold at a profit and, most always, we stayed in the Goodyear Heights area. On one particular street, we occupied four different locations. At each stop, Mom became more daring with her changes. She realized early on that one did not always need cash to bring about improvements. Through the years, she knew and made friends with carpenters, plumbers, electricians, and painters. Whenever she took on a new project, her ploy was always the same. She was negotiating.

"Jake," she knew and called each by their first names, "What'll it take to add on one more bedroom over there, a bay window here?"

Jake laughed as he asked the inevitable question, "Is this a cash deal, Rosie?"

"Hell, no!" she laughed in return. "Your talent for mine! You do those remodeling things and I'll make your wife new draperies and bedspreads."

"Damn it, Rose, I ain't made a nickel on you yet."

"Well, that's the way it is when people don't have cash. Do I have to find another carpenter or do we have a deal?"

Jake thought just a moment, saw that the wall she wanted removed was not a weight-bearing one, turned, sighed, "I must be nuts . . . deal!"

Mom never fooled herself about such things. It was Dad's day-in-and-day-out work, the steady flow of income that came from the shoe shop, that allowed her such freedom.

Shortly after a recent move to a quiet neighborhood and nestled in a bungalow surrounded by tall maple trees, Dad felt sure his Rose was settled in for good. He had not minded her moves; they had all been improvements, and their equity had grown in each case. Oh, he had fumed a few times when she bought furniture on credit. She would hide it somewhere in the house, wait till it was paid for, and then place it for all to see. For the most part, he was on to her most common hiding places. If he came home and saw one of the sofas "kitty corner" across a cornered wall, he knew Mom's new purchase was hidden behind the sofa. He nicknamed her, "Kitty-corner Rose."

"No more of that 'bullcrap,' Rose," he threatened. "I want to know when we buy something new."

One Saturday evening, after a long day, Dad pulled into the driveway of the bungalow. He was looking forward to the comfort of the bungalow and his family. As he entered the door, a strange sight appeared. None of the furniture was his and Mom's. There was a strange couple and their children dining where his own dining table had been.

"Am I crazy?" he thought, "Did I enter into the wrong bungalow?" After all, the family had lived there for only a few short months.

The woman of the family arose and greeted Dad. She said warmly, "You're Tony Pagna, aren't you?"

He grunted a "Yes." He was confused.

"We bought this place from Rose last week and only today moved in." Dad saw the unpacked boxes lining the walls. Before he could ask, the kind lady pointed across the street. "Rose moved this morning too . . . across the street into that apartment house."

Dad's anger mounted as he backed his car out of the driveway. His balding head, a remnant of the scarlet fever he had as a child, was perspiring. Once he entered the apartment complex,

Mom was there to meet him. He said nothing as she brought his supper to the table. As he ate in silence Mom said simply and confidently, "Do you want to hear?"

He looked at her in amazement and tried to keep his anger from showing itself.

"You damned right I wanna hear."

Mom unfolded the story. It was not until the morning when all was finalized. If she had not acted on the opportunity as she had done, she would have lost the deal.

"And what deal is that?"

"We sold the bungalow for $3,500 more than we paid for it, and I bought this apartment house for exactly what we earned from the bungalow. We live in the bottom two apartments that we'll enjoin and . . ." Mom paused here as she knew well it was the trump card . . . "we collect $110 a month for rent from each of the two upstairs apartments."

Dad was absolutely flabbergasted at the speed that she had made the move and completed the deal, but most importantly their income increased $220 extra a month, plus the value of the apartment house as an investment would always be a source of income.

"Still mad?"

"What a damned fool I am," was Dad's retort. "Do whatever you want to do, Rose. You make more in a week of business than my whole shop in a year." He was sincere.

"Tony," she said softly. "It's the steady drop in the bucket that fills it! You taught me that, and I know I can't do things if we don't have that cushion."

He drank his cold beer and winked at her, "Apartment owners, huh?" He had eaten now, his temper subsided, and the good fortune and judgment of his wife invoked his favorite remark: "Who's better than us?"

Our neighbor was loaded with children similar in age to all of us. Street games abounded. Aside from kick the can and hide and seek, the more serious seasonal games of tag football, softball, and basketball were played in the street every evening.

When there were too few to play a game, other innovative games were substituted. My favorite was a game they called "pickle." It was an imaginary second to third base steal where the third baseman and second baseman tried to run down or pitch out a base runner. It was the challenge of stopping and starting, faking one way and sprinting the other, outguessing the baseman. Only rarely did I get put out.

When the neighborhood got serious about football, which was on the weekends, we migrated to a vacant lot that had patches of grass and played tackle. I was always the youngest, but they let me play, since I could compete and was physically as strong as most of them.

As football season faded into basketball, the neighborhood kids gathered every Saturday morning on the clay courts behind various garages. Here we would play a game of three-on-three for the first ten baskets. The winners had to win by a margin of two baskets. There were no fouls unless you called one on yourself. Winners held the court, losers waited their turn. Again, Joe and I took part in all these neighborhood games. Though we were both short in terms of height, we had unusually quick reflexes and were ball hawks on defense and always good team players.

But suddenly Joe, now 13 and in the eighth grade, was refusing to go to school.

"How long are you staying home? You've got to go to school! Tell me what happened." Mom was concerned.

"I'm not going back, Mom."

"What if I tell your dad. Then what?"

"I'm not going back."

Mom was puzzled. Joe was very bright and never had problems in the classroom. He was holding something back. Joe missed three days of school. Dad was unaware that Joe was staying home because Mom had not told. Finally, she explained to Dad, but still didn't know the reason.

"He won't tell me anything, but he acts as if he is afraid of something or someone."

So Dad called me into the bedroom.

"You love your brother?" he asked earnestly. "Help me to help him." I told the story I knew. It was a gym class, and we were on the playground. Joe and a black boy his size got into a fight.

Seiberling grade school was almost half black enrollment. It never seemed a problem before. There was one male white teacher, Mr. Reynolds, a tall red-headed mean type of man who was the gym teacher. He pulled the two fighters into the gym and made them put on boxing gloves.

Dad interjected, "But Joe is a very good fighter, and you say this boy was his size?"

"Yes, Dad," I went on. "But this wasn't just Joe and the boy. The black girls surrounding them in the gym would rush out and grab Joe's arms while the other kid hit him. It wasn't fair."

"Doesn't the teacher make it fair?"

"No. Joe yelled at him, 'That's not fair!' But he yells back, 'Shut up, you little spaghetti strangler, and fight.'" Dad's eyes narrowed as he began to see the picture.

"And then?"

"Well, finally the black boy says, 'I've had enough' and Joe points to the gym teacher and says, 'you cheating bastard!' Mr. Reynolds carries a little shredded hose he whacks you with, and he whacked Joe a few times on the back of his legs. You know Joe. He can't stand this but what can he do? He pulled off his shoe and threw it, hitting Mr. Reynolds in the back of the head, and then ran all the way home in one shoe. He won't tell Mom or you. I feel bad you're making me tell you."

"Don't worry, Tom, you're only trying to help your brother."

In the morning Dad had his coffee but did not go to work. Joe was terrified and didn't know what to do. Dad entered our bedroom and said to both Joe and me, "Today, I'm walking with you to school."

It was winter, and Dad put on his big overcoat. Mom's mouth fell open as she watched him pull the top dresser drawer open. He picked up his .45 pistol, put a clip in his pocket, and stuffed the .45 in his belt line, right above his buckle. It was easy to see when the coat was open. He buttoned the coat.

Mom was about to say something, but Dad's eyes shot a menacing look at her, and he said quietly to her, "No one lays a hand on our kids!"

He held our hands and together we strolled through the snow. He said to Joe, "Your brother would never tell on you, but I asked him to. We'll straighten this all out."

The school principal was an elderly woman whom knew Dad quite well. He greeted her politely, and we all sat down. Mr. Reynolds was sent for. From the moment he entered, his voice was sharp and accusing, and he pointed to Joe saying, "There are high gray walls waiting for that kid!"

Dad turned and faced the giant redhead and opened his coat so that the principal couldn't see, but Mr. Reynolds could.

"I suggest," Dad said, measuredly, "you sit down and be silent. You can talk when I'm done." Mr. Reynolds squatted on a chair as though he was melting and never opened his mouth. Dad spoke to the principal at length, and all was well. Joe and I frolicked and skipped all the way home.

It was a point of pride for our Dad to arrive at Sunday Mass with his entire family in tow. But on a particular Sunday in the summer of 1940, a milestone was reached.

The priest was issuing a bombastic sermon on the evils of birth control. Mom and Dad loved each of their children and secretly became concerned with how many a family should have in order that they were all raised properly. The priest pounded the theme of "sin" and "sinful ways." Dad did not feel guilt at wanting to stop. He mentally took exception to the tirade. Only the week before, the colorless priest had ripped his congregation for their meager donations to finance the school bus. It was not the religion he had remembered from his days in Sicily. He was told that those who practiced the sin of birth control could not partake of communion. Dad became so angered at what he accepted as a personal attack that he decided never to attend again. In his heart, he had loved God. He knew his God was present whenever he invoked His name.

When we emerged from the church, and Dad had everyone seated in the car, he said softly to Mom, "This is the last time I will come here." Mom understood.

That same day was the scheduled annual picnic for shoemakers. Every year a new site was selected, and the attendance was increasing annually. Mom packed a picnic lunch, and we drove out to the fairgrounds where the picnic was taking place. There were rides of every sort, music, dancing, games and contests of every kind. We walked leisurely along, taking each new sight in view.

We stopped where a rather large crowd had gathered. In the middle of a circle of people was what appeared to be a huge wooden flagpole.

A tall broad-shouldered, youthful man, with powerful arms and tattoos on his arms, was barking at the crowd, "Win a box of cigars! Win a dozen roses for the lady!"

We stood and watched nearly a dozen strong-looking men hit a sledgehammer of wood on a platform. This would catapult a metal birdie up the pole from "Weakling." Only the young man that ran the concession was able to send the birdie all the way to ring the bell where it said "Muscles."

We urged our father to try, but he was uncertain. We didn't know what fear of failure was, and we didn't expect if of him. Only at Mom's request did he decide to try.

He removed his sweater, spit into his hands, got a look of determination on his face and swung a mighty thump. The steel bird lifted like a gun shot and easily rang the bell.

While watching the others, Dad found the trick, a subtle one. He realized that only the big man knew it. Just as a shoemaker pounds a nail, a square blow is deadened. One must hit only the front half of the six-inch stump. Dad grabbed the mallet with only his left arm and banged the birdie, then he swiftly switched to only his right hand and banged the birdie again.

The fellow in charge said, "Enough! Enough! Two boxes of cigars and one dozen roses is the limit!"

Dad gave the roses to Mom and lit up one of the cigars. His chest fully inhaled, he winked at the three of us, and said with a smile, "Who's better than us?"

Chapter 6
By the Sweat of One's Brow

As we boys grew steadily, our father brought not only Sam but Joe and me into his shop. We especially were helpful on Saturdays. It afforded Mom time alone.

We'd leave home to open the shoe shop at 6:00 AM, the long day would not end until 9:00 PM. Sam helped Dad on the jack and they prepared between them, easily fifty pair of half soles and heels. Joe and I were at the shoeshine stand all day. Actually a line had formed in waiting, and each of our four leather-backed chairs on top of the white marble stand was full. We were very good at what we did and got little rest.

Both Joe and I created a crossing hands style of brushing that looked very intricate. In reality it was quite simple if one had the proper timing. After each fifteen-cent shine (more often than not we were handed quarters or halves and told to keep the change), we pitched all our earnings into a cigar box beneath the shine stand chairs.

On one particular Saturday, an old friend walked in on Dad. It seemed he was now living in Akron and stopped weekly for a shoe shine. Sometimes he would sit on Joe's side and sometimes on mine. He was a tall sinewy man dressed rather well, with only a little hair on his head and narrow squinted eyes. He was tan and very quiet. Though it angered me, Dad whispered as he always did when the man appeared, "No charge."

As he had many times before, the man got down from the stand and reached into his pocket. I saw the gesture and could only force myself to utter, "No Charge." The man smiled an alarming smile – all of his teeth were gold. He nodded a thank you to Dad and exited.

"How come we can't charge that guy, Dad?" I asked half in disgust.

"Because," he said forcefully, "it is no charge when I say 'no charge.'"

When the rush settled down, and we had free time, Joe and I both leaned against the counter behind which our father worked.

"Why are all of his teeth gold?"

"It was," Dad said shrewdly, "the first gift he bought himself when he got a job in this country."

"What's his name, Dad?" Joe asked.

"Carpenter, Mr. John Carpenter. He's an old friend."

As we traveled home that Saturday night, a tired Joe and I took up the back seat of Dad's Packard. Thinking us asleep, Dad and Sam spoke of things that recently had been on Sam's mind.

In hushed tones, Dad said to Sam, "Sure I know what it is to have these feelings, Sam. Every man has them at your age, but to make a point, let me tell you a story the Italians tell."

"Do you have to?" Sam was half kidding his father about the many, many Italians stories told to us.

"Ah," Dad said, understanding his son's reluctance. "It's a short story and makes a good point, okay?"

"Okay, Dad."

"There was this little puppy dog with his waggly tail. He's happy and nobody bothers him, and he don't bother nobody. One day this puppy dog, he falls asleep next to the railroad track. Pretty soon comes a train. Zing . . . off comes the puppy's tail. Right away the puppy looks to see his tail and zing again, off comes his head."

"I don't get it," the confused Sam said after Dad had purposely paused.

"Well, it's how you say . . . a moral. It says don't lose your head over a little piece of tail!"

With this Sam let out a roar. Joe and I also began laughing, since we had heard the whole discussion.

"Oh, no," Dad laughed at us. "You guys are not asleep, huh? Well, that's okay. You can never learn these things too young!"

It was Sunday morning, and Dad, Joe, and I, were working in our garden. Dad put nearly an acre into vegetables. Sam was excused because he was tearing down the engine of an old Model T he had just purchased.

At this point in my early life I was sure that any word Joe spoke was both true and law. Blind loyalty in Joe's judgment guided me. Being older and more sophisticated than I was, Joe learned how to hold grudges, a talent that as yet had escaped me.

While hard at work hoeing and weeding our one-acre plot of

garden with our father, the neighbor across the street in this rural area was what we came to know as a real "hayseed" named Conrad. He was twice our size but the same age. He had foul habits and a foul mouth. He was a momma's boy who appeared never to bathe. Joe and I had little to do with him nor he us, except walking to and from the school bus stop. His mother informed him to stay clear of the "wops" and told him, "niggers are better'n wops." Conrad imitated the motion of throwing wet spaghetti on the floor with a loud-sounding "wop." In a fit of rage, Joe went for Conrad with a B-B gun he had hidden in the garden furrows. To run after Conrad was useless; he'd only run into his house with his nauseating and yet approving mother. Joe figured the B-B gun would travel faster. Dad, sensing Joe's plan, got to the gun first and planted his foot firmly on it.

"This isn't the place or the way or the time. Be patient!"

He told us that those were all insults he heard all of his life when first coming to America, but that his actions, not words, won the respect of people. "Earn his respect!" my father told us, but we didn't understand.

It worked on Joe . . . but in a negative fashion, and he plotted a deep revenge to "earn respect."

We three boys slept in the same room. Since Sam was the eldest, he merited a single bed of his own, and Joe and I doubled in a double bed. We always argued over the invisible line down the middle, and both would work to get our rumps above the other as our backs were against one another. It was a little boy's game. When we got arranged, we'd say our prayers silently but would end them with a loud "done" when we had finished. It was the signal to the other two that when all three "dones" were heard, we were free to talk.

We talked awhile, and Sam rolled facing the wall bidding us "goodnight."

It was then Joe said, deeply serious, "We gotta kill Conrad!" Though it seemed drastic, I really couldn't comprehend "kill," but I agreed with Joe.

"How?" I asked with naivete.

"We'll make friends first."

I didn't get the plan at all. Summer faded and ushered in autumn, but the autumn months became fleeting and winter was soon at its zenith. We played snowballs forts and had huge snow fights in the neighborhood. Everyone would pull each other on sleds and play ice hockey with a basketball for a puck and broomsticks for hockey sticks. I forgot that we hated Conrad long ago and was quite sure we were now all good friends.

Then spring came again, and while in bed – after "done" – Joe told me it was time to kill Conrad. He unfolded the plot. Since we all appeared good friends, Joe would invite Conrad back to the old creek and pond. Our plan was to saw a hole in the ice (let Conrad do it), and Joe would throw a rope over the overhang tree branch next to the pond. It was my job to throw the lasso over Conrad's head and Joe would set the noose with a mighty pull. The two of us would then hang Conrad. A simple plan! Even Conrad's mother, by now, was as fooled as I was and thought we were all playmates and friends. She smiled as we took fishing gear and equipment to make camp at the old pond.

All went according to plan. Conrad sawed ice. Joe threw the rope over the tree branch, and I put the noose over Conrad's head. Both Joe and I pulled as hard as we could but could not get the pleading, sobbing, and choking Conrad up off the ground.

Being innovative and able to make quick adjustments, Joe announced, "Aw, hell, let's just make him apologize." By a vote of 2 to 0, Conrad was released, but first came the humble apology and then the promise sworn in "his mother's name," he'd never call Joe and me names again. It was a deal.

Joe was elated and felt triumph. Needless to say Conrad sprinted ahead of us to his home. We saw little of him thereafter. It would be years later when Joe met Conrad through business. Conrad had missed several loan payments. Joe made the collection call personally and seeing the 6' 4", 270-pound bumpkin, Joe said, "Hope you don't hold grudges!"

Later that same spring Mom and Dad put the farm up for sale. It seemed too far out for us and from Dad's work, plus Sam was near graduation from East High School. Our house sold easily and at a nice profit. Our parents bought a very nice two-storied home with four bedrooms two blocks from their apartment house, but on the same street. The farm had been a change of pace, but Mom missed the comforts of an indoor bathroom, hot and cold running water, and really never cared if she ever saw another chicken.

For nearly the previous two years, Sam was involved in forming a ten-piece swing band. By now he was very adept at the piano and the accordion. Each Wednesday night, his high-school-aged musicians entered our basement. Mom made it into a wonderful recreation room. Sammy built ten plywood panels that were beautifully sanded and painted into music stands. As they faced the audience, one could easily make out a large silver musical note just above a scrolled "S.P." The notes and the initials in silver, sparkled against the deep blue of the music stands background.

Sam was enraptured with the big-band sounds of Glenn Miller, Tommy Dorsey, Woody Herman, and countless others. So great was his desire to duplicate their sound and maybe add some of his own innovations, he spent his hard-earned dollars investing in arrangements. Each musician Sam invited to the orchestra was hand-picked. Most of them were from East High School, but several were from other areas. All could read music.

Every Wednesday the band rehearsed in our basement. As the first sounds of the music traveled the neighborhood, neighbors would migrate toward our house. The younger boys and girls would lie on the ground and peer through our basement windows and view the performers. Older adults stood on the sidewalk or driveway and kept the rhythm by tapping a foot or clapping their hands. Some of the teens paired up and jitterbugged in the driveway and street. It always reminded me of a scene in any old Judy Garland and Mickey Rooney movie.

Times were good again! Factories were going full blast, unemployment was down, and the music mirrored the optimism of our world.

It was early in the spring of 1940, when Mom alerted Dad that she was once again pregnant. She just knew it would be a girl. The two of them didn't expect the newborn that far after nine-year-old me; still they were thrilled with the prospect.

In September of the same year, Theresa Pagna, named for Dad's mother, was born. Mom called her Terry from the day of her birth. It had a modern touch, Mom felt, and still it honored Donna Theresa.

Terry was a black-eyed, black-curly-haired beauty. More than with any of her three sons, Mom patiently took time to spend with her only daughter, spending an easy hour rocking Terry and singing light-hearted melodies. For the only time in her life, she "billed and cooed" and spoke baby talk.

Each of Mom's sisters laid claim to this daughter as her own.

It was the dead of winter now, and we were home for Christmas vacation when pneumonia attacked Terry. Mom felt her four-month-old baby's head in near panic as a fever raged within Terry. It would be at least an hour before the doctor could be there, and she became frightened and impatient. Joe and I never left our mother's sight. It was our sister's paleness and lack of movement that scared us. Sam was with Dad at the shoe shop, so Joe and I knew instinctively that we had to be at Mom's beck and call.

Pneumonia had taken Mom's youngest sister Augustine, and it had also killed her second child, Joseph. She could not lose the fear such memories brought to her. She sat in her rocking chair, holding tiny, limp Terry in her arms. She said as she rocked, "Pray to the Blessed Mother to spare your sister's life!"

Immediately and obediently, Joe and I took separate chairs in our living room and started our childlike prayers to Mother Mary.

"Hail Mary," over and over and over again.

We were jolted from our prayers by a shriek from Mom that would have awakened a corpse. So piercing and agonizing was Mom's scream that we became startled with fear. We hadn't any idea why Mom screamed or what she was doing.

She yelled out, "Oh, my God . . . she's going into convulsions!" With this, she quickly rose from her rocker and sprinted up the staircase, clutching Terry.

Afraid and startled, Joe and I followed Mom cautiously and heard her frantically pleading, "Please . . . oh please, God . . . not this one! Not this one!" Her eyes fairly overflowed with tears as they splashed down her cheek bones. All the while, she had been carrying Terry to the bathtub. She began running lukewarm water in it and was dipping Terry's entire body into the tub. We thought to ourselves even at our tender age, "Where did our mother learn to do what she was doing?"

After a ten-minute immersion, Terry's convulsive spasms dispersed. The crisis was past for now and the doctor came to the door shortly afterwards.

After Dr. Arapakis examined Terry thoroughly and administered medication, he gently laid her in her cradle, and she slept long and hard.

"Rose," he said compassionately, "not one in fifty people would have known what to do for convulsions! You saved you child's life!"

Mom was exhausted. A look of tired knowing came across3 her face. "I watched," she said wearily, "my youngest sister and my second child die. I remembered what I saw the midwives and neighbors do to try to save them."

"Thank God for that, Rose," Dr. Arapakis was touched deeply.

"I do, I do, Doctor and . . . even the boys helped me pray," she nodded at the two of us – wide eyed and mystified.

Joe and I were impressed deeply in that hour and in that day. Forever, in our minds, would we hold a knowledge few seemed to discover in a lifetime. We knew for certain that prayer was powerful and that the Blessed Mother had heard ours. Mom always said, "God didn't make death. The devil did!"

Terry would suffer pneumonia every winter for the next three, but Mom knew in her heart that this one had truly been spared. In Italian lore, anyone "spared" was thought to have a purpose and destiny designed by God. Mom fought from falling prey to the old ways and superstitions but still could not help wondering the destiny of her baby daughter.

Sammy's band began playing for high-school dances throughout the city and the surrounding area. They became more and more sophisticated and polished. They managed a sound that was highly professional, and from that sound they began to reap monetary rewards.

The imaginative Sam withheld a bit of pay from each performer, and with this money, he purchased matching gold blazers to be worn with a white shirt and dark tie over dark blue trousers. They looked and played quite professionally, and Sam shortly opened his band's bank account, setting aside money for travel and new music and uniforms. He arranged all the music now, played it, rehearsed it, led the band, tended the bookings and payroll, and kept their books.

Sammy's band, with Sammy, far right, and Joe, next to him, are seen in this studio shot. They were true professionals even at this age.

Joe took drum lessons from the fourth grade onward. Though he was not sharp at reading music, Joe owned a sense of rhythm that seemed phenomenal. By the time he reached the eighth grade at Seiberling, he was the lead drummer in the school band. He hungrily watched and listened to every drummer he could.

When Gene Krupa played the Palace in Akron as a drummer, first with Tommy Dorsey, and later as his own leader, Joe skipped school and spent the day peering from the balcony. He would beat out rhythms with open palms on his thighs trying to match the mastery of Krupa.

As Joe increased his skill and after the formal rehearsal was over on Wednesday nights, Sam always invited him to "sit in" on their informal session of swing. It was a big moment every time Joe seated himself behind a set of drums. The marching band and the staccato of a snare drum seemed far removed from being the "beat and heart" of a real band. He was good, there was no doubting it. He was creating a style and a flamboyance that encompassed all he had heard and all he had seen plus all that he had to add.

After one such display of drumming behind the big band, each member applauded him heartily. The shy Joe could not force himself to look up. His somber black eyes were hidden by the black wave of his hair that unfurled over his eyes. Inside, he was pleased. Inside, this was an identity he savored.

No matter what the outside activity we boys were caught up with, there was always the shoe shop. It was far from a despised duty to work in our father's shop. It was an experience that permitted each of us to become more of an adult. Sure, there were menial tasks to do – sweeping the floor, hauling the trash, cleaning the huge white marbled shine stand, washing the windows, and stocking the shelves with merchandise; but also Dad saw to it that each of us had our turn on the jack and then the machines.

"With a trade, you'll never starve."

As Joe migrated to the jack and the finishing machines, Sam moved to the dry clean and pressing portion of the shop. He became our "presser." It saved Sam's hands and made room for the next trainee.

I think the most memorable moments were our lunches. It was here where many of the lessons of our lives were taught us. Dad, pretty much bald now in his early forties, would pull the shade on the window to our entrance door. It said simply on the outside-showing shade, "Out to Lunch, Back at 1:00 p.m." Many people, impatient with the wait, would pound on the windows as they peered in.

Dad always yelled amiably at them, "Hey . . . it'sa lunch time.

That'sa why we work, so we can eat!" He would smile as he pointed to the sign's "1:00 p.m."

Our lunch was a Saturday afternoon ritual. Joe or I would go to the corner store, buy the cold drinks and maybe some fruit. Dad would unpack the picnic basket Mom packed and line up the food from it on top of a recently cleared counter. There would be two loaves of Mom's homemade bread, unsliced, a large jar of huge black and oily olives, cucumbers, radishes, tomatoes, and lettuce. Wrapped in waxed paper or tin foil, fresh lunch meat of ham, salami or prosciutto, and pepperoni. Always there were cheeses, provolone and Swiss. The last items Dad would remove were the salt and pepper shakers wrapped in a linen tablecloth Mom provided. It was never just lunch; it was always special. Dad insisted on it.

With a flair and a ritual, Dad would invoke a blessing, make the sign of the cross on the new bread loaves, and slice them into good-sized hunks.

One could make a sandwich if one wanted, but it was far better to have a bite of cheese, a piece of salami, a bite of that wonderful bread, an olive . . . and a swig of the cold pop. Once you made the rounds, you could repeat it as often as needed.

For dessert, Dad would pull out his pocket knife, used only for this purpose. Each piece of fruit, whatever the day offered, was peeled in a unique way. No two different fruits were ever peeled the same. He delighted in his artistry and in turn, we all copied the feat mentally. All of our lives we would replicate the style we had all learned.

More than the food, though, Dad granted it high importance that we all eat well to work hard. There was always a thirty- or forty-minute recess after lunch.

It was talk time, Dad said. "There is a time for work, for eat, and for talk. Don't try to do more than one at a time!"

It was this time when we boys would tell jokes and stories with our father. Sometimes the subjects were deeply serious and sometimes light and airy. In this way, Dad was learning of his sons and we of him. Often, he would enthrall us with a story from the old country. It all seemed so unreal, so vastly different with their old customs and beliefs, their morality and violence. Choice pieces of wisdom it had taken a lifetime to learn were given us freely. It was never "advice." It was always a story with a hidden logic and a subtle value left for us to figure out. If you unlocked the secret, he'd affirm it!

In more modern times, people would give the work, play, laugh, cry, sharing of families a name. They would call it "bonding," but it truly was more. It was the mortar, the common link of a team that was forming. As Dad viewed his three sons, he could not help but know our strengths and weaknesses. Each of us was different in personality. Each had skills and qualities that he thought would mark us as fine men. Physically we were much the same. Dad thought often about how maybe one brother could add to the other's makeup, thereby doubling or tripling strengths and overcoming weakness.

Looking at Sam, Dad saw a reserved, polite, humble youth. He had great respect for Sam's leadership. Sam would never be trouble, Dad knew. He would always do the right thing when it needed to be done. "This one," Dad thought, "was always a little man, but so compassionate others might take advantage of him."

When he evaluated Joe, Dad would laugh to himself because Joe, so like Mom, had a wild flair. Not only could you not know what he was thinking, he was never predictable. Dad and Joe shared friendship that differed from the one he had with Sam and me, for Joe always showed enthusiasm to work with Dad. Sam had a mind outside the shop, and I was only present because I was told to be.

I loved sports and played all of them in the street, whatever the season might be. I was such a "rough house," Dad thought, like a baby bull, tripping over things, colliding, breaking. Of the three, it was I who most often would receive a blast of Dad's belt across my butt. I was bright, sassy, and mouthy. So were my brothers, but they were wiser and knew when to be silent.

This particular Saturday morning, as with every one that preceded it, we boys were busy cleaning the shop. It would be nearly 9:00 AM before the heavy flow of traffic began. Dad was preparing shoes, Sam was pressing pants, I was cleaning the shoeshine stand, and Joe was dusting and cleaning the counters.

When Joe finished, he'd find something new to do. I would just say "Now what?" and had to be told. The three years between us showed in these responses.

Joe brought out the steel wool and began an inside and out-side cleaning and polishing of our relic brass cash register. From a dirty, dusty colorless box, Joe was making a shiny brassy show-piece. He loved what he was about. When he opened the register drawer, he sought to open it even wider.

"Maybe it comes out," he said. As he probed and pushed and pulled it, Joe triggered a spring lock that held the drawer in se-curely. When it triggered and was loosened, he extracted the en-tire drawer. In the rear of the dark and dusty cavity was a clutter of debris, probably as old as the machine itself. Joe brought a flashlight to shine in and swept the contents out on the floor. His eyes widened as he got a closer look. They were old and faded high-numbered bills. There were 5's, 10's, 20's, and several 1's.

Elated, he yelled out, "Dad! Dad! Come here quick!"

With amazement Dad looked at the heap Joe had swept out of the register. Always in the past, the drawer had pushed in hard; now it glided to its proper position. An amazed Dad un-folded the bills and laid them out . . . $140 in cash.

At lunch time, he told Sam and me, "You guys I worry about, but Joe . . . he can smell the money."

Later that evening, Dad took great relish in relaying the cash-register story to Mom over dinner. Sam and I were never envious. We had our moments, and we both knew that Joe al-ways did remarkable things. It was his way.

But there were times at the shop when discoveries worked against Joe. One day, as my father popped a cigarette into his mouth and fumbled for a match or lighter in one of his pockets, he looked at Joe, whom he had suspected of indulging in ciga-rettes, who alertly reached into his pocket and produced a lighter. Once the open palm was offered, he dared not put it back. To my father's great credit, he remained calm, took the lighter, and lit his cigarette. He puffed leisurely and resumed his work, placing a pair of new heels on a pair of work boots, then said aloud, almost to anyone, "Today, I learned something about my son Joe!" It would be brought up Joe in private.

In the quiet of her heart, Mom too had a knowledge of her sons. She also knew that she would never be able to convey these thoughts to anyone. It was too hazy to put into words, too complex to frame into thoughts. Unlike others she had known and watched grow into adulthood, these three pulled for one another and not against. They never seemed jealous of what each accomplished. How this came to be, Mom was uncertain. She only knew she was grateful for the bonds we were forming. It was true we fought "like cats and dogs," but these were trifles that ended when the day did. If it were really a major thing, Dad would intervene before we all went to bed. He would make the opponents face one another and with unwitting psychology shame the anger out of us:

"You love your brother?" he would ask of the first.

"Yes," he would say, with a reluctance that could not lie. To the other he posed the same query.

"Yes," again reluctantly.

"Shake hands with your brother!"

We would reluctantly shake, but it wasn't over yet. "Now kiss your brother."

We would slowly kiss on the cheek.

"Now hug your brother."

At this the anger was broken. We boys would embrace and laugh.

Dad would end it with, "Your family is everything! You hear? Everything! They are the best friends you'll ever have! Never! Never forget that!" Then the argument was erased and vanished!

In this fashion, even though our ways would be separate, we could always draw strength from one another whenever and wherever we needed. It was as though we knew from the very first heartbeat that we had to look out for one another. It was never a burden, and always it was a saving grace in the mountains of trouble we would all come to know.

Each of Mom's sons helped feed our sister, change her diapers, and do housework. Mom was a "neat freak" for her family. Her personality was highly assertive, unless she was speaking to Dad. When she would forget and raise her voice to him, his eyes would flare. She knew it was time to be silent. I was learning from my Mother. When there was a strained silence between Mom and Dad, the three of us would hold court.

"Stand up," Sam ordered our mother and father. They both played the game as Sam ordered. "Look at one another!" They looked. "You love you wife?" A nod yes. "You love your husband?" Another nod yes. "Shake hands. . . . Kiss your wife. . . . Kiss your husband. . . . Hug each other!"

It always worked, and Sam would end his judgeship with, "Never . . . never forget that!" We never forgot, nor did they.

It became apparent to Mom, long before Dad knew, that I had a gifted mind for reading and remembering. In just a few years of reading, I developed a thirst which would never leave me. I delighted in stories and sagas of great deeds, with strong and courageous heroes.

While in the fifth grade, my teacher read to the class a story about Charlemagne. Beyond the great king, my interest was toward Roland, the son of a warrior, fallen in the defense of Charlemagne. I loved to hear how Roland grew straight and tall, was a mighty warrior with great courage and strength, and vowed as a boy to his mother at his father's funeral, "My hands will wait upon you, Mother" . . . how, as he grew, he was loved and admired in stories and songs as a legend and hero.

It was this story that caused deep emotion within me. In an era when radio and movies allowed only a "good guy" to win, when the hero overcame all adversity and never sacrificed principle, I was smitten with the image, and it remained indelibly etched in my memory. Taking care of one's mother was the noblest deed!

During regular school days, Dad arrived at home about 6:30. Dinner was served promptly when he arrived. Mom had her rules for us boys. "Change your school clothes! Hang them on hangers. Shine your shoes. Do your homework. Set the table!"

Down to the way our shirts hung in our closets and the socks, hankies, and underwear were folded into our drawers, Mom was organized. Between her husband and three sons, she ironed as many as twenty-eight to thirty shirts a week . . . each one starched and pressed to perfection.

In the orders she flung at us, she had no patience with questioning her authority or delay of any kind. With her wash hung on the line, her daughter in one arm, and stirring dinner on the stove with the other, she ordered Joe, "Take the wash down before the rain comes!" One day Joe forgot, and the weight of the rain brought the whole wash down in a muddy heap. Mom was smoldering at this error, and when dinner was over and Dad asked his inevitable question, she would be ready.

"And Rose," he began it, "how did your day go?"

The seating at dinner was always the same. Dad at the head at one end, with the two older sons to his right and left. Mom at the end nearest her kitchen with me at her right and Terry's highchair at her left.

She was animated; she couldn't keep calm in the telling of her story about Joe. She became so furious that she reached to her right and smacked me across the cheek with her open hand.

Dad waited till she finished and said with a sense of justice, "Why, if this one did it," pointing to Joe, "do you hit that one?"

Mom was flustered and confused, but said quickly to summon a defense, "Because," she stammered, "they're brothers!"

Dad roared with laughter at her logic and even I could not be angry at my mother's reflex. Dad said to Joe. "You see what you got coming?" Joe nodded. "Don't let it happen again." With this, he pointed at me, "You . . . you don't wipe dishes tonight, Joe does!"

Whenever we playfully wanted to do an imitation of Mom, it was always with quick staccato orders: "Don't track in on my carpet! . . . Damn you, I just mopped there! . . . Here, hold the baby! . . . Feed the baby! . . . Rock the baby! . . . Where is Tom? Let's slap Tom!" Even Mom would burst into laughter as she recognized her own expressions and style.

Sometimes Mom's sisters would witness these outbursts. "They're such good kids, Rose, show them some love and affection."

"Oh, hell," she'd fire back. "They know I love them. Besides, who has time for all that?" Or more frequently, "I can't be bothered."

At day's end after she had washed and ironed, scrubbed, cooked, mothered Terry, and sometimes babysat for a niece or nephew, she would reflect on the thoughts of her sisters and say with near exhaustion, "God, let them know I love them!" Everything she did was evidence enough.

After the birth of Terry, Mom and Dad quit going to church completely. They could not withstand the guilt heaped upon them from the pulpit about birth control.

"Maybe," Dad had whispered in Mom's ear while they slept in a bit on Sundays, "we don't go to church, but we will always love and believe in God." They left it at that.

Some evenings and some mornings, when they were by themselves, they would talk about their family. From her childhood, Mom remembered a priest saying these things: "When you raise children, pray to our Lord that each of them be tough but not toughs, hard but not heartless, and relentless not ruthless." She always remembered the phrase and knew no way to improve on that prayer. She had no way of knowing that each of her sisters and all of Dad's side of the relatives spoke of the Pagna boys with great admiration. We were well groomed, polite, respectful, and obedient. It dawned on none of us to be otherwise.

Mom knew we were tough enough. Reports from the school or other children in the neighborhood would fill her in on Joe and me combining to fight much larger boys who had insulted one or the other of us.

"They stuck together," was the most frequent report, "and whipped so and so."

"Who started the fight?" Mom wanted to know.

"Not Joe and Tom," was the reply.

"Tough," she thought, "not toughs." She was proud of us but never allowed us to know what she knew.

Before Terry had her first birthday, America was involved in a war. Within three months' time, World War II was declared. It was December 7, 1941.

Dad was somber, sitting in front of his radio, as it blared out the bombing of Pearl Harbor.

"How could anyone attack such a country as America?" he asked. To his sadness he learned of the Italians joining with Hitler and Japan against America. He was furious for Italy ever thinking to go to war against his beloved adopted country. His thoughts turned to a long ago friend, Fr. Trivassano. In only a few years after he arrived in America, he had paid back the priest. Dad worried and wondered of Father Trivassano's safety.

He listened anew to the voice coming through the airwaves. It was Franklin Delano Roosevelt saying that "Yesterday, December 7 . . . a day that will live in infamy!" The U.S. was at war!

Mom's and Dad's worst fears were confirmed as Sam, along with several of his senior classmates, wanted to enlist. Huge posters with Uncle Sam pointing to you, said it all. "Uncle Sam Wants You!"

To Sam's heartbreak, and Dad's and Mom's hidden joy, Sam was classified as 4-F. He had one perforated eardrum that kept him out. Distraught over the news, Sam volunteered his highly polished orchestra for USO tours. Within his travels, he played background for some of the day's superstars.

Sam asked Dad's permission to seek employment in the war plants. Goodyear had just organized the Goodyear Aircraft and manufactured Navy Corsair fighter planes. Sam was accepted and became a maintenance mechanic for repairs. Whenever he could, however, Sam helped us in the shoe shop, since we were swamped with work.

At no time in the history of America, before this time or after it, would the atmosphere of patriotism reign so supreme. Almost daily, flatbeds pulled by tractors brought Hollywood and radio stars into major cities. They were selling war bonds for $18.75. Your bond would be redeemed for $25 in seven years. Citizens were helping to finance our fighting men. Rallies and fund drives were daily occurrences.

Rationing was invoked by the government because all the priorities were given to the troops. Some of the items rationed were gas, butter, meat, oil, coffee, silk, rubber, and leather. An entire nation lived out of ration booklets and made do. At least once a week a blackout would be hailed by loud sirens. Each home would turn out all lights and pull draperies tight to conceal the smallest of lights. Volunteer fire marshals and block wardens patrolled the streets. Curfews were enforced. Bomb shelters were constructed in every schoolhouse.

Patriotic, sentimental tunes and songs flooded the airwaves. The lyrics spoke of love, parting, someday returning and loving again. Other songs spoke of lost love or lost lives, with gold stars hung in the windows of those bereaved by the loss.

Everyone knew what a "Purple Heart" was. Heroes abounded. War movies and stories lit up the screens. Mothers left their homes to replace the men in factories who were gone to war. Aviation was the future. The factories worked either three eight-hour shifts or four six-hour ones. They never shut down. Money flowed, and products exploded. Everyone had money, and everyone wanted to do their share. There were no riots, no protests, and very little crime. Everyone was too busy with the war effort.

In 1941, Dad was up to his ears in work. When rubber and leather had been rationed and the factories going all the time, people needed shoes. Repairing them was important, since new ones were almost non-existent. With Sam in the aircraft factory, Dad hired another cobbler, and the two of them prepared work all day until Joe and I came from school to finish their work on the machines. Dad arranged huge boxes across the back of his shop. Each box marked with a black marker stated a different day of the week. Every box was overflowing.

Joe and I had little free time. Sam held his band together, and the demand for their music grew greater and greater.

In the summer of 1942, an article appeared in the paper that stated there would be a formation of the North Eastern Ohio Bantamweight Association Football League. It would be sponsored by the factories to give opportunity to boys aged of thirteen to seventeen to play football. These, because of weight, probably could not or would not play in high school. You weighed in at 120 pounds for the first game and were allowed to gain a pound per game, or nine pounds by season's end.

What most people would never realize about the formation of this league, spanning over three counties and nearly a million people, was that it was financed by the corporations. They would provide the finest equipment, coaches, and facilities available to anyone. Each squad would carry only a thirty-three-man roster. They would play in the Rubber Bowl (doubleheaders) on Sunday or at a local stadium nearby. The Rubber Bowl held 36,000 for the season's opener. The press had caught on to the ramifications this had for schoolboys, for community attendance and morale. Clever names were given the teams, most of them correlated to the war effort. The league was comprised by geographical area and the names given were as

1. North Akron Commandos
2. South Akron Rangers
3. West Akron Hornets
4. East Akron Corsairs
5. Kenmore Gremlins
6. Kent Bearcats
7. Barberton Barons
8. Cuyahoga Falls Buckeyes

The top four teams would make a playoff, and the final two would vie for the championship. The last two teams having a nine-game schedule. Football was truly king!

Joe and I often sat through two Sunday double features, just to catch a few second highlights of the newsreels showing the nation's top collegiate teams and players. Always, there were breakaway runs by Tommy Harmon of Michigan, Les Horvath from Ohio State, Choo Choo Charlie Justice of North Carolina, etc. We thrilled to these moments, locking in moves and styles of running mentally, focusing a mental picture of how the great ones did it.

In the months following the announcement of the Bantamweight league, the movie *Knute Rockne, All-American* came to our local theater. I could not leave the movie. I was so enraptured of Rockne, Notre Dame, and George Gipp, I was stricken for the remainder of my life to play and coach at Notre Dame. I knew in that movie house that this dream matched my special desire, and that desire decided the path my life would follow.

July 1943: At the tryouts, three hundred young boys lined the practice field site of the East Akron Corsairs. It was a park area next to Seiberling grade school, with plush ball diamonds and practice fields. There were four coaches who split the three hundred into four groups. Each of the coaches were running sprints to see who had natural speed. Size too was a consideration so long as the weight barrier could be met. After the sprints, thirty three were selected to be issued uniforms. Those without

No longer the "clumsy little bull," here I am in 1943 at age 11, and already a Corsair.

could still participate in the drills, but if they were without uniforms and pads, contact drills became a hazard. More than a few disgruntled fellows walked away and headed for home. Nearly another one hundred stayed, however.

The groups had divided now into two. There were two coaches observing each group. At the one end of the field there were backs and receivers; at the other, linemen. I fell into a line, one of two that were formed on both sides of several centers. The centers would alternate snaps to alternate punters. Downfield, backs and receivers were to field the ball and try to evade the coverage people coming downfield from the two formed lineups. Two at a time, the defenders would attempt to corral the ball carrier.

I was only eleven years old, but I had played against larger boys all of my life. I had not once doubted my own ability. Each time I was one of the two to go down for the tackle of the ball carrier, I made the tackle. Back in the lines, many boys milled around, reluctant to go without pads to tackle a fully padded player with football spikes and wearing a helmet. In this fashion, I appeared far more often than would normally have been my turn. I caught the eye of one of the coaches, Les "Swede" Olson, a

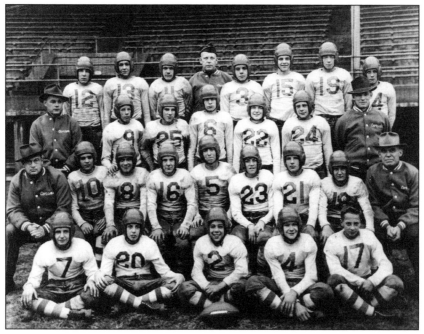

The East Akron Corsairs of 1943. Yours truly is the one with the toothy grin in front of the football.

former lineman for the Washington Redskins, who pulled me from the lineup.

"How old are you, son?"

I thought myself caught – that I would be sent home.

"Eleven," I replied truthfully,

"Where'd you learn to tackle like that?"

"I been playing a lotta years in the street."

"A Lotta years?" Swede chuckled, then called over a rather tall fellow who had won several sprints and had been awarded a uniform. He put his hand on the player's shoulder and said simply, "Son, this really isn't your game." The young fellow nodded in agreement.

"You two boys go in the shelter house over there and change clothes."

"Chesty," he said to me, not knowing my name. "You've earned the right to a uniform."

"He's no bigger than a peanut," Olson told his wife that evening, "but every time he'd crowd the line and go down and whack the ball carrier! Why, hell, he showed more heart in ten minutes than I've seen in years!"

"Will his age prevent him from being selected?" Mrs. Olson had asked.

"No, there's only a limit on the high side at seventeen, but who would ever figure an eleven year old?"

When I brought the incredible length of canvas practice pants home and showed my brothers all of my new equipment, none of the family had any idea what I was involved with. Mom cut out nearly ten inches of material and tailored the pants perfectly to my body mold.

After several weeks of practice, game uniforms and numbered jerseys were handed out. Mom, again form-fitted my tiny uniform. I weighed 88 pounds and stood 5 feet even.

I would stare often at the uniform in my bedroom chair and dreamed mighty dreams. The uniform sported blue satin pants with white narrow striping down the sides, my own knitted white game jersey with a large blue number "2" on the back and a smaller one in the front. There were what I had come to learn were "pro" socks, ones that came up past the knees. They had no toes or heels but only a stirrup. On these were to be worn fresh and new white sweat socks that rose half way up the blue pro sock. My helmet was padded blue leather all around, with a white dome of hard plastic with an inside suspension. I was very proud to be an East Akron Corsair.

At such an impressionable age, I listened intently to every word the coaches said. Every clich and thought pierced my soul. These things would mold my whole philosophy of life.

"Always run on and off the field . . . never lean on others in the huddle . . . never swear, show anger, or emotion . . . never showboat or hotdog . . . never give in, never give up . . . a champion plays with heart every play . . . greatness is consistency . . . a team that won't be beaten can't be beaten."

These concepts became ingrained in my soul. The coaches spoke of politeness, humility, loyalty, and team players. All of it, I tried to absorb.

Because the players on the teams played two ways and the quarterback became the safety on defense, I was positioned at quarterback. From a toddler I had thrown the ball, and passing it became second-nature. The Corsairs went from a T formation and shifted into a box or single wing, right or left. From the shift the quarterback was only a yard behind the center and off to the side. A side snap to the QB would allow a pivot and faking or giving the ball to the other backs.

All in all, the year was a great learning experience for me. I had found a niche and knew with certainty that I wanted to coach. My grades remained very high. I was less mouthy and less a braggart, more attuned to my personal actions and imagined them being watched and evaluated constantly.

At the year's end, the Corsairs received personal gold footballs to be worn as trophies. We were also awarded Bantam jackets designed in red, white, and blue with the team name on the front left lapel and on the back. In the lower right bottom of the jacket was stitched the player's name, "TOM PAGNA." I was very, very proud. It would mark the first year of forty years I was involved with organized football as either a player or a coach.

The opening day at Rubber Bowl, August 1, 1943, witnessed the Pagna family in the stands among 36,000 people to view our first doubleheader. I got in the game several times, and Mom and Dad felt pride in my achievements. Dad could only see that beyond any doubt, I was the smallest player on the field. The fans thought me cute at such a size, but Dad worried about my well being. As the game went on, Dad was struck with my dexterity with the ball, my sharp reflexes and nimble feet.

"What became of that clumsy tiny bull?" he thought, smiling to himself.

The war years were very prosperous for the workers in

America. Sam was still working in the Goodyear Aircraft and maintaining his orchestra. Dad's shop was bustling. We too were prospering.

A troubling word came to Dad that the government had formed investigative teams of FBI to seek out information on anyone naturalized of Italian, German, or Japanese heritage. Several of East Akron's businessmen and professional people were of those extractions. All of them underwent investigation. Dad passed with flying colors and was told so, much to his relief.

It was evening now, and he had just locked up his shop and started to walk to his car. He usually parked in front of the store, but this day, finding no space, parked further up the street near Annunciation Church. The neighborhood was well aware that investigations had been going on, but they didn't know the findings and outcomes. As Dad spotted his 1938 Packard in the lot, he felt the presence of others in the shadows.

Though it was not fully dark, he could make out only a scuffling sound of feet on the pavement of the parking lot. When he approached closer he saw the complete scenario. On the ground, bloodied from the blows of a baseball bat, Dr. Kaufmeyer was crumpled and groaning. Seven young toughs led by an older man had attacked him as a "Nazi," The older man was still holding the bat, and the young punks still looked on.

"Hey," one of them pointed and yelled at Dad. "He's a wop and one of Mussolini's boys. Let's show him what we think of foreigners."

In an instant, Dad was surrounded. He was certain that this would be how and where he died. His mind flashed to his wife Rose, his boys, and Terry. As the enemy tightened their circle, a voice spoke clearly, not loudly, but very distinctly. It was a tall man in an overcoat. He was smiling with an alarming grin of gold teeth.

"I too am a wop!" he said. "Teach me your ways!"

With this, John Carpenter swiftly drew his pistol from a shoulder holster and fired it into the air. The crowd of thugs ran, screaming in every direction.

Dad looked at his old friend and said only one word, "*Grazia*."

"No charge," John replied, as he smiled at his little joke.

Both men helped Dr. Kaufmeyer to his car and went their separate ways.

Chapter 7
The Illusion of Someday

M any "somedays" found their way into Mom's internal hope chest, but none so solid as that place in her mind's eye that would be acknowledged as "home." This would be our place to grow roots and there would be no more moves or seeking, just . . . home!

With Sammy's steady job and Joe finding outside employment at a metal plant, also critical to the nation's defense, we had several paychecks. Since Joe was now sixteen, Dad rewarded his efforts with a '41 Ford coupe. Mom was quick to capitalize on Joe's new freedom and gave him gas money to help her run down "homes for sale." It was a day of intermittent rainfall in mid-April of 1945 when Mom ordered a willing Joe to take her to the outskirts of Akron. She had read the description of a home for sale, and it sounded like one Mom was seeking.

They took the highway out of Akron, driving eight miles due south toward Canton. It was truly country in atmosphere, but the home that was advertised, though it had acreage, was reputedly, very modern.

Mom spotted the "for sale" sign along the roadside and directed Joe to turn into a long gravel drive. She read the address on the mailbox and said with some satisfaction, "This is the one!"

From the highway, the gravel drive traveled up a slanting hill about a quarter of a mile, where it bent slightly to the right, entering to a garage connected to the house. The entire home sat on the crest of a hill. It was a long flat bungalow of red brick, with a green roof and trimmed in white woodwork. At the level near the highway and at the base of the hill where Joe entered into the drive was a small lake of about two acres in size. From the lake level and up to the front of the house was a neatly trimmed fifty yards of lawn. There was a small white bridge from the lawn into the lake, anchored there on a petite island. In the center of the island was a large weeping willow tree that appeared to hang its limbs in such a fashion that it created what appeared to be a private room upon the island. The rain kept true visibility of the home from keen inspection.

Off to either side of the home, at a distance of no less than 300 yards, were other homes. Mom's eyes could hardly acknowledge these, since she was entranced by what she saw. As they sat in the Ford at the end of the driveway, it became apparent that behind the home was what seemed like an endless expanse of wood and fields. Nothing else appeared. The rain softened to a soft drizzle, and she rolled her window down. A small arch of a faint rainbow was forming over the fields in the back. It gave the illusion that one end of the rainbow fell on the rooftop of the bungalow.

"It's lovely," she said, half to herself and then to Joe. "What do you think?"

Joe saw the rainbow and kidded her; he knew his mother was smitten with the place. They left shortly, but Mom was determined to see the inside of the home and find out the cost. She knew getting Dad to move was becoming increasingly harder.

Mom knew that our overall cash flow would never be better. With Sam and Joe holding full-time jobs, Dad's shop thriving during the war years, and me ready to leave Seiberling grade school, it was evident to her that the iron was hot to strike again. She approached Dad. He was not averse to the idea of a move, but knew his wife to be impetuous in the actions if not harnessed.

Terry at the home with the lake.

As they met the real-estate lady, they realized that she also was the owner of this home. Dad and Mom examined the pin-neat brick bungalow. It had a large living room with fireplace. On both sides of the fireplace were two huge picture windows giving full view of the lake and highway. There were only three bedrooms, a bath, a kitchen, a dining room, and a large solarium attached at the back. The driveway led to double garage doors with a walk-through into the basement. Over the garage was the master bedroom.

Upon seeing the interior of the house, Mom fell in love with its possibilities. Dad liked the idea that it sat on ten acres, with plenty of room for a garden, fruit trees, and grape arbors, and backed into endless elbow room. He liked it immensely!

The price shocked the two of them. It was nearly four times what they had paid for their current home. In 1945, $3,500 had bought that home. The selling price of this one was $12,500. It seemed such a great deal of money. The lady owner liked the looks of this warm family and offered them a personal note she would hold at a small rate of interest. If they could put $5,000 down cash, and pay the woman off in three years at $220 a month, the home could be ours.

Mom and Dad calculated their holdings. They sold off the apartment house and the equity of the one we were living in. It was mid-summer 1943 when they realized this long, elusive goal and moved into Springfield Township and the "home with a lake."

In the months that followed, the Pagnas enjoyed the rare air of fulfilling a hard-earned dream. Dad surely did plant his grape arbor, a dozen peach and plum trees, and a wonderful vegetable garden in which he loved to work. In mid-summer, we boys would take long hard runs down the grassy green hill and dive from the bridge into a spot of six to eight feet of spring-fed water.

In the evening, Dad would show us how to bait a hook and fish for the panfish that filled the lake. Often, he would view the back woods with little Theresa holding his hand. He loved the scenery, the pristine view of God's handy work.

On the side of the house, Dad inlaid 4 x 4's into the dirt and erected clay boxes for horseshoes. It was a skill we all picked up readily. Often, Dad and Mom would sit inside the solarium in the evenings and watch the romping brothers play catch or basketball.

Mom purchased a fairly new chicken coop. "Not for chickens," she assured the family. She scrubbed it inside and out until it was all but sterilized. When she was sure it was devoid of germs, she whitewashed the outside and had Dad reroof the top in the same green roofing as our home. Once inside, she wallpapered throughout and placed wall-to-wall carpeting. She then furnished the playhouse with children's furniture: a sofa, a rocking chair, a play stove and refrigerator, a table, and chairs. It was, she said exuberantly upon finishing it, a doll house for Terry! Terry would play there for hours with her little girl friends from the neighborhood.

Weekends became festive affairs, since our grandpa Joe Crimaldi visited often. Always, Dad brought his mother, Donna Theresa. All of Mom's sisters visited periodically, but we always came together on holidays. Uncle Mike brought whatever wife he was currently married to, and Mom's sisters brought their own husbands and children. It was always a major picnic outside. There would be the grilling of hamburgers, hotdogs, steaks, or chicken. There were long wooden tables with enough folding chairs to seat everyone for the feasts. After meals were the horseshoe contests, swimming in the lake, or softball on the open grassy fields. All of the aunts and uncles of the Pagna clan took part in the events. The older relatives sat in chairs and observed the good fun. Wine was plentiful, as were fruit, nuts, and fresh vegetables. The dream of family and togetherness ignited deep affection and memory in all of us forever.

Within families, there are shades between "inlaws" and "outlaws." The outlaws entered into the family knowing about it. In their hearts, they knew no family of their own would come to mean as much. Their children looked upon Mom and Dad as the "grand" mother and father of all of them. It was their hospitality given freely, their hard-earned dollars that made the "home by the lake" a family paradise.

The feasts and athletic contests dimmed with oncoming evening and the mosquitoes. Each of Mom's sisters would pitch in to help her tidy up and move the outdoors to indoors. In the evening, there was music – Uncle Mike at the piano, Sam with the accordion, Dad on the guitar, and Joe with his drums. While the other men busied themselves with poker, female voices would lift themselves. Dixie and Flora could harmonize. Betty and Ann, Mary and Mom, they all sang the tunes of the day. With a few more drinks than she needed, winsome Aunt Dixie, whose voice held that pure tone of a professional, honored the crowd with a tear-jerking version of "I'll Be Seeing You" and "Mexicali Rose." It was great fun for all of Mom's family, Donna Theresa, Dad's brother Gaetano and sister Mary plus their children. Those who knew the struggle, the planning, the vision, and raw energy of Mom and Dad honored them and wished them well. Some, invited on just a few occasions, had jaundiced eyes.

"Where does she get the money?"

"She probably owes on everything they've got!"

"Maybe Tony's a bootlegger."

"Or Mafia."

Donna Theresa saw and heard all of this and though she spoke only a few English words, understood much that was spoken. She told Dad in Italian, *guardarsi eh mallocu* ("beware of the evil eye"). Those who have not earned the right are jealous and would dance at your downfall!

Dad, anxious to leave the old ways and superstitions, could not believe that all of our guests were not happy for all of us.

Mom too had heard the remarks her sisters brought to her from visiting strangers.

"They think you're rich."

"To hell with them," Mom answered, "Our life is what we've made it." Mom would give to anyone at anytime and could not comprehend such smallness in the nature of people.

In the fall, Sam got accepted to the Cincinnati Conservatory of Music. He was thrilled at the prospect. Joe and I were to enter the small country high school where enrollment was not quite six hundred. Since the eighth grade was included with the high school, Joe and I would have a few classes near one another and some together. It was a time in our lives (Joe was sixteen and I was thirteen) when we rivaled each other at every turn. We argued over clothes, girls, duties, and chores. Mom was sick and tired of the constant fighting between us. Joe wanted his freedom from my tag-along ways. Mom told Dad she could not stand the "rough housing" between us two. Dad understood. He could easily see that in size we were very similar and that we both fought for a limelight of our own. Rather than show anger, he gathered us together. When he spoke, we listened!

"Someday . . . you gonna be great friends . . . but that someday . . . until she comes . . . your mother is a nervous wreck. You wanna fight? Go in the woods! Go fight until its all gone!"

On his advice and with our next heated argument, Joe and I tramped into the woods. Watching us was like watching someone fight himself. Each of us was quick, strong, knew all the same holds, and tried them on each other. We feigned real anger and never put our fist to the other's face. After a knock-down-drag-out, breathe-heavy, sweaty, all-out encounter, we both lay exhausted on the ground, gazing skyward.

"You're a tough little bastard," Joe admitted. "I'm glad I beat you."

"You didn't. I beat you!"

"You want more?"

"Do you?"

There was no answer.

Joe thought silently to himself, "Few battles in my life time will be tougher than the one with this guy . . . and he's my brother!"

I thought as well, "Even if I could win . . . I cannot. He's my older brother, and I'd follow him to hell!"

"C'mon," Joe said kindly. "Like Dad says, someday we'll be best friends. Why not now?"

Touched with the concession of Joe, I shook my head yes, and we stood and hugged one another, breaking into laughter. We would never fight each other again . . . and would always be best friends.

Both Joe and I now played for the East Akron Corsairs. Joe was a fullback, swift and sure-handed on offense, and a linebacker on defense. I played the T quarterback position, and it was fun to be included. When our teammates piled into Joe's coupe for a lift, Joe always said, "Just save a place for Tom."

As teammates, Joe and I formed still another bond. We had a great year going and had a memorable laugh at the official weigh-in at our season's opener. Each player had to produce a birth certificate and submit it to the league. Prior to the first game, the commission that ran the league would enter the playing teams' locker rooms, call out each player's name, weigh him in, and rubber-stamp his wrist, certifying his eligibility.

The head of the commission would bark out a name from the

certificates. When he yelled out "Gaetano Pagna," neither Joe nor I knew who that was. The birth certificates had been sealed in an envelope.

"Hey," Joe nudged me. "I'm pretty sure that's you! Either that or our Uncle is on the team." We both laughed about it, and when we told Dad, he legally had affidavits drawn up with the names Sam, Joe, and Tom (instead of Salvatore, Giuseppe, Gaetano). Until we heard "Gaetano" and "Giuseppe" called out, neither of us ever knew our real names.

It was during the fall practice of 1945 when the Corsairs were getting ready for a game that the booming main plant of Goodyear sounded its siren. Coach Steve Sitko called us around him to address us. This in itself was unusual because practice was only half over.

"Fellas," the ex–All-American at Notre Dame smiled broadly. "You know what that means?" He was shouting through the sirens. "Victory in Europe! The war is over! Take off and see you tomorrow!"

A half dozen guys to a car, our young teammates headed for downtown Akron. The streets were teeming with people. There was confetti spilling out of office buildings, and traffic was at a complete standstill. People got out of their cars and hugged one another. Strangers kissed strangers on the lips, and bands came out of nowhere. You could hear strains of "Johnny Doughboy" and "Stars and Stripes Forever." Groups were singing "God Bless America."

A pretty red-haired nurse still in her uniform, with cape and hat all in place, stopped next to Joe's coupe. She opened the door and pulled him out. She was at least a foot taller and perhaps fifteen years older. She cradled him in both arms and swooped her lips onto his, thrusting her tongue down his throat in a long and passionate kiss. She let go then and searched out another and another. Joe spit into the street and said, "I hope I'm not pregnant!" Everyone laughed. The war was over!

The celebration lasted until the wee hours of the morning only to resume again the next day. Schools were unattended. It was a national holiday. VE, or Victory in Europe, meant "our guys" were coming home.

Women who were riveters and tube builders, painters and

taxi drivers would give up their masculine garb of slacks and head bands. Once more they would put on their "feminity," anxious to welcome back brother, uncle, sweetheart, or husband. Never before and (probably) never again would there be such an absence of crime, such an abundance of esprit de corps in the United States of America.

Mom and Dad had rigid ideas about the way their kids were raised, the way we dressed and acted. Being a shoemaker, Dad forbade us to wear tennis shoes or, as he called them, "overalls" to school. Mom saw to it that each son had clean neat shirts, sweaters and pressed gabardine pants and shined shoes.

On the first day of high school, we had no idea what to expect. Because of the way we were dressed – with the rest of the boys in boondock work shoes, overalls, and plaid shirts – the Pagna brothers appeared as "city slickers." With our dark hair, well groomed and combed back slick, we were soon dubbed "Hood" for Joe and "Slick" for me. In my first classroom, I sought to sit down in a chair. The chair was jerked from beneath me. I fell backward and hit my head on a table edge behind. My scalp was oozing blood, which I felt with my hand. I looked upward to see an adversarial grin on a boy my own size.

"Yeah," the boy croaked with confidence. "I did it. Whatcha gonna do about it, Slick?"

It seemed all too familiar. Pick on the new boy. With all the moves the family had made, there had been a lot of first days and a lot of "Whatcha gonna do about its?" The "Slick" part was new. Since class was ringing in, I said to the boy, "After school, we'll settle this!"

In high school when the bell rang, you went on to your next class. By lunch time, the rumor had spread throughout the school that the little brother of the "hood" who drove the neat '41 Ford coupe was going to catch an old-fashioned "country shit kicking."

Joe spotted me in the cafeteria, brought his tray to the table, and sat down next to me.

"What the hell happened?" he asked as he saw the bloodied handkerchief with which I was dabbing my head.

"Same old thing," I said. "Let's test the new guy!"

"Which one?" Joe asked.

"By the door in the green plaid shirt!"

"Can you take him?"

"Take him? Hell, I'm gonna kill him!"

"Hey, be cool and don't let anger blind you, okay?"

Indeed, it was always the same wherever we had been. We acted differently; polite, alert, mannerly. We dressed differently; neat, shined shoes, combed hair, clean nails and hands. Always we were called "wops," "hoods," "mafioso." Always one or the other had to take our turn at stemming the tide.

The last bell rang out clearly, and there was a rush to lockers; a throng of bodies filled the hallways only to exit at the staircase and bee line it to the parking lot. Before too long, the entire student body formed a circle to view the new kid's initiation.

I always wore a religious medal on a chain. I entered the circle and took it off, slowly handing it to Joe. The boy I was to fight stood arrogantly in the middle of the circle.

He uttered to me, "And now city boy, you're going to get yours!"

Though I appeared casual, adrenaline was throbbing through my body.

"Hit first," Dad always said. "Get in your best shot and first."

We sparred around, sizing each other up a moment. The crowd egging Kemp, the boy in the green plaid shirt, to "get 'em Kemp . . . get 'em."

When we boys had boxed all those years, Sammy had taught us a slight reaching feint with the left hand to an opponent's stomach. It was not an intended punch but merely a feint to register opponent attention there for a split second. From the left hand going forward, was an easy up and hooking swing to the right jaw of the opponent. I feigned the left, changed the direction and left-hooked Kemp's jaw. Not a hard blow but a setup and a second later a straight right hand to the mouth and nose. This one had full power; Kemp crumpled to the ground, cupping his face in both hands to stop the onrush of a bloody nose.

The crowd grew hushed. Kemp wouldn't get up. Joe grabbed me as we walked to the Ford Coupe.

"Damn," Joe said admiringly, "That was a tough spot, and I'm proud of you!"

In my freshman year, with four years of bantam football under my belt and Joe beyond the age limit for bantams, I was having trouble making the weight limit, so I went out for freshman football in high school. The teasing of "here comes the big bad bantam!" started. The coach was eager to see what this compact 145-pounder could do that was so different. He aligned me as a safety on defense, and they punted the ball to me. I was cocky, believed in myself, and was proud of my ability. My defensive team was eager to teach me a lesson, so they rigged the play on the punt return and purposely missed their blocks. I fielded the high ball and instantly took a thunderous shot to my chest. Everyone was set to laugh at the lesson. Instead they were stunned. I took the blow and spun off it, scampered to my right, hip-faked the first tackler, straight-armed another, planted my right foot sharply, and cut straight up the field piercing the line of tacklers spread across to corral me. I outsped them for a neat 60-yard punt return and touchdown.

"I'll be damned," the coach spit on the ground. "The kid's for real!"

In the weeks that followed it became more and more apparent that compared to their inexperience, I had incredible balance, great leg strength, and lightning reflexes. Though I was not super fast, my quickness and savvy were far in advance of my teammates. Four years of Bantam football served me to great advantage.

I tried not to showboat but really did believe in myself. I said, "I'll score if you give me a chance."

I guess the coach thought I needed humbling. What no one realized but me was that my utterances were not boasts; they were cries for approval and acceptance.

"If I'm good," I thought, "they'll accept me."

The freshman coach, a twenty-year retired major from the Army and a stickler for discipline, kept me out after practice one day. He said he wanted to help two of his lineman learn to double-team block. I knew nothing of line play, but in my naivete did what I was told. The two lineman outweighing me by 60 or so pounds apiece lined up in opposition. The coach snapped the ball, and they came to block me. Time after time, I split the two, dodged the two, outsmarted and out-maneuvered them. I began to tire but was resolved to stay until it was over. They lined up again, and one player went low for my knee. While warding off the blow, the other blocker uncoiled a solid blow, full force, to my thigh. It snapped the plastic thigh pad and sunk deep into my thigh muscles. I screamed out in pain while writhing on the grass, my leg was hemorrhaging within and beginning to swell quickly. Scissors had to be used to cut off my practice pants.

Remorse filled the face of the freshman coach. He didn't want this, nor did he expect it. It was only meant to be a lesson. He picked me up and after I showered, all three drove me home. It had not once dawned on me that learning a lesson was the purpose of this experience.

With the injury I missed the freshman season altogether. I remained bed-ridden, two weeks with traction and four more just in bed. The doctor said that the blood was clotted between the layers of my quadriceps. It would be months before my body could absorb it all and maybe half a year before I could fully bend my leg.

In the evenings, after work, Dad would stop in the bedroom to see me. The doctor told him that my muscular development in the thighs was that of a twenty-five-year old, While my waist line measured only 32", my thighs were 24" each. There was something else he had told Dad. "There is a Mediterranean-inherited tendency to bleed in some of the young males. Yes, he could grow out of it, and no, I'm not sure he has that trait, but from the history of this bleeding from tooth extraction, a broken nose, and other normal bruises, I think there is a good chance he may have it."

What Mom could not forget was when Dr. Arapakis said, "Clotting time for a bleeder is crucial. If a bleeder were to be in an auto accident, he could die before they could ever arrange emergency help."

"You are saying . . . he should not play sports?" Mom was troubled.

"No, Rose, but be aware that if he has this tendency, that he takes all precautions. Very often, boys mature out of this weakness. To say he cannot play is to break his heart. For this, there is no cure."

Dad sat on my bed. Mom moved me to the single bed to sleep alone.

"Tom," Dad shook his head no, as though not understanding. "This game . . . is so important to you?"

I nodded yes. He patted my head.

"Well," he sighed deeply. "Sometimes we gotta do what we must do. This I understand, but I hate to see my son in bed with pain. Your mother, she hates this for you too."

"But," I was fighting back tears at the concern of my father, "I'm good at this game. It may be the only thing I'm really good at."

"Okay," Dad patted me again and said in a resigned way, "you sleep now, get well. Tomorrow, she's another day."

My father was not feeling well, and his hay fever was giving him sneezing fits. Dr. Arapakis prescribed a vacation. Mom kept correspondence with an old school chum through the years, who now lived in Colorado. Connie wrote Mom often of the beauty of Colorado and in every letter invited her out for a visit. Dr. Arapakis thought the high altitude of the mountains, well above the pollen line, would be a tonic for Dad. Since I was out of school anyhow, and Terry wasn't enrolled yet, they would take a leisurely drive out west to visit Mom's friend, Connie. Mom asked her sister Flora to come along and help drive. Flora too had a baby girl close to Terry's age, and the two of them would keep company.

The six of us drove out in Uncle Mike's 1946 Buick. It was brand new, large, and luxurious. Uncle Mike had done well these past years, parlaying two beverage stores into a one-third ownership of a bingo and keno casino and restaurant. Flora's husband Nate was also a third partner. The trip would accommodate everyone.

When we arrived at Connie's small spread and cabin, all of us were struck with the beauty of Colorado. The drive out was scary in places with increasing altitude, hairpin curves, and no guardrails. We encountered one heavy snowstorm while engaging Vail pass through the mountains, and though we were quite shook with the experience, the grandeur of Colorado softened our fears.

Connie was ecstatic to see old friends. She was remarried these past few years to a ranch hand named Pete Duncan. The Duncans were the caretakers of a 400-acre cattle spread and lived high up the mountainside outside of Rifle, Colorado. They lived sparingly in a small cabin built as a storehouse for hunters.

Dad immediately stopped sneezing at the 7,500-foot altitude. Though stiff-legged, I went with Dad and Pete to hunt and fish the area. It was like a romance novel in high gear: the radiant sunrises, the indescribable sunsets, the wind and warmth, the lack of humidity and the incredibly gorgeous landscape of sky, mountains, trees, and water – all of it punctuated by the complete spectrum of wildlife.

In only a short time, Pete had pointed out quail, sage hen, pheasant, jack rabbits, coyotes, grouse, cougar, bear, deer, elk, and antelope. The trout fishing was magnificent. It may well have been the only time some of the streams were ever fished. All of us fell in love with Colorado.

When the Pagnas and Aunt Flora returned to Akron, Mom and Dad decided to make a venture with Connie and Pete. The owner for whom the Duncans were working was offering them the section where the cabin was, plus 165 acres of land. The Duncans had no money and Connie made a proposal to Mom.

"You buy it with the money down . . . let Pete and me work it with the money crops and cattle, and we'll make the payments. It'll always be yours to visit whenever you like. You'll own it, and all we want is the cabin to live in." Dad and Mom made the down payment and sent monthly checks toward a dwelling they wanted built for themselves. The land was quite cheap and building costs not too high. It seemed a sound investment and future vacation spot.

Returning to "the home with the lake," as we all called it, Mom was grateful for our good fortune. She and Dad were well rested and our home was a showplace of domesticity. There remained one particular item that would fulfill a dream for Mom. She always envisioned a large grandfather clock in her living room. It would be placed opposite the grand piano and counterbalance the room. It would be her gift to herself and the family.

"An heirloom," she was fond of saying. "It will stay in our family and be handed down to each generation. One day," she chortled at Terry. "It will be yours and then your children's."

Indeed, it was a beautiful piece of furniture made from mahogany and teak wood. It chimed out melodiously on the quarter hour and boomed out its hourly time with forceful but harmonious accuracy. The day the movers delivered it, Mom sat on her sofa with a cup of coffee. She could not keep her eyes from the symbol. For one of the rare moments in her life, she was truly happy.

When Sammy made it home from music college and the family all came together again, our "home with the lake" glowed with warmth and love.

We sat at the dinner table enjoying Mom's homemade pasta and meatballs. Dad surveyed his children. He too was very happy. When Mom served her special apple pie and coffee, he would utter with open pride, "Who's better than us, eh?" And just as fast, "God is good."

When Joe was a senior at Springfield, and I was entering my sophomore year, my leg was well again, and I was very involved with school and sports. When World War II ended, and while still at our home with the lake, many visitors and friends visited our home and paid their respects.

At the time it seemed insignificant, but I remember a particular group of men who visited our home one Sunday morning. There were four of them in all, and they all appeared cut from the same mold. Each was a well dressed (dark suits and white shirts with ties), properly trimmed, and shaved. Even though I was oblivious to company at my age, I was told to be present and on my best behavior. I remember that my mother asked all of us to be properly dressed in our best Sunday clothes and help her prepare a great breakfast.

As the men were seated, my mother presented them with hot coffee, rolls, eggs, and bacon, along with home fries and fresh fruit. Once they were into the meal that we all helped to serve, my mother gave us a sign to exit the room. These men, representative of some organization, wished to speak to my father in private. Bits and pieces of that meeting were picked up by the remainder of the family, but it would take years for each of us to understand the tremendous impact of what really transpired.

The visiting gentlemen represented the Italian Consulate and were requested by the Italian Government to call upon my father. It seemed that Father Trivassano held the deeds to over twenty lots surrounding the church. The deeds were given to the church as gifts in the pre-war days. By now, all of these lots were diminished to rubble. Many of the deeds were made out to Father Trivassano and not the church per se. It was always his intention to correct the error, but he never made the effort because of the war. These same lots were held in his personal estate and listed in his will.

After his recent death, Father Trivassano's estate and will were explored. Since he had no one family member remaining alive, he bequeathed any and all of his personal belongings to Antonio Pagna.

Several years had transpired before the province of Messina could straighten out the problem. Since my father had corresponded with Father Trivassano through the years, several of his letters were kept by the priest. The consulate found the letters and identified my father, now living in the United States.

The committee entertained at breakfast that Sunday morning presented my father proof of ownership. They were concerned because the rubble was cleared and buildings appeared, but ownership of the land the buildings rested on was lost in the estate. To clear all the legal ramifications the committee was here to offer my father compensation so that the homeowners on the property would own both the land and the buildings on it.

After hearing the proposal they made, all of the men sighed with respect and relief when he told them simply, "Whoever lives on them, owns them. They now own the land." My father could not bear to profit from an oversight and knew Father Trivassano would understand the generous act.

"Bravo, bravo," the four men clapped after my father's statement.

My mother and all of us heard the applause and saw the laughter with each shaking my father's hand as they rose up to leave.

"What was that about, Tony?"

"Nothing, Rose, a little unfinished business from the old country."

It was over and not until nearly thirty years later would we know just what business it was.

Joe no longer had time for sports; he was too busy in the adult world. Uncle Mike saw in the handsome Joe a trusted soldier and brought him into his own circle. He arranged for Joe to help manage an after-hours gambling spot owned by Uncle Mike. Joe wore full suits to school and drove a used Cadillac Uncle Mike was able to procure cheaply. Joe became thirty five long before he was twenty.

Dad's shop, with the extra cobbler, gave him some freedom. He and Mom planned to visit Mom's sister, Mary. Aunt Mary had remarried, sold her beauty shop in Cuyahoga Falls, and moved with her new husband to Phoenix, Arizona.

More and more, Dad's high blood pressure led to dizziness and headaches, and the stress of his work needed to be relieved. While they were visiting Aunt Mary in Phoenix, Dad became quite ill. They hospitalized Dad, and the doctors found that he had a diseased kidney. It probably was the work of his childhood attack of scarlet fever. The doctors felt confident that removal of the kidney would solve the problem. Mom stayed until Dad was well on his way to recovery. Aunt Mary's husband urged Dad to stay several months extra, since the sun and air seemed to agree with him. Mom agreed that Dad should stay, but she felt strongly that she had to return to Ohio.

Only Mom really knew the real quandary of our family finances. Returning from college on a holiday weekend, Sam found her weeping. It was not often anyone saw this of our Mom.

"Mom," Sam asked. "What's so wrong? I've rarely seen you cry?"

She stifled her sobs and cleared her throat, looked directly at Sam, and said as though a confession: "I never thought that your father would not be able to work. Everything we've done, all our plans, your college, our home, the business, all depends on his steady drop in the bucket. I've never told him, but with the doctor bills, the property in Colorado . . . yes even the furniture we've bought," she gestured around the room. "Sam we're broke!"

"Does Dad realize?"

"No!" She spat out in anger – not at Sam but the concept. "He has no idea! I had no idea! Where the hell did it go? And what's coming in?"

That evening Sam and Mom talked into the night. At long last, Sam grasped the situation fully. He painstakingly had rooted out our status in every aspect of the family. Mom broke down and cried again when she told Sam she had even borrowed money from her own father to pay his last tuition.

"I couldn't let your father know."

"He has a right to know!" Sam insisted. "I have a right to know!"

"He's sick, dammit . . . he's sick, and I didn't know where to turn."

Sam turned full focus on his tiny mother. He thought how well she had run our family and what a marvelous upbringing each child had as a result of her hard work.

How could she be blamed for the complexity that pressed them? She had made each move with calculated good faith. Her positive attitude never considered failure, illness, or bad timing. He hugged her close and kissed her.

"Mom," he spoke gently. "I've had an idea going through my head that could help us. See what you think." He continued, as Mom sat in silence. "I'm a damned good musician, but I doubt I'll ever be great. There have been times at the conservatory where I've seen so many people with so much talent, I've questioned my own. I'm a showman though, Mom, and I love to entertain. There was an ad I answered to be the accordion accompanist for a very renowned, world famous, ballroom dance team. Their names are Veloz and Yolanda. They are to go on tour shortly. If I make the audition, I'll leave school."

"That's not what you want!"

"Maybe it is, Mom. Maybe this situation makes the decision for me . . . I've been struggling with it anyhow."

Within the month, Sam received notice that he had been selected. There were many talented people, but Frank Veloz saw a flair and showmanship in Sammy Pagna. He liked the stocky lad and his black wavy hair, the clean-cut face, and, most of all, he liked the sense of humility that he knew to be real.

At the start of my sophomore year, I debuted on the Springfield High varsity. The high school aligned in a T formation and ran many plays from it. Sometimes however, they would shift from the T, and the quarterback would shift to the tailback in the single wing. From this formation, the tailback could be a run, pass, or kick threat.

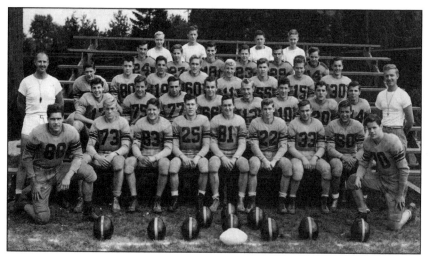

The 1946–47 Springfield team, during my sophomore year. I'm in the second row (#17). It was during this year that I was the Metro leading scorer.

I was listed on the roster as the no. 2 quarterback, but played as a starter as a defensive safety. In two days, Dad would be flying in from Arizona. I was elated that he would see our opening game.

When he was driven up the drive by Uncle Mike, the sound of tires on the gravel alerted us that he was home. Mom had made all the preparations and food. All of us resolved not to rush our father. Terry would go first, as he came through the door. It had been three long months since his operation. Uncle Mike opened the door, and Dad stepped inside to view his family. In a rush Terry went to him. He bent a bit and placed a hand under each of her shoulders, swooping her up to his face. He kissed her face all over and fought tears for a moment. He put her down and hugged Mom . . . a long, loving, God-it's-good-to-see-you hug. He went to Sam with a bear hug, then to Joe, then to me.

Uncle Mike, watching Dad and his family, felt the genuine love flowing through each and was himself touched deeply.

Dad had lost nearly forty pounds. His once round torso had given way to a svelte waistline. His face was thinner now and very tan from the Phoenix sun. Never had he appeared to be in better health. His eyes shone brightly as he flashed a grateful smile and said "*Deo grazia*. It's great to be home!"

True to his promise, Dad brought Mom and Terry to watch me play. After only a quarter, the chill of the night air got to Dad, and they had to leave early for home.

Late in the fourth quarter, I intercepted a pass and returned it for a touchdown. Learning that they all left early, I went directly home, my elation tempered at my father's illness.

Mom had already put him to bed. He was shivering and said he did not feel well. Mom read the disappointment in my eyes.

"He saw you play a little while, Tom, and he was very proud."

The next morning, a Saturday, our family held a meeting. Dad had a very bad night and through the night suffered a hemorrhage in the region of the eyes. It had blurred his vision and though he could focus at a distance, he had lost the capacity of fine focus. Alarmed, Mom sent for Dr. Arapakis.

"He looked so well on his return, Doctor," she said.

"Rose," Arapakis interrupted her. "Get him back out to that climate. It agrees with him." As Dad slept, Sam, Joe, Terry, and I spoke with Mom.

"We'll have to sell the house," she said resignedly. "And the shoe shop," Sam added.

"I'll take him to Colorado," Mom spoke. "If he can live best there, then that's where we'll go!"

Within six weeks, Mom had an offer to buy at $35,000. She broke the news to Dad, and though it saddened him, he agreed. Terry would go with Mom, Joe and I would live with Aunt Flora, and Sam would be our lone breadwinner on tour with Veloz and Yolanda.

Joe and I sat on the wall overlooking our drive as people went in and out of our home, a great sadness fell upon us though we maintained our composure in silence. Mom was selling off her cherished possessions. The baby grand piano went quickly, as did most of the furniture.

As Joe viewed the lake, he recalled the special kick he got out of tossing a fistful of oats in the lake while we waited on the school bus. Panfish bigger than a large man's hand – sunfish, blue gill, bass, and pike – all lurched at the oats in a frenzy. Then Joe reminisced about the morning he and I landed the longest and largest muskrat ever caught in the area. It had been dangerous, and the muskrat was still alive when Joe pulled the chain from the trap to a stake in the ground. A thin veneer of ice became darkly shadowed as the giant swam under it.

Joe ordered me to whack the giant muskrat as he pulled hard on the chain. A couple of near misses with a baseball bat, and we were half-laughing and half-afraid we would lose this trophy.

A huge pull by Joe, and the muskrat, with gnashing teeth and whipping tail and claws, exited out of his sanctuary on to the island bank. I caught him squarely on the back of the head. Once stretched, the water rodent measured forty-four inches. We received $10 for the pelt and another $20 for the largest muskrat of the season.

In the meantime, I was thinking of our first winter there, when we had kids over to play ice hockey on the lake. We created makeshift goals out of chicken wire and poles. Our puck was a smooth old basketball and the hockey sticks old brooms. It had been great fun in the cold of winter during Christmas vacation. We built a bonfire on the bank, and Mom prepared hot chocolate and cookies for all the contestants.

These daydreams vanished when the people at the auction carried out the grandfather's clock. It was the last large item auctioned, and Mom's insurance man had eyed it earlier as he inventoried the house. He was gleeful as he directed its move to his awaiting pickup truck.

We understood the symbolic significance the clock had held for Mom. It had been one of her "someday" items . . . maybe THE item. It was gone. *Someday* had become *yesterday*.

In the minute we watched the truck exit the long driveway carrying the clock, both Joe and I had finalized drastic decisions. Though made separately, they were made in silence together.

"I'm quitting school," Joe announced to me. Though he had only a little over a semester to go to graduate, Joe knew he could work in the factory during the day and Uncle Mike's after-hours spot at night.

It was a hard decision for me also. Even though it was only mid-season and I was only a backup quarterback, I was leading the league in points scored.

"I'm going with them to Colorado," I answered back to Joe. "To hell with the season . . . they need us." It was settled. Mom did not try to dissuade either of us. Her mind was too full of other concerns.

There were three weeks of making arrangements and packing before Uncle Mike would take Dad and Mom, Terry and me out to Colorado. A week earlier was the opening of Veloz and Yolanda in Cincinnati.

Dad rallied himself, telling Mom, "I want to see him on stage."

Veloz and Yolanda would appear in Cincinnati for three performances. It was the third performance the Pagnas were to attend.

Though Sam had not mentioned it, his first performance had received mixed reviews. Mr. Veloz arranged a fast-moving and diverse act that showed off the variety of entertainers in his troop. A comic, after finishing his own act, pointed to the wings and introduced the young accordionist, Sammy Pagna.

As the comic passed Sam on the stage he whispered, "Your fly is open." Sammy stood sideways, wearing the forty-pound accordion and performed his solo. After finishing, he nodded once and walked offstage. When he discovered his fly was indeed not open, he became furious. After the show was over, Sam chased the comic from the dressing area into a locked room next to Mr. Veloz's. Mr. Veloz heard the commotion outside his dressing room. When he saw the livid Sam pounding on the door and threatening the comic physically, he at once knew what had transpired. He calmed Sam down and he explained that it was an old show-business trick that troupers had played on one another for years.

Mr. Veloz knew Sam's mother and father would be at the

third performance. He stated calmly to Sam, "Put that behind you and perform the way you can . . . no anger . . . no retaliation. You have a naturalness, Sammy. It exudes warmth and crowds sense it! Do nothing that destroys that!"

When Mr. Veloz saw the comic exit his door, he said only, "Choose your target well, my friend. Some have great memories and this one," he pointed at Sam, "is a Sicilian! No more bull-crap!"

When Dad and Mom, Nate and Flora, Mike and Marie seated themselves in the large auditorium, they were center stage and about ten rows back. Mr. Veloz had seen to their seating and tickets.

The lights dimmed, and a hush fell upon the audience as a light samba beat came from the orchestra pit. Slowly the curtains parted, and a bright spotlight hovered the left center stage. In an instant the spotlight stopped and focused on Sammy. He picked up the melody to match the samba beat and the tune "Brazil." His black shiny hair gleamed in the spotlight. Sam's flashing smile showed the pleasure of a performer in his own element. He was dressed in black tuxedo pants and a white fluffy-sleeved silken blouse with a red sash around his waist. As his dexterous fingers glided the keyboard, the expanse of accordion across his chest, his feet took miniature samba steps to the melody he provided.

In an instant, at the back of center stage, another larger and brighter spotlight focused on the flawless dance team of Veloz and Yolanda. Yolanda was swan-like in her beauty. Her raven-black hair was pulled back severely, like that of a ballerina. She was dressed in a form-fitted white gown of intricate lace design. At her knees, the gown flared out into a normal gown. Veloz was dressed in a black tuxedo with a ruffled shirt and brilliant red tie. They literally floated and bounced, gyrating to the rhythm and becoming part of it. They owned the dance, the music, their art, and the audience. With sensational ease and mastery they covered every inch of the stage area.

Toward the end of their theme song, they came to a center position on the stage and in a crescendo of intricate accordion chords ended in a twirl and abrupt stop, their right arms flung to the ceiling, their left ones embracing. The applause and reception was thunderous. Mr. Veloz greeted the crowd warmly and singled out young Sammy for his own share of applause.

The evening was a rare treat for audiences that loved the Latin American rhythms and could appreciate the artistry involved with every dance step displayed. Midway into the show, while Veloz and Yolanda underwent a costume change, the comedian spot arrived. He was a very funny man in looks, motions, and delivery. After his bows he introduced the next act, "The brilliant accordion soloist Sammy Pagna!"

Sammy selected a tune for his solo that called for all the diversity an accordion could display. It was a semi-classical presentation of "El Ricario." It provided him the opportunity to show his dexterity, timing, and flare. He had rehearsed it for months and rendered a flawless delivery. He trebled the accordion with his powerful arms and made it look like pure pleasure. In actuality it was quite hard. The crowd, sensing the difficulty of execution, applauded mid-song and followed at the ending with another solid applause.

Dad grasped Mom's hand, "Excellante," he said with excitement tingling his voice.

The total performance was a huge success. My parents had been transfixed, as were the others in the arena. Just before the finale Mr. Veloz called out each member of the troop. His introduction of the members was presented lightly and in good humor. When he came to Sammy, he asked first that Sammy's mother and father rise in the audience. A spotlight shined brightly on them as they stood proudly and waved.

When it was over and they were waiting to speak to Sammy before heading back, Dad whispered to Mom, "I could not be more proud." She felt the same. Sam would be on tour now for nearly a year, with a second one pending. The troop would weave itself across the U.S. and parts of Canada. In the second year, it was scheduled to visit Central and South America and perhaps Europe.

Veloz and Yolanda had been touring nearly twenty-five years in all. This was to be their last full swing before retirement and perhaps a spot or two in the movies.

Chapter 8
"And Watch the Things You Gave Your Life To, Broken."
Rudyard Kipling

My father weathered the car trip to Colorado fairly well as Uncle Mike did the driving. Mom's good friend Connie and husband Pete were to meet us in Grand Junction, Colorado.

On the last day of the trip, Dad told Mom that he had seen small blood patterns in his urine and stool, and he was beginning to feel very weak. As these symptoms became more and more apparent, Mom decided to admit Dad to the Grand Junction hospital. Connie's and Pete's cabin and the property we had purchased was forty miles away, outside a small community called Rifle. Mom decided she would go back to see the progress being made on the living quarters of the small ranch and try to prepare it for Dad's eventual coming. On the weekends, Connie and Pete drove her to Grand Junction to visit. It gave a fairly renowned staff of medical doctors a chance to run a multitude of tests on Dad.

When Mom, Terry, and I were settled in with Connie and Pete, Uncle Mike headed back on the long drive to Akron.

From the town of Rifle, one had to traverse thirteen miles of rugged mountain country to reach the 165-acre ranch. The plot of ground sat at 7500 feet of altitude and was quite lonely and remote from other neighbors.

Three miles before reaching the ranch there was another, larger one, and adjacent to that, a one-room schoolhouse. One mile before entering our gate lived our nearest neighbor who ran a small saw mill. The last three miles from the school house up were steep and treacherous, full of grooves washed out of the red clay road. It was slow going in the pickup.

When we arrived at the gate and drove through the winding quarter-of-a-mile driveway, we spotted the small hunter's cabin Connie and Pete called home. It was solidly built with rough-hewn logs on the exterior and a mud mortar sealing the seams.

Inside was a huge cook stove and a wood-burning pot-bellied stove. Though it was a large one room, it was only one room.

The entire cabin was surrounded on three sides by three large mountain peaks. The open side faced downwards toward the town. Beyond the cabin was a corral, rather large, made from cedar posts. Off to one side of the cabin was the foundation for our home to be. Several walls had been erected but, as of yet, the completion of the roof was far from finished. Upon inspecting it, Mom made a mental note that the roof was a top priority if Dad were to be moved here. Only the kitchen area had been roofed and enclosed. A pot-bellied wood stove was inside, but the rest of the house was unframed.

Dad, Pete, and Mom, with the 16 lb. Jackrabbit Dad shot in Colorado.

Where the house sat, one had a full view of the three mountain sides. The middle mountain slope had 60 acres of hayfield, showing a bright green. The expanse of mountains it ran into were a potpourri of color and majestic design. It was breathtakingly beautiful at sunset or sunrise.

Sleeping arrangements were made, and Mom, Connie, and Terry took the hunter's cabin, while Pete and I slept in the bedroom framed and sided but not roofed. The evenings were quite cold in early fall, and we both slept fully clothed, with plenty of extra blankets. Often upon our waking up, there was a thin layer of snow across our blankets.

With Mom on the scene to direct them, the carpenters framed in three completed rooms and were busy roofing them. She wanted it at least livable when Dad would be dismissed from the hospital. Each weekend all five of us took the trip to Grand Junction to visit him.

It was the end of the third week when the Doctor in charge of the medical staff pulled Mom aside.

"Mrs. Pagna," he began slowly. "Your husband's bloodstream is completely filled with cancer cells. It is as though a floodgate were opened from one source and spread throughout." A saddened Rose took the jolt courageously, still of the mind that this bull of a man could not be dying.

"Are you saying that he is dying?"

"Yes, and within a short time."

"How long?" she asked somberly.

"Two weeks, perhaps a month. If it is easier on you, I can break the news to him."

"Thank you, Doctor, but no. We've always been very open to one another, and I want him to know as soon as possible and from me."

"Whatever you think best, Mrs. Pagna."

Mom asked Pete and Connie, Terry and me to allow her a few moments with Dad alone. She looked at him, but her expression betrayed her, and Dad read her eyes accurately.

"It's okay, Rose," he said softly. "I think I knew the night I had the first hemorrhage that the end was near."

"It's not okay," she felt anger. "My God, Tony, you're only forty-seven years old!"

"Listen to me . . . listen," he calmed her down. "When they removed the diseased kidney in Phoenix, they explained that they thought they got all of the cancer, but they also explained that there was a great possibility of exposing any remaining cancer. Rose," he continued, "let us do what needs to be done. If I have only a little time, then let me see what we're building in the mountains, and then get me back to Akron before I die, that I might say goodbye to my mother and the rest."

The doctor, after learning of his plans, told Mom that airplane travel would lessen his time, as the altitude would cause his blood to thin and bleeding would be enhanced. He suggested a train and perhaps a nurse to administer blood plasma if necessary. Immediately, Mom called her brother Mike, whose third wife was a registered nurse. Her name was Marie. Marie was a tall attractive Texan whom Mike had met while visiting Texas. Their marriage, her first, his third, seemed providential at this time.

"And Mike," Mom added by way of an order, "notify my boys," she could not say the words easily, "their dad is dying."

In the few days it took for Marie to arrive by train to Rifle, Colorado, Mom brought Dad to the small ranch. The first day he arrived, we sat him in a large soft chair, warmly wrapped in blankets and looking out a wide picture window facing the ascending mountains. The picture window and the living room adjoined the kitchen. At Mom's insistence, these two rooms were the first to be completed. Beds were brought into the living room, as the pot-bellied stove from the kitchen could easily warm both rooms.

Dad gazed at the mountains from early morning till noon, at which time Mom fed him broth. He slept in the chair off and on, but when he awoke, again resumed his gaze of the landscape.

I filled twenty-gallon milk cans with spring water. It was no small chore lugging the heavy cans almost one hundred and fifty yards to the spring and then back again, full. Pete and I cut plenty of firewood and made sure the fire in the stove wouldn't go out. Mom wanted to heat water and bathe Dad. The second evening, after Terry and I had fallen asleep, Mom shook my arm to awaken me.

"Your father's in trouble," she whispered with urgency. "I need your help."

Dad awakened during the night to a sticky mess of blood. From the side he was laying on, the internal bleeding had formed a huge pouch below his jaw and in his neck area. The external blood was oozing from every opening – his belly button, his rectum, nose, and mouth.

With painstaking care and remarkable control, Mom bathed

away the crust of blood left as residue. Dad was very weak and his eyes were dim with dwindling strength.

"Like a baby, eh?" he said to me, as my mother toweled him down and put a fresh pair of pajamas on him.

"No, Dad," I was quick to reply. "not a baby . . . a man!" One hell of a man, I thought.

Through the night, between scattered moments of sleep in a nearby chair, I watched with awesome admiration the constant care my mother administered to my father. She bathed him, took his pulse, his temperature, fed him broth, held his hands and reassured him everything would be fine. In the span of the one evening I broke the bonds of childhood as I witnessed the adult world of reality, and saw heroic moments from both my mother and father. It would etch itself deeply in my memory forever.

"Once," I would always be able to say, "in this less than perfect world, I saw perfect love!" I was so touched by the unabashed caring my mother gave to my father, I buried my head, hiding the tears that filled my eyes.

In that instant, I had the knowledge that I would never be a boy again. I was 14when morning light appeared and at long last, Dad was asleep. I tended the fire. Connie and Pete were off to meet Marie at the Rifle train station. The very next morning, armed with plasma, pain killers, and other assorted medicine, we left for Akron. Connie and Pete assured Mom they'd see to the completion of the house, and they bid us all goodbye.

Dad was placed in a sleeping compartment where there also was room for Marie. In an adjoining compartment were Mom, Terry, and I. It seemed a long, exhausting trek back to Akron – the train, with its endless clacking and rocking, and the time, broken only to make a pit stop at some small shadow of a town. It would take two complete days and nights, plus a transfer in Cleveland, before we were back.

Aunt Marie was an ex-WAC in the nursing corps. She was masterful in her care and patience. She made all the arrangements with doctors along the way and the conductor on board. Only rarely did she leave Dad's compartment for a break or a visit with Mom.

It was the second evening, and Marie was showing signs of fatigue. She was just opening the door from the compartment when I asked her if I could stay with Dad for a while. She was visibly grateful for the break.

For a long time, Dad was asleep, and I merely sat and watched his breathing pattern. My eyes surveyed the intravenous plasma entering his bloodstream. For a moment, I dwelled upon his face. It was a strong, honest face. This was a man who laughed easily and loved life, family, and America. He was always so incredibly strong in his prime. This once–215-pound man had dwindled to less than 140. His skin hung loosely from his once powerful arms.

His eyes flickered open, and he caught my presence. He smiled slightly and said my name, "Tommy." He took my hand in his, "How long you been there?"

"Just a while, Dad, just a little while."

"You gotta be a man now, Tommy," he said as he saw my eyes brimming with tears I fought to hold back.

"I know Dad . . . and I will be, I promise. I haven't been much . . ."

"Sshh . . ." he stopped me in mid-apology, "you are my son, and I love you like the rest . . . that's all."

With this, I laid my head upon his chest, hugging him dearly for a long time, all the while sobbing gently. He patted me fondly on the back . . . no words were necessary.

We arrived in Akron at the train depot where both Sam and Joe were there to help carry the litter supporting our father. Uncle Mike and I manned the other two corners. We brought him directly to the Akron City Hospital. Once in Akron his condition rallied. Donna Theresa was sent for, and Dad spent several hours talking with his mother.

On the third day back, the doctors suggested that Mom summon a priest, that the rally was indicative only of the end. Dad asked to see Terry, and Mom brought her for a brief moment. He gazed upon his darling daughter, kissed and hugged her, saying with a half smile, "Always listen to your Momma." His five-year-old daughter, not sure of what the situation was, nodded affirmatively and hugged her father one last time.

Dad sighed heavily and said as Mom was leaving with Terry, "Send in the boys, Rose."

She came into the hall and said simply, "Your father wants to see his sons."

When we entered, Sam stood at Dad's right side, Joe on the other, and I at the foot of the bed.

"I wanna," he began, "say a few things to my sons. First . . . I don't think I'm going to make it . . . and . . ."

Sam interrupted, "Sure you will." We all three chided in together.

"Okay," he acknowledged the hope. "If I don't make it . . . there are some important things I must say." He looked directly at Sam and said, "The home with the lake . . . buy it back for your mother."

"I will, Dad," Sam said. He had no idea how, but he agreed eagerly.

"Good . . . and now you three," he gestured with his hand encompassing all of us. "Promise me three things."

"Anything," we responded in unison.

"See to it always," he was fighting back his own emotion, "your mother is always taken care of."

"We promise."

"And your sister."

"Yes. Yes, we promise."

"And,". . . he paused, "Never . . . never fight among yourselves." With this he raised his right fist, and we covered it with our hands.

He was very tired and seemed to know we received his message. He eased back to his pillow and formed a pleased, proud look with his lips and a slight nod. "I sleep now."

Mom was staying with Aunt Flora along with Terry and me. Early the next morning, Aunt Flora received the call. Dad died that night.

Mom sat in a chair and gazed through the living room window out into the world, seeing everything and seeing nothing. She was stunned that he was gone.

"How could it be?" she asked of herself. "This once-powerful man reduced to nothing, in just a few short years."

The impression of our father's funeral left two impacts on our family – first, that he was so widely known and so well thought of. Hundreds of people came to the wake. A tall man with gold teeth put his hand upon Sam's shoulder as he passed through the line to wish the family condolences. "Today," he whispered to Mom and Sam, "we lose our best friend."

Though familiar, no one seemed to know the man, except Dad's brother Gaetano, who answered him, "Indeed . . . our best friend!"

One of the women visitors from an adjoining wake, seeing the huge crowd, said, "He must have been some big politician or something."

Sam overheard the remark and said almost triumphantly, "No lady, just a little shoemaker!"

The second impression we received was the stark and shocking reality that our leader was dead. Until seeing him in the coffin, it had all seemed unreal.

Mom was in control of herself outside, but within, she was totally inconsolable. "Tony . . . my Tony," she almost blamed him, "How could you do this to us?"

Uncle Mike and Uncle Nate helped Mom put a down payment on a newly constructed home that was only a few blocks from where they lived. Aunt Dixie and her daughter Donna would live there as renters. Also Betty, who recently divorced her husband after he had physically abused her, was to rent a room. In this way, the three sisters, Donna, Terry, Joe, and I would have a home. The rent from Aunt Betty and Aunt Dixie nearly made the house payment.

Realizing Veloz and Yolanda would soon retire, Sam formed his own quintet. His travel and solid bookings would be the mainstay of our income. Joe too was bringing home a salary. At 39 years of age, with the hospital bills and charge cards that equaled nearly $30,000, Mom was penniless. The only equity we had left was the 160-acre ranch. That would have to wait. Terry and I enrolled back into school. It was 1947.

Dad's loss affected my mother and the three boys more intimately than Terry, she wasn't sure what death meant and that was a good thing. Sam, Joe, Mom, and I had major adjustments to make. Terry was too young for the total impact. It would reach her later.

Joe became enraged at the world. He trusted no one and disliked people easily. Sam was on a mission and set out to do what he knew best. A heavy responsibility fell upon his shoulders.

Joe, yours truly, Rose, Terry, and Mike during our transition time.

Re-enrolled, I went out for basketball when I returned to my old high school. Though I no longer lived in the same high-school district, I returned to Springfield Township, since they waived a small tuition. Under the same roof, Donna, nearly the same age as me, would attend a different school, the one in the district in which we lived. It was called Ellet High School, arch-rivals of Springfield Township.

It was a thrill for me to be back in the element of school and athletics. I made the team, and it was to serve me as a diversion from my recent loss.

It was only the first Friday game of the season when I, deeply involved with a basketball game, intercepted an errant pass from my frontal defensive position in our zone defense. I scampered with a few dribbles and arched the ball to my teammate across the floor. The ball was returned, and I grabbed it, took one giant step and was going in for a lay-up when an opponent also went up for the block. The opponent's knee caught me fully in my left thigh and I crumpled to the floor. It was the identical place of my earlier injury.

Once again, I was bedridden. The ice packs and the constant care of Dr. Arapakis had me pretty well mended, although limping around, within a month's time. By now it was the heart of winter, with ice and snow everywhere. On the first day of my return to school, I was very protective of my leg. I wore leather-heeled dress shoes and was careful with each step. My first class was study hall in the gymnasium. I started to ease down the aisle ramp. There was a bit of ice and snow on the heel of my right shoe. When I placed it on the ramp, it slid straight out in front of me and the left leg, the injured one that could not yet completely bend, doubled under me and my full body weight. I screamed at the knifing pain and lay there moaning only seconds when the ex-major coach heard me. He ran to me and gently picked me up, unknowingly putting one arm under my knees, thereby bending it again. The pain was excruciating and the coach carried me to his own car and brought me home.

Dr. Arapakis rushed to our home as soon as he could. He wished not to hospitalize me, since he knew we were deeply in debt. He sent his office nurse out on an every-other-day schedule. She administered to me various intravenous prescriptions. She saw to it also that Mom learned how to bathe me while bedridden. In a week or so the great pain subsided, but the tremendous swelling the internal wound had forced left a throbbing ache that seemed never to end. In the evenings when sleep would not come, the pain intensified. My mother could barely stand the heart-wrenching groans I must have made while asleep.

"That damned ball," she would swear to herself. "If it weren't for that damned ball."

Awake, I'd ask God to transfer the pain to my other leg just to give me a break for a little while. I would know emotional pain that was deeper, but no physical pain ever equaled what I underwent this time.

Once I heard Dr. Arapakis speaking with my mother outside of my bedroom door. I feigned sleep and listened intently. "He should not play anymore sports, Rose."

"I don't want anymore. I can't stand anymore!"

Then he added, "Don't tell him this now, Rose. Let him have all the hope he can, to recover."

Joe always stopped in to visit awhile when he came back from work, "How's it going?"

"Okay . . . better."

"Good." It could be that only Joe truly understood my great desire for sports. After two tough months of winter, spring broke, and I could get around on crutches. Mom allowed me to leave the bed and come out to the living room. I sat with my left leg extended on the couch. In this way, I could gaze out the large picture window and view the outside. Aunts Ann, Betty, Dixie, Flora, and Mary all visited and brought me reading materials. I began to read everything they brought. From Aunt Betty's collection, I *discovered The Great Snow, Moby Dick, David Copperfield.* These and countless others inspired my mind, and I read throughout each day.

I read many things in those recovery days, but two very special stories stick with me. I really didn't understand the significance or the essence of the subject matter until I was well into my sixties.

The first notable impact made on my impressionable mind was a treatise written on faith by Bishop Fulton J. Sheen. At the onset, he pointed out that the gift of faith was bestowed upon the very wise and the very humble. The three wise men and, in contrast, the shepherds in the fields. The distribution of faith was both practical and symbolic. It was obviously a plan designed to dramatically emphasize who the recipients would be. It was not coincidence, but something pre-ordained, for a reason. Bishop Sheen saw the division as one that would always be present in the world – the two extremes, separated by a majority middle. He observed candidly that as the world grew older, it would undoubtedly move from simplistic to more complex. Knowledge would blossom and flower, discovery would increase, and technology would replace the old with the new. The irony presented in this view also existed within the realm of men's thoughts. Thoughts, beliefs, habits, and customs would change. Sophistication and worldly pride fostered arrogance. Though the very wise and the very simple may always trust in the faith of scripture, the vast middle would be too caught up with living life to see or understand clearly. These, would always be hovering between the two extremes.

To illustrate this, Bishop Sheen fashioned an analogy that imprinted itself on my mind. He likened the whole of faith to the face of a clock. At 12:00 o'clock were those he labeled as "Don't Think." It was not a derogatory label. He knew that a certain group of people would never doubt God, question their faith, or impugn the sacred scripture. It was a kind of pure faith untainted by the world; hence the shepherds! Forever in the world, there would be those of simple faith, believing and living it until the end. I believe my parents easily fit this category. That isn't to say that they are simpletons who never doubt, ask questions, or get troubled or stymied. It is to say that, despite the consequences, they would persevere in the faith. They never even had to think about that!

Moving from that point halfway around the clock, we find a large part of humanity at 12:30. For these people, who can be described as "of the world," there begins to be a reliance on practicality and expediency.

The recording of personal lifetime experiences begins to taint their innocence with rebellion, greed, corruption, false pride, and arrogance. A kind of; what's-in-it-for-me? mentality flowers. Material things, wealth, trappings, possessions crowd out any spiritual blessing of faith. These depend more upon themselves, believe more in themselves, and discard anything that does not meet their own concept of right, comfort, pleasure, etc.

Knowledge of the world, is not wisdom. It does not harbor fertile ground to nurture faith in God. It is "of the world." Anywhere from 12:00 o'clock to 12:30 o'clock are degrees and measures of breaking away from pure faith. So far removed by false premises and concepts, is this grouping, it becomes easy and natural to create schisms and splinter groups, even to the point of one's own personal gods.

So 12:30, diametrically opposed to 12:00, the bishop called, "Those who think they think." These are worldly people, some very bright and gifted, some well educated, but all self-assured of their own prowess are as far away from truth and faith as they can be. Within this grouping, at this precise juncture, is where wars are made, blood is spilled, life is cheap, and corruption the norm . . . people led by people. "The blind leading the blind."

But the world or fate does not decree that all are blocked and dead-ended at 12:30. A very few, a rare breed, through life-long searches and traumatic and humbling experiences, reach a point of such humility they overthrow the trivial distractions of the world. They fight through the world's knowledge and emerge into a crystallized wisdom. From 12:30 o'clock, they walk, creep, and crawl toward a new time.

It is not 12:00 o'clock anymore, it is a new time, but it contains the same pure faith. It is for them, 1:00 o'clock, paid for in full by the endless effort of seeking truth. These become "wise men"; these are inspired by the dispenser of wisdom, the Holy Spirit. These are those souls who fell to the temptations and enticements of the world. Perceiving the deceit and illusion of this temporary condition, they fight to rise above it. When they arrive, they are filled with awe and amazement by a mere glimpse into the Divine mystery.

The only way to 1:00 o'clock is by way of 12:30. Bishop Sheen calls these, *Those that truly think.* They have gone full cycle; they are very few.

The most unforgettable novel I ever read, was presented to me by my Aunt Betty. To ease the pain of my recovery she gave me a copy of A.J. Cronin's, *Keys of the Kingdom.* Years later, I would see the story presented in a great movie starring Gregory Peck. No matter. The novel left such a remarkable impression, the movie was just a visual confirmation.

I had always seen life as unrelated slices – a piece here, a fragment there. This story spoke of a total life, not only comprised of slices. The whole loaf was everything!

The story is of a young boy, orphaned at twelve and raised by grandparents, who soon die. Somber from this and his parents' accidental deaths, he migrates to the ministry. He is not blessed with a handsome appearance, he is a bit slow of speech and not gifted in any particular way. He plods and grinds through his novitiate and makes his final vows, becoming a priest. With little or no outstanding traits, he is marked for missionary work in China by the hierarchy, wishing to avoid any future embarrassments. Almost his entire priesthood is served in China. Completely unknown to himself; his work is powerful, meaningful, and infuses great faith in his followers. He baptizes, marries, buries, and, in general, fulfills all of the priestly functions. Spanning almost fifty years, his work entails the building of a church. It is destroyed by war and rebuilt. It is destroyed by flood once and fire yet another time. He survives it all and rebuilds. To himself; he is an abject failure.

There are tiny victories and major setbacks. He is humbled at his apparent inadequacy, never realizing his own worth to man or to God. Through his efforts, thousands are baptized, more thousands are converted. He is a doctor, an advisor, a co-worker, a soldier, a priest, and whatever he has to be for his people. As age begins to burden him through sickness and infirmity, he is called back to America and given a small, very poor parish in New England, where he had spent his childhood.

His church is old and sorely in need of repair, but loving his own little parish and congregation, he works daily to do what he can. Because the parish is always in the red, mismanagement is suspected. An auxiliary bishop is assigned to it for an inspection. The bishop is a very young man rising rapidly to hold such a high position. He was born into wealth and was afforded the best education and all that went with it. He arrives at the parish and speaks to the old priest in condescending tones, born of a practiced arrogance. He proclaims the Church's disfavor with the priest's managing of the parish, saying that his report will recommend relieving the priest of the responsibility and suggesting he be placed in "the rest home for their order."

The elderly priest is devastated, his total life's work and a desire to fulfill his days in this small parish are rapidly crumbling. The auxiliary bishop announces that he will stay the night before returning to his headquarters in the morning. The old priest, now quite gray and bent with age, remains a priestly priest to the last. He offers the bishop the comfort of his own bed and bedroom upstairs, insisting that he often sleeps on the couch in the downstairs study. The bishop's demeanor and actions convey that he expected as much. Haughtily, the bishop says "Goodnight," saying he is retiring to the bedroom to write his report.

He obviously sees the old gentleman as an incompetent, a dried-up and used-up old man. His report will reflect this.

When the bishop enters the bedroom, he removes his coat, sits on a chair near a desk, and removes his shoes. In his bent position, he views a large tome of papers neatly packaged between leather bindings, underneath the edge of the bed. Curiously, he slides the book out from its place and opens it. Though it is early evening, he becomes so involved with the content, he reads it from cover to cover. It is a daily log, kept by the old priest from the day of his ordination until the very last entry . . . the day before. It is a record of the man's thoughts, his actions, his insecurities and doubts. It is the summary of his life. It is one way he converses with God. The sun was well up when the bishop finished reading.

The bishop's mind reflected upon this half-century of dutiful service, immense humility, selfless servitude, and enormous amounts of prayer and fasting. It was never complaining but accepting, never prideful; rather it was self-reproachful for not doing better.

A shock wave of awareness poured over the young bishop's consciousness. Such an insightful look into a man's soul caused in him a revelation he would never again be able to equal. Within an instant, he no longer saw an old and bumbling priest of questionable worth. A new and profound knowledge of the man formed for him. The man had lived an almost saintly life, and where others may have found nothing, God had found a priestly priest!

The immensity of this full realization brought the bishop to sobs, so ashamed was he of his snobbery and pre-judgment. A gentle knock upon the door startles the bishop as he composes himself and says, "Come In." The old priest enters carrying a tray of a freshly prepared breakfast. He himself had made the bacon and eggs, kept the toast warm, the coffee hot, and saw to its delivery by climbing the steep staircase.

The bishop, again losing composure, began a tearful protest. His face contorted he exclaimed, "No! No! my dear, dear man. It is not for you to serve. I am not worthy to kiss your shoes!" With this the bishop bent to all fours, kissing the aged priest's. Needless to say, the priest maintains his own parish and truth triumphs. That book, that scene, filled me with great inspiration. It taught me a truth at an early age that I would often hide amid my personal baggage but, thank God, never forget. The truth is that one day, or one success, or one failure, or one mistake, or one sin, or one person, or one act of kindness is never the total of a life. The book of life must be judged by all the pages and the later chapters can surely balance the earlier ones if one just keeps on trying.

When Donna Theresa visited me, she handed me my first rosary and said in her halting mixture of Italian and English, "You pray . . . hear me? You pray . . . firsta . . . St. Anthony then St. Rocco . . . then," she pointed to the rosary as though it were the biggie, "*Benedire Maria*" ("Blessed Mary"). Whatever you pray, she hears! She maka you wella, and your prayers alla coma true! *Capece?*"

"Yes, Nanna, *io Capece!*" ("I understand").

In the next four months, I had read all about Lourdes and Fatima. I never missed the lectures on the small television that my Uncles Nate and Mike brought me. My favorite was a brilliant theologian, Bishop Fulton J. Sheen. Bishop Sheen said that prayer was the single most powerful thing anyone could do on this earth. He stated convincingly that to pray to Jesus Christ and to his Mother Mary was to bring them into your very own presence and that they heard every word you said.

Daily, I prayed the rosary. I truly believed the good bishop and prayed daily to be well, play football, and win a scholarship to Notre Dame. One day, I was sure I might even play professionally and rid my mother of her debts.

Mom was distraught over our financial picture and knew deep down that what little investment we held was in Colorado. Either that investment had to be harvested by sale, or we should return there to live. Each evening her mind turned to this decision.

Years back, when my parents fought the conscience battle about birth control, they stopped going to church. Though Sam had received a first communion, Joe, Terry, and I knew little of formal religion . . . other than prayers.

It was a warm spring day, and I was resting on the sofa gazing out the window, when I saw a young priest making door-to-door stops.

"Mom," I called to her, "could I talk to him?" She summoned the young priest. He made arrangements to stop in to see me on a periodic basis.

It was in this way that Mom felt the pull back to the church. For nearly twenty years she had stayed away. Now she saw the hope in my eyes. She watched me pray my daily rosary, and she knew it had all gone full cycle. She would return to the church when I made my first communion. Joe too saw the change in our grieved mother. He witnessed the hope I had, and slowly the bitterness of Dad's death melted in him. Joe and I took our catechism lessons together.

Nearly a year had passed since the basketball injury. Having dropped out of school, it seemed unlikely I'd ever rejoin. Slowly I was allowed to move on crutches, putting just a portion of my weight upon the injured and wrapped leg. I was very thin, and my legs quite atrophied from inactivity, but my arms and shoulders, from handling the crutches, matched the spurt of growth I had at age 16.

One night, while watching TV, I heard the announcer mention a young Akron boy who played basketball for Miami of Ohio. Miami was playing Western Reserve University on one of the first basketball games televised. The Akron player, a short, stocky, dark-haired chunk of muscle was Ara Parseghian. I remembered the name because of its uniqueness. I also liked the aggressive play of young Parseghian. I'd remember him for the future.

Joe, still working in the metal factory, caught on with a large local dance band. Several times a week and always on weekends, he played the drums for extra income. This was his element, the one place that was a refuge. He loved the sound of a big band and felt he was the steam that pushed the band. His natural style improved with every outing. His sense of rhythm and innovative skill blossomed. He was truly a drummer and loved the action of it all.

Joe doubted that he'd ever return to high school. It held no meaning for him any longer. He ran with Uncle Mike and friends of Mike's. He was introduced to bars and show girls, hot cars and sleek-looking clothes. Never outgoing, and with an inner anger that would take years to subside completely, he lived life recklessly.

Sammy wrote home to Mom that, while in Tulsa, he met a girl he thought he could love and marry. He was bringing her home to Akron. When Virginia arrived, her beauty struck a chord with all. She was one-eighth Cherokee, and her high cheekbones and symmetric face fit her incredible carriage and posture. She walked as though she were a model. She had only a mother to raise her and made a hit with all of us. We too had made one with her.

Mom flew to Tulsa when Sam and Virginia were married. Virginia would travel with the band, much as an agent. Not only did she keep the books and arrange payroll, social security, etc., she made all the arrangements for rooms and future bookings.

Sam had wrestled a long time with the idea of marriage. He doubted strongly that he had the right, and though Mom assured him, "Of course you do," he was not convinced he should cut off income to Mom. Sam recalled Dad's admonition to the boys, "One parent can raise many children, but all the children cannot support one parent." Sam saw the truth of it and, without the push of Mom, would never have married.

In many ways, that marriage made a decision for Mom. She wanted to settle our property in Colorado, one way or another. Aunt Dixie and Aunt Betty assured Mom they could handle the house, and she should do whatever she needed to do. Plans were being made. Mom was on the move.

Shortly before Easter of that year, I asked Dr. Arapakis whether he thought I'd be able to bend my leg for first communion. He made no promises. Both Mom and Joe would also be taking communion. For Mom it was a return after may years, for Joe his very first. Before we left, I tried to bend my leg. No matter what I did, I could not. The deep clots were slowly dissolving but not enough to allow the muscle fibers complete flexion. A massive lump on my lower thigh prohibited the bend. Resigned, I went to church. I guessed that I would take communion standing.

When the priest elevated the host, saying the sacred words, "This is My Body. This is My Blood, Do this in remembrance of Me," we rose with our aisle. The three of us walked in the line that moved at a steady pace. When we arrived three abreast at the communion rail, both Mom and Joe kneeled down. Almost in a reflex action, I knelt beside them. The priest placed the wafer on our tongues. We stayed a moment, arose and walked back to the pew.

When we arrived at home, Mom said simply to me, as I was unaware of the act, "You kneeled at Communion."

Astonished, I said "I did?"

"You did," Joe confirmed it. Immediately I tried to kneel again. I could not.

"What does it mean?"

Mom spoke, "It is your sign that, if not now then later, you'll be able to bend it."

I would never know for sure if I had been part of a miracle, but I was happy with the accomplishment. It would be yet another year before the leg was fully healed and able to bend completely. Colorado was in our future for the next year. None of us knew what it would mean for any of us.

Shortly after Dad's funeral, Joe told me, "Whatever we do, we must never turn one hair of her head white," indicating Mom.

"I agree." I knew the depth of what Joe said.

It was Joe, very close to Dad, who would emerge as Mom's worst critic and greatest ally. "I can't let her go out there alone to live," he told Sam. "I'm going with her."

"I'm losing my drummer in a month, Joe," Sam said. "He's going into the Army. You could join me."

Joe was torn, but be had to see Mom settled, so he declined the offer. Shortly thereafter, Mom, Joe, Terry, and I returned by car to Colorado.

Chapter 9
"And Stoop to Build Them Up with Worn Out Tools."
Rudyard Kipling

A very happy and smiling Connie Duncan greeted us in the lobby of the only hotel in Rifle, The Pioneer. Mom wrote Connie and pre-arranged where we were all to meet. Connie introduced Pete to Joe; they had not met before this time.

Because there was several feet of snow on the ground, it would be virtually impossible to drive all the way up to the ranch. Connie instructed Joe to follow her pickup. We would all park near the barn of the ranch three miles below our own. Connie further arranged that Mom look at a large flat wagon for purchase. We already purchased a plow horse team earlier in the year with money sent from Mom, and the team was wintering here. The team would come in handy, and the wagon, of course, would convey all of us, plus the luggage, that remaining three miles. The drive upwards was slow going because the dirt had shifted considerably in places, and some of the bare patches that thawed were muddy and treacherous. When the pickup truck and Joe's car pulled into the area of the neighbors barn, Pete seemed hurried and quickly got out and ran, seeking the rancher.

The rest of us just got out and stretched. Within five minutes or so, Pete came out of the barn with the neighbor rancher, leading a huge pair of white horses.

"This here is Prince," he announced, "and the other one's Jerry. These are your horses, Rose . . . you bought 'em." They were gorgeous animals, both white, large and gentle.

"I also just made a deal for the wagon we'll be needing," the nervous Pete mumbled. "It's a good deal too for $40."

Mom searched through her purse and found two twenties and handed them to Pete. He disappeared into the barn, returning shortly, tugging on the wagon tongue to position it correctly so that he could hitch up the team.

Joe walked into the barn and met the rancher. "That's a fine-looking team of horses," he said.

"Yep," he replied. "They'll make your Maw a pretty good'un."

"And the wagon," Joe was feeling his way into a warmer conversation. "That was nice of you to sell that to us for . . . what was the price again?"

"Twenty five dollars. It's a real good wagon . . . sturdy."

"Well, we sure appreciate your kindness," Joe spoke in an obliging voice while he extended his hand. The rancher smiled and shook Joe's hand.

While Joe and Pete began to load all their luggage onto the wagon, Connie brought Mom and Terry up to the rancher's house and introduced them to Claudia, their new neighbor and the grade-school teacher, who taught all eight grades in the adjoining single-room schoolhouse. They were busy chatting, and Claudia was making small talk with Terry who would soon be her new student.

As soon as the rancher was out of earshot, Joe stopped his loading and turned to Pete, "Okay, you son of a bitch," he chewed the words out, enunciating each one without raising his voice. "You owe us $15. The wagon was $25. God only knows what the horses were!"

"Why . . . why . . ." Pete was flabbergasted at the accusation and the quick turn of Joe's temperament. "I . . . thought maybe we could get us a chew or maybe a beer when we got to town," he drawled out quietly. Reluctantly, he fished into his pocket and handed over a ten- and a five-dollar bill.

"Did you think I'd cheat my own mother?" Joe responded. "I won't say one word of this, but you damned well better straighten your ass up and deal straight with us because there won't be a next time! Understand?"

Pete nodded yes, sheepishly. I almost laughed out loud, but that would destroy Joe's effect. Here was Joe at 18 years old, bawling out a wrinkled old cowboy of 42, twice his size, and damned near had him in tears. It was exactly what the shrewd Joe wanted. He wanted to set everything straight and send a threat to Pete for the future. He had accomplished all of that.

About half-way up the mountainside, a light drizzle turned into a heavy downpour. The luggage was all unprotected, as were Mom and Terry. I, though completely stiff-legged, could get around pretty well, and with Joe, tried to protect our mother and sister with a small tarp we brought along from the car. The road became red mush from the already dampened clay, and it clung heavily to the large metal wheels of the wagon. Progress was very, very slow, and the incline of terrain seemed even steeper.

Almost at a standstill, Pete yelled out at the dismal crew of soaked passengers who remained grim and silent. Each was wondering what we got ourselves into and worried about one another.

"They can't pull the load," he yelled over the noise of the rain. "You'll have to get off till we get better footing!"

Joe and I helped our mom and sister off the wagon, and Connie also jumped down from next to Pete. She was a large woman and knew her heft would lighten the load considerably. Each of us tracked alongside the wagon, the red clay mud covering our ankles.

"Giyap," Pete was urging on Prince and Jerry. "Giyap ya durn fool animals, or we'll all drown."

The rivulets of water mounted in size the further on we went. The spring thaw was now gushing a flood of water down every crevice, and the new rainfall only intensified the flow. Prince and Jerry came to a halt on the steepest part of the last incline before it leveled out; just around the bend and we'd be at the ranch. When the two large horses halted, the ground gave way beneath Jerry, who was the left side of the team. He was swallowed up to his belly. The underground currents of water had eroded through the mud and allowed a hollow spot beneath the road but appearing level on the surface. Prince, although on normal ground, would not pull so long as Jerry was entrapped. Jerry refused to try and all of Pete's urging could not convince the horse to save itself. In a very short time, it was conceivable that the whole wagon and both the horses could be overturned and washed away with a major mud slide.

Joe assessed the situation quickly and was pulling an upright stake off the flat wagon. It was a 2 x 4 plank of about 6 feet high.

"You can't whip a horse with that," an excited Pete screamed at Joe when he read Joe's intent.

"The hell I can't!" Joe yelled back, "Just shut up and steer."

With this, he raised the 2 x 4 high over his head and with all his might brought it down on the buttocks of Jerry. He did it over and over until Jerry began a frenzied struggle and, with it, Prince also began to pull. Joe had whacked the horse no less than a dozen times in the same spot. He had repeated the blows so rapidly the poor horse could only think of escape. In that instant the two powerful horses pulled clear of the washout.

Once we were on board again and closing the last quarter of a mile, Pete whined to Connie, "You can't treat a horses like that, honey."

"Shut up," Connie yelled back. "He saved the horses' lives and maybe ours!"

Mom and Terry had not uttered a sound as they watched and grimaced at the scowling Joe. For just a fleeting moment during Joe's explosion, Mom read the look on his face and knew she was watching my father. It was exactly what he would have done. Everything – yes, everything – was expendable when it came to family.

Once into our boundaries, the ride smoothed out. We unloaded the soaked luggage at our uncompleted house, and Pete put the horses into the barn with the wagon. He was drying off the team when he ran his hand over a long and tender welt of Jerry's butt.

"Sorry ol' boy . . . I didn't do that to you."

Joe and I were carrying in the luggage, and Joe spoke softly to me. "He's an idiot son of a bitch, and we don't trust him as far as we can throw him!"

Connie Duncan was an even six feet of woman who probably tipped the scales at 250 pounds, though no one would ever know. She was not fat and certainly not pot bellied. She was a pioneer through and through, but born out of time with her life. She was a jolly gal, always with a bright hearty laugh and smile. She surely loved life, Colorado, and the way of life they lived. She ould out-ride, out-shoot, out-fight, and out-swear any man. All ll, she was a loyal friend to Mom in every way. Connie knew was much less a man than she needed or wanted, but in ways she herself needed to be needed. Pete certainly fit that bill. Had Connie known less freedom than she had in these mountains, she would have left Pete in an eye wink.

"Rose," Connie was explaining without the question being raised. "He's a good sort, and we keep each other from being lonely. He'll help out a lot . . . I promise."

We four Pagnas prepared for our first night in exactly the same three rooms where Mom had nursed Dad in what seemed years ago.

We gathered in as much wood and water as we could before dark. The semi–log-built cabin was wired for electricity, and it was ignited by an outside generator and ran on white gasoline.

Mom saw to the unpacking and made ready the sleeping areas. She had difficulty looking at the chair in front of the windows. This was where Dad spent his last days. She could not keep from dipping back into the past and a sense of grief revisiting her.

We were awakened in early morning by a pounding at the back door. It was Connie, and she was screaming her war cry to the mountains and anyone else who could hear, "Oh . . . it's a great life if you don't weaken!" Quickly she followed that with, "And I ain't weakening!"

When Mom opened the door, Connie rushed in with a huge plate of homemade muffins she had just baked. "Welcome to Colorado, Rose."

Mom laughed at her friend's exuberance and was delighted that some of it was rubbing off on herself. We all sat down to a fresh pot of coffee, and Terry began dressing, eager to taste the muffins.

Two carpenters arrived and felt sure they could finish off the rooms and roof of the house within the next two weeks.

Joe and I worked hard at cutting down trees, trimming them and cutting them into logs. As one of us sawed the timber into logs able to be used in the cook stove and heating stove, the other split them upon a stump. We were building up a huge supply. Getting water was the toughest of the chores, since the spring was still a pretty far distance and the two feet of snow would add to the difficulty. Even though neither of us knew how to ride, we saddled riding horses that went with the ranch and rode side by side carrying a twenty-gallon milk can between us. In this way we could dip out of the well into the milk can and once filled, deliver it to smaller containers. In all, we sometimes made a half dozen round trips for water, each time swearing the milk can got heavier.

"Does she have to bathe every day?" I was complaining.

"Hey," Joe answered, "Whatever she wants, she gets, okay? I gotta agree with you though, Tom. It would be a helluva lot easier if we could channel this spring to run in front of our house."

Mimicking Pete's style of talk, I replied, "Come nex' spring, and we'll just pint the bastard toward the house!"

"You got it, brother," Joe laughed, "Come nex' spring."

Eager to win the favor of the carpenters, Mom made them luncheon daily and invited them to sit down with us as a family. They were almost done with their work, and the one man was telling Joe that there were some extra rough-hewn cedar planks that would make a nice back porch and steps. Joe made a mental note that a porch made a lot of sense, and he'd get right after it.

As the men sat down for lunch, Mom held a large stew pot and put it down in the center of the table, the dipper inside the pot.

"I sure hope you fellas like fresh deer meat," she said rather proudly as we had just shot one and Pete showed us how to dress it out, into hind quarters, filets, steaks, etc. Pete did know about game and the outdoors. When Mom said, "fresh deer meat," a roar of laughter echoed from the two men. Joe and I looked at one another quizzically.

"What the hell is so funny?" we thought.

"Rose," one carpenter began as he chuckled after each word, "We're not laughing at you . . . because you probably don't even know that deer are out of season, and there is a $500 fine for killing one. And Mitch here," he gestured to the other carpenter, "is a game warden!"

"Don't worry. Don't worry, Rose," Mitchell persuaded Mom, "I'm off-duty, and I love venison stew. Rose, never say 'fresh deer meat.' That way no one knows when you killed it!"

We all laughed about it together and the somewhat hurt look on Mom's face changed to a lighter one. She brought out a fresh-baked loaf of bread with butter and jam. While she poured their coffee, she asked timidly, "how about rabbit stew or . . . are they out of season?"

We all laughed again and the men assured Mom that no game warden worth his salt would fine a resident who ate the meat, only an out-of-state "sportsman poacher."

Within two weeks, the carpenters finished the roof and supervised Joe and me in the construction of our porch. They were trying to gather their tools up, since the weather forecast told of a large snowstorm a few days away. When they finished, the two men shook Mom's hand. They had come to know her and admired the way she was working out her grief.

"With those two fine boys, Rose, you'll be fine," Mitch assured her.

"Thank you," she returned, "I'm afraid they haven't had much chance just to be boys."

When the porch was completed, Joe became "antsy" at the quiet life and early evenings around the cook stove. He missed the variety his life had known, but mostly he was aware that we had very little cash. Just this morning, Connie brought a letter from Sam and Virginia. It contained their expression of love and a small check that Sam managed. Joe could not help but wonder that he could double the size of that check, since Sam's letter mentioned they still had not replaced their drummer and he'd be leaving in a week.

"Mom," Joe approached her. "There's only so much I can do here. Let me call Sam to see if he'll take me on as his drummer. I'll send a monthly check."

Mom thought about it awhile. She knew my leg was stiff but I could do everything there was to do and that Joe was right. She knew very well that this mountain life was never going to be his cup of tea. After breakfast the next morning, they placed a call to Sam.

Sam was thrilled to know Joe would join him and was glad to hear his mother's voice. It was agreed, and Joe would pack his car and leave the next morning. The snowstorm watches were now warnings, and he didn't want to be snowbound.

At daylight, Joe dressed, had breakfast, and hugged Terry,

"Be a good girl, Terry," he admonished her, "and I'll write you once a week." He hugged his mother a long embrace and rocked her slowly a short side-to-side motion.

"I'll be all right . . . and you'll be all right. It'll all work out, Mom."

I walked him to the car, but just before entering he turned and saw the lost and hurt look I tried to hide. It was saying almost aloud, "My God, Joe, you're leaving us alone?"

"Look," he said to me frankly. "I can't help us here. You can do everything that needs to be done. I'm going to work to get your asses out of here!"

"Don't let Mom hear that," I interjected. "She thinks we're going to make our lives out here!"

"You're not. Trust me."

We two peas in a pod hugged each other. We were the same height and weight, and we knew what the other was thinking long before it was ever spoken. Joe whispered in my ear as his voice cracked with emotion, "Take care of yourself . . . and them," indicating Mom and Terry.

"I will."

"And remember what I told you about Pete. You be the dad!"

"I will."

Mom, Terry, and I waved as the car drove slowly down the mountainside to the gate. Within three days Joe would be in Texas with Sam. It would be a year and a half before Joe would see us all again. He wept as he guided the car toward Rifle.

Within twenty-four hours of Joe's leaving, the largest snowstorm of the year came over the mountains. Eight-foot depths swept around the corral, and the animals were kept in our lean-to barn. Somehow grain and hay had to be brought to them, along with fresh water, or they would perish. Pete and I saw to it, with much adversity.

Connie could yell across the way at us, but the snow was too lightly packed to hazard trying to walk. Pete could get to his own wood pile for their cabin, and I could get to ours. Since the snow would not support body weight, I would roll over to the pile of logs, grab two or three and roll back to the porch. Mom pulled the logs from the porch into the cabin. Melted snow would have to do for drinking, cooking, and bathing. No one could possibly make it to the spring well.

On Monday, Tuesday, and Wednesday of that same week, I attended Rifle High School. I rode a horse the three miles to ranch, and from there hitched a ride with the rancher's son. The morning Joe left was a Wednesday, and the storm hit that same night. I gave up on the idea of further school; it was out of the question.

In the month that followed, even though we had managed a path to Connie's cabin, we were totally snowbound.

"Cabin Fever," she had called it. "It could bring down an elephant if you let it."

Mom merely thought that an expression. She hadn't the slightest idea of what being walled in would be like. Our only touch with the outside world was a small radio we packed from Akron. We had plenty of food. That wasn't a problem, but when we clicked the radio off, the howling wind, with its lonesome wail, brought Mom a deep melancholy. Most evenings, she sat in her rocking chair after Terry and I had gone to bed. She could not sleep. She spoke to herself, sometimes critically, sometimes reassuringly, "Did I get us into this mess? Was it my spending ways that brought us to debt? Is God reaping a return on me for my lack of humility? Didn't we earn all that we had?" There were no answers to her questions, and soon there were no questions.

At 40, she was entering a change of life, brought on prematurely by the stress of her plight and the grief of Dad's death. She seemed to forever look out at the mountain peaks as it was an ever-changing scene from different angles of light.

It was as though somewhere out there, among the white-rumped elk or deer, there was an answer. Sometimes her mind turned it all off, and she rocked quietly, sadly, lost and bewildered . . . replaying scenes of her past.

"Tony," she uttered at no one. "Can you help us now?"

In an attempt to bide time and maybe find some answers, Mom read late into the night from her leather-bound Bible. She felt inadequate for the first time in her life.

"I read," she said to herself, "but the meaning doesn't come to me. Please God, help me to understand." In the instant she fingered her Bible and said "please God," her Bible fell open to a page in Hebrews, and she glanced at a paragraph in the middle of the page. There, written in bold print was a promise from God. It stood out in red-colored ink as every one of Christ's quotes were printed in red. It said simply all she needed to read: "I shall never leave thee or forsake thee."

Gratefully she knew what she had to do, and no longer felt alone. Throughout the month-long siege of howling blizzard, Mom looked forward to the evenings so she could have the quiet time to read her Bible. Slowly, her mind began to see what had been hidden. Her lack of attention and faith had fallen away with the one line.

In early May, the weather broke, good and warm. The snow was melting easily now and even the horses could make it to the corral for their own feeding. With the sunshine, the days became a gorgeous array of scenery, and it was all too alive and vibrant to hold any depressing thoughts. Early one morning, Mom beat Connie to the punch, and opened her door yelling at the neighbor cabin, "It's a great life if you don't weaken. And I ain't weakening."

It aroused laughter in Connie as she yelled back, "You got it, Rose. You got the spirit now!"

Every day was full of just the work it took to survive. There were potatoes, flour, and sugar in the storehouse. Connie made butter from the cream of the cow's milk and had a real stock of jellies and jams she had prepared a year or two before.

Pete and I hunted again, and we always seemed to bring home a jack rabbit or sage hen. One of these days, we'd get another deer. With all that Connie had canned, with Mom and Connie baking, with the eggs from twenty or so hens, we'd never be out of food. Mom saw this clearly. We could live here with virtually no money at all. If a crop were raised and we sold eggs and a few cattle, we could make a decent living.

"We'll make our lives here," she said frankly to me.

"We got through the toughest winter they've had here in thirty years. If we can do that, we can get through anything."

"Yeah, but Mom," I countered her. "What about Ohio and school and . . . and . . ."

"That damned football?" she screamed at me. "And that reminds me, mister. If you don't stop throwing that ball at the chickens, we'll never get another egg, you hear?"

I made a reminder to myself, but they had been such great moving targets.

"Look," Mom softened her voice. "Do you think I don't see you measure how far back your leg goes? Do you think I don't know what's in your heart and what you pray for with your daily rosary?"

She paused here. "Tom, there is no going back. There is nothing back there. We're broke. This right here is what we've got. It's all we've got! We're not just going to pull out so you can play that damned football. There's more to life than that!"

She knew she was scolding me again. She reached out and hugged me close, something she had not done in a long while.

"You're happy here, aren't you?"

I admitted that it was almost like playing a movie role. It was far, far different from my previous life, but the film had to end sometime, didn't it?

"Yeah, Mom, I'm happy." I knew that she was making a breakthrough from her grief, and I didn't want to upset her. This last month was more the 'old Rose' I knew than had been since the death of my father. "I cannot mention Ohio again," I said to myself.

As more and more of the snow melted and spring brought its early colors, Mom too lightened up, anxious to be rid of the winter doldrums and the melancholy that Dad's death had brought her.

I shortened the stirrups of one of the saddles, then padded the stirrups by binding burlap sacks folded many times. In this way I could hoist Mom into the saddle and take her on short walks through the mountain trails. Terry too took to the horses and the excursions. Though she was thoroughly afraid of horses and horseback, like things all her life, Mom overcame the fear to reap the experience.

I laughed at her constant coaching of the saddle horse. In her plaid shirt, cowboy hat, and jeans, she chattered, "Easy horsey, be careful, horsey. I'm your friend. Are you mine?" Secretly, she loved the rides and saw the unlimited grandeur of Colorado from mountain peaks that would have been denied if she had not overcome her fear.

Mom with my Aunt Mary, wife of Gaetano.

When the weather dried out the moisture, and the days warmed to the point of normal temperatures, Pete and I started our assault on a strand of cedar trees halfway up one of the mountains overlooking the cabin. Mom watched the two of us working at this task through binoculars. She saw now that my leg was not only completely healed but the hard winter had changed my boyishness to manhood. I reached my full height of 5'10" and tipped the scales at 195 pounds. Through her binoculars, Mom focused on my bare back and saw the rippling muscles carved there by long hard hours of work. Pete and I cleared nearly a thousand cedar trees. Each one had to be cut down with an ax, stripped of its branches, and cut to the length of twelve feet. About six feet would be buried into the ground and the other half stand upright to hold barb wire strands. It was our plan to fence off the 160-acre plot. Each post called for the digging of a six foot hole. At day's end, Mom welcomed me, nearly exhausted, back to the cabin. In the evenings, just before sunset, I would allow Terry the luxury of riding one of the more gentle of the saddle horses.

"Now, you can't run him, Terry," I warned. "If you run him, he'll get a nosebleed from the high altitude!"

"Aw right, aw right, turn him loose." For as long as she was within my sight, she walked the horse. The second she made the turn around the cabin, I could hear the hoof beats of a run. I smiled to myself and when she re-appeared at a walk I asked her, "Did you run him?"

"Nope."

I dearly loved my sister. I wanted her to have fun, and she loved the thrill of riding the huge and gentle gelding. I also knew she couldn't run him too far around just three sides of the cabin. Terry waited for my return every evening and took delight at the independence her horse ride afforded her. Mom always smiled at the total denial her daughter affected each time she issued her "Nope."

The meat reserve was pretty low for the freezer that ran off of the generator, and Pete and I talked about getting a deer. We spent most of the day in a thicket, carving out the cedar trees that were becoming more difficult to find. We were well above the reservoir nearly 9,000 feet high and peering downward, the cabin appeared the size of a match box. Mom was following our progress with her binoculars, and within a half hour would ring the dinner bell to tell us the time.

I told Pete I was planning on staking myself out in a tree as we knew from all the tracks that the deer would move to the water hole about sunset. If I could get a clean shot and kill, we would have venison before tomorrow evening.

Pete left me resting on the lower branches of a tall pine tree that overlooked the reservoir. My horse was tied and grazing nearby. Pete kept on the trail and headed back to the cabin. I waited a long time for the deer to shift out of the high country and come down for water. They may have caught my scent, however, because none showed, and soon it would be too dark to find the trail. Reluctantly, I climbed into the saddle and slid my rifle into the leather scabbard and was heading for the trail home. In the dim light just minutes from sunset, I arrived near the corral just in time to see Pete helping my sister out of the saddle.

Apparently he had given Terry her much-awaited riding time. I pulled my horse up and stood still as I watched Pete reach to help Terry off her horse. His hands slipped under her dress, and he lifted her from the waist toward himself, letting her body slide down the front of his, a long elongated slide. I was in a livid rage but had not moved a muscle, though my body was trembling with anger. I fingered the scabbard that held the carbine and, for a fleeting moment, thought about putting a shot through the head of Pete. I watched my sister hit the ground and run into the house, Pete shuffled off to the barn to unsaddle the mount.

"The dirty son of a bitch," I spoke softly to myself in disbelief. "You could do that to a six year old kid?" The rage which I felt sent my frame into quirky moves. "I'll kill that son of a bitch," I repeated it over and over and over.

When I entered into the house, they all greeted me and set a plate. It was one of those evenings we were all dining together. I had little to say, but it went unnoticed, since Connie and Mom were full of humor and conversation.

I could not take my eyes from the gnarled and wrinkled Pete. He ate like an animal, with food drippings all over his face. When he laughed, I saw myself in fantasy, shoving the shotgun into that gaping mouth and blowing off that ugly head.

After chores, I excused myself, saying I was very tired, and went to my bunk. After what I had just witnessed, I asked myself what Joe or Sam would do. I knew what Dad would have done, but shooting Pete on the spot would not solve the dilemma. Most of all I did not want to upset Mom. If Connie had known, she would have shot Pete! Up until this episode I had found myself halfway liking the bumbling ex-bronco rider. He taught me about mountain life, how to ride, shoot, fish, hunt, cut down trees, and put up fence, plow, harrow. There were any number of woodsy tricks Pete had shared with me. Deep down, however, I knew that liking Pete could never be, for now a deep mistrust of the man had sunken into me. Joe had been right from the first with his intuition. It was a knowledge one has without knowing the source.

I knew I had to work with Pete day-in and day-out, and the sun would be rising shortly. I slept fitfully. Soon, it was time to rise up for another day in the cedar strands. We hardly spoke as we rode upward and began our cutting. I wasn't quite sure just how, but I knew that I must confront Pete. I would not let it pass or be unspoken or forgotten. It was too big a thing. Multiple scenarios were playing in my head. They came and went in a flurry, as I buried my ax into the cedar over and over again. The thought entered my mind, "If I approach Pete, he'll deny it was anything. Don't let him deny!" The command came to me.

Finally, as we stopped to eat lunch, I approached the topic. I was only sixteen years old but quite mature and quite grown. Joe made me the protector for Mom and Terry.

"Look, Pete," I began unsure. "There's nothing more sacred to me than my mother and my sister."

"Yeah?" Pete acknowledged.

"Well, last night I saw you do something that has me pretty upset, and I just want to tell you that it can't happen again."

"What the hell are you talking about?"

"I'm talking about the way you slid Terry out of her saddle. I saw your hands go up her dress!"

Pete's eyes narrowed, he hadn't realized anyone saw.

"Aw, bullshit," he objected. "You're seeing things!"

"Pete, I'm telling you that if you ever lay a hand on her again, I'll put a bullet between your eyes."

"You don't have the balls for it, kid, nor can you shoot that straight."

I felt my face grow warm. I thought a moment and then said straightforwardly with cocksuredness, "You underestimate me."

We worked that afternoon in near silence. That evening we ate our meal pretty much the same, even though Mom and Connie were again full of conversation.

"We need a deer!" Connie yelled to anyone who could hear on the empty mountains. She had risen with the sunrise. "Oh it's a great life if you don't weaken!"

It was decided that Connie, Mom, and Terry would drive the pickup. Pete and I would lie across the cab. Deer were attracted to lights. We knew that this kind of hunting was illegal, but nevertheless, Connie drove up Peance Creek. In a forty-mile stretch of creek with hayfields and mountains on both sides and sage brush with a railroad track running through the valley, 40,000 deer had been counted. We were going to poach a deer in the name of food.

Connie slowly eased the truck along the dirt road, noises and shiny eyes peaked at us. All of a sudden a huge buck ventured into the road and froze in the lights. Pete let ring out a quick shot with his .30-.30. The buck jumped, began to wobble and break for the sage and cover. Deer usually won't go up in altitude if they are hurt. Connie drove off the road so we wouldn't lose it in the darkness. Her beams found it in a hump. Pete jumped out of the truck, leaving his rifle behind. The buck wasn't quite dead and at the kneeling of Pete, lashed out a hind leg. I squeezed off a shot from my Winchester, inches from Pete's hand. It found the deer's neck.

"Jesus Christ," he shouted with fear and anger. "You almost kilt me!"

"That's true," I said out of the darkness. "But I hit what I was aiming at this time!"

As Pete drew his hunting knife, he was visibly shaken as he started to gut the buck.

Back in the house, alone with Mom and Terry, Mom asked me, "What was that all about?"

I told her the whole story. "I was looking for a chance to throw him a scare, Mom."

The ends of her mouth turned up slightly into a half smile. "Good," was all she said. Later, she said to me that maybe God allowed the snowfall so that I couldn't attend school, and that it was good that I was there to keep an eye on things.

Because of my frankness and my overnight maturity, both physically and mentally, Mom saw me in a different light. We had always been mother and son, and we would always be that, but now there entered in a dimension that rarely has a chance to emerge – we became good friends.

In the evenings we spoke about things we heretofore had held inside ourselves. She watched me nightly lie on the floor and fold my knee to measure with the span of my hand how far back my heel came to my butt. With a steady pull on my toe with my hand, lying face down on the carpet, I could touch the heel into my butt. It was forced, but it reached.

"You got your miracle, didn't you?" she was pleased.

"I never thought it would happen."

"Why not? You prayed for it! Surely you believe it could happen, or you wouldn't have prayed for it."

"Yeah. Well, I pray for a lot of things, Mom, and I don't know that they are all going to happen."

"What are your prayers, Tom?"

"I'd tell you, but I don't want to make you angry."

"You mean Ohio?"

"Yeah."

"Do you still think we'll go back to Ohio?"

"Aw, Mom, I do . . . I really do. I see pictures behind my eyelids. I know we will."

"What kind of pictures?"

"Just pictures, Mom. like I'm in high school among my friends and . . ."

"And . . . playing football and basketball?" Mom asked. "You promised me," she said it, softly. "Would you break a promise to your mother?" I was silent. "We'll see," she said.

"Do you ever see pictures behind your eyelids. Mom?"

"Sometimes," Mom answered, "but they're never clear enough for me to know if it's past or future."

After cleaning the supper dishes, she quietly scanned her Bible. She rested it on her lap and gazed out into the night.

"I wish I understood," she said.

"Understand what, Mom?"

"The Bible. I want to, but I don't have the education, the schooling." She stopped here, remembering I was no longer attending school. "I wish I knew what God wanted us to do."

"It would be simple if He'd just tell us, huh?" I said.

"Listen to this," she said, as she read aloud from Matthew, chapter 18, verses 19 and 20: "Again I say to you, that if two of you agree on earth about anything that they may ask, it shall be done for them by My Father who is in heaven."

"That's a promise, made by Christ," Mom said insistently. "When I was a little girl," she continued. "my mother taught us that if we all prayed for the same thing, and we all prayed to Jesus Christ, He would ask His Father and it wouldn't be refused. She looked upon that as the secret to life . . . praying together."

"Maybe we should," I said.

"What would we ask for?"

I thought for a moment. I didn't want to blurt out, "To get us the hell out of here." I knew my mother would blame herself.

"Maybe," I said hesitantly. "We should pray that God guides our lives, Mom, and then let Him."

She was silent, and we retired to bed. The next evening, as the sun sent its copper rays, spreading shivers of light through the rocky crevices at the mountain's peak, she spoke of it again. "I thought about what you said, Tom. Maybe there is a great secret in not praying for all the little things, and maybe He'd love to hear several people in agreement say, 'Help us, guide us, do with us what you will.'"

While Terry was asleep, we prayed together that God would show us what direction to take.

At long last, by late May, the snow was gone. We were all tired of melting snow for drinking water and I plowed a deep furrow from the spring to the house.

"Hot Damn," I yelled for Mom and Terry to see, "running water."

Each evening Mom and I spoke about faith in God, of her dreams as a little girl. We spoke about Dad and of Terry, Joe and Sam. We placed our faith in the prayer that God would lead us where He wanted us to be.

It was one of those spring evenings, almost a year to the day that Pete and I completed the fence project, and Mom was giving Terry her nightly hair brushing. Terry in turn would brush Chummie, our black-and-white collie shepherd. Terry had the rich thick black wavy hair that women envied. She had a natural curl, and her dense hair was sometimes difficult to brush. She winced hard as Mom swept the back of her head.

"Ow, Mom," she whined with tears filling her eyes.

"It shouldn't hurt that bad," Mom said matter of factly. "Come here," she commanded Terry as she walked under the kerosene lamp and the brightest bulb we had. Mom searched Terry's thick hair.

"My God," she exclaimed. "Her head is all red and swollen. Her head is burning up!"

I got a flashlight and zeroed in on the middle of the deep dark red blotch.

There it was, a tick the size of a button. It was embedded into Terry's scalp, swollen with the blood it had drained. Mom took

Terry's temperature. When she read it, she panicked. "Oh God, Oh God," was all she would say. "It's 103."

We were all told there was no cure for "Rocky Mountain spotted tick fever." Mom's heart sank. Pete and Connie had gone into town with the car to visit Connie's daughter, who was passing through. The pickup truck was out near the barn, but I didn't know how to drive it. I offered to saddle a horse and ride to the nearest neighbor.

"No!" she yelled sharply, "There isn't time. You know how to start it and you know how to steer. Get the truck!"

It was with herky-jerky movement and grinding sounds that I sought to find the gear paths. The truck moved forward. I knew the road at least, with all its danger and curves. When we made it to the neighbor's home, the neighbor being the school teacher, her husband drove us in the rest of the way.

"I'll teach you to drive," he whispered to me.

The doctor was angry at us for removing the tick and not saving it for him to look at. I had removed it the way I had been told. Mom held Terry's head, I heated a pin over a candle and placed it on the rump of the tick as it backed its head out. I then grabbed it with a Kleenex and squeezed it dead.

"Did it have spots on the back like a lady bug?" he asked me.

"I don't know!"

The big country doctor, even though he resided in town, knew of ranch life. He sensed Mom's trauma.

"Now look, Rose," his voice was calm, "she may not have spotted fever. Children often run temperatures with normal tick infection." He brought medicine and gave her a schedule. "If the fever breaks in forty-eight hours, it's not spotted fever."

As the neighbor drove us back up the thirteen-mile road, Mom was in a trance. She held Terry on her lap wrapped in a blanket as Terry began to have the chills the doctor promised. Once home, we thanked our neighbor. Mom sat up at night, her voice pleading over and over, "Please God, make her well, and I promise I'll leave this place."

Mom suddenly had a belly full of ranch life. It had threatened her baby's life. She rocked Terry through the night. I slept on the floor next to the wood stove. On occasions Mom would prod me with her foot. She was silently saying to tend the fire. In the morning we were both exhausted. Terry was hungry, and at about noon her fever broke. After Mom fed everyone, we all went to bed and slept. When we awoke, she had finished writing a letter to her brother Mike.

"We're going home," she said to me quietly. "This wasn't meant to be our home."

Chapter 10
Some Crooked Lines

It was not easy for Joe to be subordinate to Sam both as an employee in Sam's band and also as a younger brother. He wanted the freedom to do as he pleased, and this very often conflicted with what Sam had in mind. Though the boys sent money to their mother regularly, sometimes resentment over their relationship was ready to explode.

Not only was Joe resentful of Sam's supervision but that of Sam's wife. It was as though she assumed responsibility for Joe's education in both manners and propriety. Joe wanted no part of it. The rift between bandleader and younger brother flared so high that there were moments when they nearly forgot our father's words, "Never fight among yourselves."

The band was playing in a typical night club in the south of San Antonio. Sam and Joe were at odds over Joe's gambling sprees, and they were barely talking. The show had to go on, however, so they played out their roles. Late one Saturday night, a tall Texan approached Sam's wife Virginia at a nearby table. "Le's dance, queenie," the slightly drunk giant swaggered as he attempted to pull her onto the dance floor.

"My husband is the bandleader," Virginia spoke sharply, "and I don't dance."

With this, the lanky cowboy approached the stage area and proceeded to talk to Sam while sticking his fingers in the open bellows of Sam's accordion while he played. He playfully pulled them out just in the nick of time.

"Hey, you-all won't mind if I dance with that pretty little filly, will you?"

Sam, slow to anger, except that the Texan had hit upon two items in his life that were pretty sacred, his wife and his accordion.

"Yes, I mind," he grunted not trying to be nice. "We'll talk when the set is over!"

"Oh," the Texan got the drift. "You and me gonna go outside in the parking lot and settle it, huh?"

Joe overheard the whole scene and realized that this guy was talking eye to eye with Sam, but Sam was on a 15" high stage.

"My God," he thought. "Sam's in trouble!"

At the set's end, Sam put down his accordion, told his wife to "stay there," and took off the standard blue coat of the band. His short frame jumped from the stage and went for the exit along with the jeering Texan.

Joe removed his coat also and ran after the two. In the parking lot Joe watched his oldest brother mix it with this lanky and tough Texan. Sam could usually handle himself, but this guy was a tough hombre and much too large. Besides, Sam was tiring. Joe watched as the Texan got a good lick in, which sent Sam sprawling alongside the car where Joe was crouching. In the dark the two brothers, both being in white shirts with the same stocky build and black hair, looked identical.

Joe grabbed Sam as he started to scramble up.

"I got him awhile," Joe said and dashed at the Texan with fresh energy.

Between the brothers secretly alternating, they overcame the big guy, and he stumbled to his car saying, "I've had enough." He peeled his convertible out onto the highway, never aware there were two opponents.

Sam and Joe looked at one another. Each was bruised and dirty from the tussle. They broke out into a simultaneous laugh and hugged one another at their deception and victory.

"It's hardly fair," Sam said.

"Screw fair," Joe said. "We're brothers, man, that's fair!"

When Mom got her call from Sam as she usually did every few weeks, she asked as she always did, "Are you taking care of your brother?"

"Yeah, Mom," he replied, "he's fine, and sometimes he takes care of me."

"That's good," she replied.

Only a down payment had been made on the Akron home, where Mom's sisters were making a monthly payment. She had planned never to return to Ohio. This last trip to Colorado was to finish the ranch, she started, and make it a paying proposition. None of this was to be. When Uncle Mike drove in the drive and gate of the ranch, we were so thrilled to be leaving we all shouted "Uncle Mike!" He drove us back to Akron where we moved into the house with my aunts.

Uncle Mike opened up a supper club and offered the Sammy Pagna Quintet as his feature attraction. Both Terry and I re-entered school. For that one year, as a second-semester junior, I was not eligible for sports. The state mandated that I must be in school the semester before participating in a sport. It was autumn, and the high school season was well underway. I could only watch the games from the sidelines. The team had an eight-win, no-loss, one-tie season and the championship.

After the season's end, the coach held an intrasquad game, pitting his graduating seniors against the remaining squad. Since it violated no rules, he invited me to play for the underclassmen.

I was aligned as a tailback and engineered a 13-12 win over the champions. Mom never knew I played. Only Joe watched me play.

He told Sam privately, "We gotta talk to Mom about letting him play next fall, Sam. He's too talented not to, and I really think he's outgrown his bleeding problems."

Mom had no quarrel about me playing basketball, and as the semester changed, I joined the varsity. My new physical stature and overall maturity were welcomed by our coach.

For awhile, with the brothers living at home and working locally, Terry and me in school, things smoothed over for Mom. She became the hostess in the evenings for Mike's supper club and welcomed the chance to dress and act the part. It also allowed her to see Sam and Joe entertain with their music.

The summer of 1949 passed, and as fall approached again, an inquiry into my eligibility was made from the opponent teams. The State Board of Athletics was questioning whether I exceeded eight semesters of eligibility. An investigation at the small high school in Rifle recorded only three days of enrollment and attendance. A complete week would have constituted a semester and would have in turn rendered me ineligible. As it happened, that huge snowstorm and snowbound Colorado days became a blessing in disguise. I had one semester of fall eligibility left.

There was only one obstacle to overcome now, and that would be my formidable Mom. Sam, Joe, and Terry pleaded my case with Mom, and she responded as one determined.

"We owe $20,000 in medical costs for your dad. Will this football help pay that? He needs to get a job and help out!"

The money wasn't the part that bothered Mom. She was re-membering the pain and anguish I had with the blood clot in my leg. She remembered too well the bed-ridden days and changing sheets daily from my sleepless and sweaty nights. She also re-called me on crutches or in a wheelchair and the voice of our own family physician saying, "Rose, he should never play a contact sport again. He has that rare Mediterranean trait of being a bleeder under trauma. A car accident and he could bleed to death!" The words still rang in her ears.

"No," was her answer and she pointed a finger at me. "You promised!"

Sam and Joe went to her, "His only dream, Mom, is to earn a scholarship to college. This is his chance. He'll never have it again."

Joe urged her, "Mom, he's 195 pounds of muscle and not playing ball will leave him empty."

She called me into the kitchen late that summer morning. "You've been praying to play, haven't you?"

"Yes, every night."

"How do you pray? What do you pray for?"

"I pray that my leg will grow strong, that I win a scholarship to Notre Dame, that I play pro football with the Cleveland Browns and make enough money to pay off our mortgage."

She softened her voice and sat down at the table with me.

Tom," she spoke sincerely, "It isn't that I want to hold you back from anything, but I remember the year and a half where you were stiff-legged. I know the pain you had, and I think of what the doctor told us. Is football so important to your life?"

"You remember the pictures I'd see behind my eyes, Mom?"

"Yes."

"These were the pictures, Mom."

"They're not behind your eyelids, Tom. They're in your heart," she paused. "Go play. Play the best you can and with my blessing."

"Thanks, Mom," and I hugged her hard. "Oh God, thanks. I don't want to do anything without your blessing." I cried openly, and the tears were foreign since I held so much in for so long. She cried too and was full of my happiness.

"I'm not sure your father would have allowed this."

"I always thought he was behind it, Mom," I winked.

"Maybe."

In 1949 the word "isometrics" had not yet been created, but the isometric of me holding my weight in the stirrups of a saddle, riding the mountain sides, developed my legs into muscle. More than just physical maturity, my personality was altered also. This was the time to carve my niche and make any dreams I had, come true.

In the ninth and last game of the year, Springfield Township High School was scheduled to play its biggest rival, Ellet High School. The build-up was created throughout the season, and both teams by year's end were undefeated. Springfield Stadium was overflowing with nearly 10,000 people.

I lived in the Ellet district but elected to finish high school where I started. My cousin Donna, who lived with us, attended Ellet. One night during the lead-up to the final game, she came home in tears. My mother, trying to console her, asked what was wrong.

"Aunt Rose," she cried, "they had a pep rally at the end of classes today, and they performed a skit. During the skit, six players carried in a coffin with a dummy in it wearing Tommy's numbered jersey. They want to kill him! They spit at it and threw things. It was awful."

All of this was kept from me until after the game. On the opening kickoff, I was hit hard. We had to call time-out, since two of my teeth were loose in my lower front jaw, and I thought my nose was broken. The Ellet coach had stressed, "Stop Pagna, and you beat Springfield. Hit him hard early, and we'll see what he's made of."

Springfield ran a few plays without me, while I was being examined by our physician on the sidelines. I re-entered shortly and was amazed at the booing crowd from the opposition.

We won that game 44-6. I broke away for two long-run TD's,

and we rolled from that point forward. We were awarded the Mythical Class B State Championship. It was Springfield's first undefeated, untied season in its history. The following Monday at school, they dedicated a three-hour pep assembly to award us our trophies.

We were a much smaller school in size than most recruiters bothered with. Our graduating class was about 100 people. Small though we were, word spread through the papers and radio about our team. This attracted several major college recruiters. One of the assistant coaches was a Miami of Ohio graduate, and he made sure they were informed. At least a half-dozen players on that squad were given athletic scholarships. It was a storybook finish for us and worth waiting for.

In January 1950, many colleges visited me and invited me to visit in return. I met the same Ara Parseghian, whom I had watched play basketball years ago. In those earlier, crippled, bedridden days, that snowy television set introduced me to Ara Parseghian. I finally met the man with the stocky build, the quick reflexes, and dark hair. I also knew of Ara when he played half-back for the Cleveland Browns. I heard his name once more as the freshman coach under Woody Hayes at Miami of Ohio.

"Miami," my Uncle Jim used to say. "It's a hot place, no?"

"Where the hell is Miami of Ohio?" everyone asked me.

Ara wanted me to matriculate immediately, but I deferred, explaining that my father had recently died, and the family needed my help. What I needed was a good job.

Ara called upon an ex-Miami grad who was a vice-president at Goodyear Tire and Rubber Company and got me a job there. I worked twelve-hour shifts at Goodyear. I loaded and unloaded crude rubber and compounds from the freight cars. Eventually, on the Goodyear Trainee Squadron, I worked in every department, including the active building of tires. I was pale from lack of sunlight, but at 195 pounds I was big enough and strong enough to be confident.

Mike's nightclub went under, and the boys with the band were mapping out a road trip to keep working. Sam, his wife, and Joe would drop me off at college in the fall of 1950. When we entered into the lonely dorm at Miami of Ohio, I carried one small suitcase. Miami appeared to be an abandoned campus. The players reported for camp two weeks before school started.

When Sam entered my assigned room, and I put down my small suitcase, his eyes showed disbelief at the cell-like closet where he would leave me. There was a scrawny mattress rolled up on ancient bedsprings, no curtains, one light bulb in the ceiling and one rusty chest of drawers with a tarnished mirror. A small desk was the only other piece of furniture. Depressed, Sam tried to be light-hearted. "We'll send you some carpeting."

I sensed their feelings and, as they were about to leave, told them with a feigned braggadocio in my voice, "Hey, don't be worrying about me. When I leave here, I'll be a legend."

We all laughed at my boast and then a serious mood fell upon us. Both of them hugged me and said in unison, "Take care of yourself."

When they got to Sam's car, he turned to Joe with a small chuckle, "I'll be a legend," he repeated my phrase, "He's got balls, and I for one would never doubt it!"

"He'll be okay," Joe affirmed, "and he does have balls!"

They were very quiet as they drove off, each saddened.

Not knowing much of college and being totally alone for the first time in my life, I tried to embrace what was around me. The first two weeks of practice were very tough because the summer of 1950 was very hot and humid. When two-a-day practices came to an end the dorm assignments took place. I drew a three-man dorm room. One roommate was a bright young Jewish fellow from Cleveland, named Charles Pasternak. He had been a bat-boy for the Cleveland Indians and obviously came from a family of means.

The other fellow was another Italian halfback from a small school near where I played, named Joe Rosato. We knew of each other by name and reputation. Not only would we be room-mates, we would be competitors for the same position. By now, I knew my own major skill was that of a ball carrier. My height would almost rule out the quarterback position.

It was registration time, and I entered a long line. At the end, they requested $65 for books and fees. It was all the money I owned in the world, but the coaches told me this would be reimbursed. After two weeks of waiting, and no one offering a reimbursement, I packed my suitcase and headed for the highway to thumb the 250 miles back to Akron.

One of my frosh teammates spotted me and ran to Parseghian with the information. Not ten minutes later a green Pontiac pulled along side the curb. I got in and faced Ara Parseghian, "So you're going home to Momma?"

"Yeah."

"How come? You've got a future here."

"I'm broke," I said, ashamed.

"But you worked all summer. Hell, I got the job for you!" he was intense.

"I didn't keep the money. It went to my Mom, and the little I had was spent on registration. You guys told me you'd reimburse me, and nobody has."

"Room, books, tuition, and fees," he said, "that was our promise." With this he made a U-turn and brought me to the dorm.

"You'll have the money tomorrow, or I'll drive you home."

It had been an oversight, and it was truly part of the scholarship. Both Woody Hayes and Ara made it right.

Within two weeks, my Italian roommate proved to be a bit of a practical joker. Not only did he short-sheet my bed, he put in a three-foot rubber snake about an inch and one half in diameter in it. Little did he realize that he had hit upon the only thing I feared.

As I slipped into my bed and struggled with straightening my legs, I reached down and pulled out the lifelike rubber snake. With the lights out and only the glow of moonlight in the room, the underside of the snake's silver finish glowed and wiggled. I let out a panicky scream. My two roommates burst into laughter as one flipped on the light switch. I was enraged, my neck swollen and eyes bulging. I attacked the Italian halfback. I threw him to the floor, sat on his chest, and proceeded to bang his head on the floor. The ex-batboy, seeing how serious it had become, screamed for help.

Hurrying into the room came a tall slender youth, several years our senior. He was a dorm counselor in his junior year.

Both the counselor and the batboy tried to pull me off of the helpless boy on the floor. I took several swings at them and, wild-eyed, returned to punish the roommate.

The counselor, a fellow by the name of Dave Shanafelt, kept yelling at me, "I'm a counselor, a counselor!" as though that had authority."

I never knew the word. I thought that was his name. I stopped the banging for a moment and screamed at the counselor, "Look, Counselor! This is none of your business! Get the hell out of here, or you're next!"

The counselor again grappled for my arms. With this, I left my opponent on the floor, grabbed Dave Shanafelt and threw him through two swinging doors and down a flight of steps.

Appearing before the dean was the last thing I would do before leaving Miami of Ohio. The dean called Ara Parseghian and Woody Hayes.

Woody told Ara, "He's your recruit . . . see to it."

"Dean," Ara spoke to the man in private, "this kid is not a troublemaker. He may be troubled, but he's not a troublemaker. There has to be more to the story."

With this, the two men called me into the dean's office.

"In your own words, Tom," the dean said gently, "tell us your side of the story. We've heard the counselor's side."

I explained what had transpired. I spoke of my fear of snakes, my dead-set goal of getting an education, and the fact that I didn't know what a counselor was. I thought that they were just ganging up on me, and "Counselor" was the boy's name. I said I never played practical jokes and didn't want them played on me.

Both the dean and Ara listened intently. They asked me to wait outside the door. The dean spoke, "We throw this kid out, and we wrong him."

"I believe him," Parseghian said.

"It only confirms the story the counselor tells. Let's see if we can get him into a single room." They did.

It was a shaky start for me, but I weathered the first semester, did pretty well for grades and had a terrific frosh football season. We played a very hard four-game schedule and managed it in undefeated style. I was elected captain and proved to be the leader of the team. Parseghian was glad he salvaged the tough little halfback that Sid Gillman said ran like Jackie Robinson (bow-legged and pigeon-toed).

In the off-season, my teammates could often be found drunk on strong "three-two" beer. I had difficulty understanding this mania to "chugalug" and drink and get blasted. It made no sense to me. I became so intent on being the best I could be, I resolved two things with great tenacity never to drink while I was a player and never to cut a class and cheat myself of one moment of college.

Though my clothes were always clean and neatly pressed with shoes shined well, I had few clothes, and none that were considered "stylish" for the college atmosphere. Christmas vacation was a godsend.

When I entered our home and greeted my mother and sister, I held them tightly and wept tears of joy. I inhaled the familiar scent of home.

"Don't cry," Mom said as she wiped away her own tears.

"I'm just so glad to see you guys," I said in unashamed fashion. It had always been this way with each of us and would be all our lives.

Terry had grown taller, got prettier, and was doing well in the third grade. On Christmas Day, Uncle Mike and Mom's sisters came over for dinner. They brought along Grandpa Joe Crimaldi and Dad's mother, Donna Theresa.

Sam and Joe, still on the road, were unable to make it home. They called late in the afternoon and announced that Joe received his draft notice for the Army.

The next spring in Oxford, Ohio, highlighted fraternity life on campus for me. Soon it would be Mother's Day, and Mom made plans to visit. I thought it wonderful to have her on the campus. I took her to early Mass, and we walked the picturesque slant walk to town for breakfast. It was a fun Saturday for her as she attended a fraternity sing on the library steps. The entire songfest was beautiful, and as luck would have it, my fraternity won.

Mom spent the night in the fraternity dormitory with all the other moms. She told me that, since she was one of the youngest, they elected her to an upper–double-bunk bed. She said several of the ladies had to help each other up and down. They all had a good laugh. It was a warm feeling to have her see what I was about, even though I was only a freshman.

When we entered one of the typical little spots that adorn college campuses, I ordered her bacon and eggs, a toasted roll, and coffee. When we were eating, she said as gently and sincerely as I ever heard her say anything, "Tom, there's something I needed to ask you, and we need to talk about."

"My God, she wants to remarry!" the thought struck me. It was always like this between my brothers and sister and our parents. We could say two words and know exactly what would follow.

When Mom's voice said, "We need to talk about," her eyes leveled with me. We both stopped eating.

"What would you say or feel if I wanted to remarry?"

Tears well up in my eyes, but I fought them back. It was my turn to speak and I searched myself for fairness in what I spoke. I was in college now, and supposed to have some kind of judgment. We were too great of friends by now from our trials in Colorado. I needed to know what she knew or feel what she felt.

God, how I loved this woman, my mother, my friend, my idol for courage, strength and faith. She was my reason for being or trying to be anything. Surely she had the same effect on both Joe and Sam. It was only slightly different with Terry because she was so young. It was as though we all knew we were in this life together and must look out for one another. We couldn't rely on anyone else, not even trust anyone else. This bond went to the core of our existence.

"Mom," I started slowly, "it isn't that anyone can ever replace Dad, I know that. I also know you are a young woman and have a full life ahead of you. Every one of us wants your happiness. Terry will be raised in a few years, and you shouldn't be alone. If you want to marry out of the need for love and companionship, God bless you! I can understand that! It doesn't lessen your love for Dad, and it doesn't diminish what any of us feel. But Mom, and I say this from my heart, if you marry because of financial security, afraid you'll have to depend on the boys for support, I'll never accept it. As long as I'm alive, I'll work, I'll do anything. You'll never want, I promise you."

She lowered her head and avoided my steady gaze. We were both quiet, as I waited for her response. She shifted her head slowly, tears blinding her eyes.

"You see right through me. We see through each other. We always have. Okay," she said in a way that seemed to settle it in her mind. She'd been wrestling with this a long while, "I'll do what I have to do."

"Do what your heart tells you to do, Mom. Remember, all of us – Sam, Joe, Terry and I – are all on your side."

She never mentioned it again as I walked her back to the dorm to get her packed for the noon train.

"Are you happy?" she asked me.

"Yeah, Mom, I'm happy." I was so broke and shabbily dressed compared to the other students and hoped she wouldn't notice. "Don't worry about me, Mom. All I have to do is study and play football. That's why I'm here."

When we got to the train, I held her close to me and breathed the personal scent of my mother. There was none in the world that could be her but her. She seemed to have mellowed these past years. She could now show her feelings, and she hugged me back and whispered, "Take care of yourself, Tom."

It was our special way of saying it all, and I said, "I love you too, Mom. Take care of yourself."

When she boarded the train, I was very grateful for the time we spent but saddened at her leaving. A deeper resolve filled my heart. I wanted to play pro football after college. The money would secure her future.

My Aunt Betty secretly was dating the younger brother of Nate Weiss. When Nate married Flora out of the Jewish faith, his family "sat shiva" for him (that is, held his wake). He had married a Gentile! Shortly, Uncle Mike married Nate's sister. Within years they were divorced, but they also had done the same for her. And now, Betty and Herb Weiss would enter matrimony. Betty was moving out, and Mom's father came to live with us. Mom and Terry, Dixie and Donna, plus grandpa Crimaldi - now occupied our home.

Mom found employment sewing for one of the department stores. Dixie worked nights, so there was always one to watch over Terry and Donna and grandpa.

At this stage life seemed nothing more than a grind for Mom and Aunt Dixie. They worked and cooked and entertained their families, and were always eager to see Mike or Ann from Cleveland, Betty and Flora from Akron, or, on rare occasions, Mary from Phoenix.

Summer came, and with it my arrival at home. Mom at least had someone to do yard work. I worked the first shift at Goodyear and was done at noon most days; then I played hardball in the evenings twice a week. There was a 20-and-under league that the church entered, and I pitched. I rarely spoke of things that happened in my life, never wanting to burden Mom. The next year, my second, I would make a strong bid to start for Miami. Woody Hayes, after completing a fine year, took the Ohio Stale job. Ara, on the basis of his undefeated freshman team, became the new Miami head coach.

Two weeks before I would be going back to Miami, Mrs. Calderone, whose son Jules played catcher for our team at St. Matthew's, called Mom to tell her a story of our game against St. Anthony's. A player from St. Anthony's, bully by reputation, played dirty. Even the three or four priests on St. Anthony's coaching staff were intimidated by "Midge." It wasn't that he was so big or so tough, but that he went berserk when things didn't go his way. Once, and it served to heighten his reputation as a tough customer, Midge had bitten off an opponent's finger while engaged in a fight.

According to Mrs. Calderone, Midge was on third base with the tying run. I took a windup, and he attempted to steal home. The throw was perfect, and Jules stepped up to tag Midge easily. After the tag, Midge, in passing behind Jules, made his left arm stiff, doubled his fist, and with a mighty swipe, backhanded a fist to Jules's neck. Jules fell like a tree and was out cold.

Without a moment's hesitation, I came off the mound with full force and threw a cross arm-and-body blow to Midge's face. It violently upended him. For a second, his entire body was in the air about five feet high, parallel to the ground. He dropped flat and lay there gasping and sucking air, his body in convulsions. The players and priests jumped to his rescue.

One priest shouted at me, "Get out of here, before he gets up. He'll kill you!"

My neck was swollen with rage, my veins and eyes fully enlarged. Full adrenaline flowing, I grabbed a bat and screamed, "Get up, you son of a bitch, it's time you learn a lesson!"

Midge would not get up, the game ended, and Jules revived. Then the team left the field. Jules had told his mother, and she in turn told my mother.

Mom wrote to Joe in the service and relayed the whole story. She did not mention it to me, and I never mentioned it to her. She was very proud knowing that I never seemed to start anything or bully anyone but that I had a strange balance of justice in my makeup. I was a kind of Roland to myself. In her heart Mom was always fearful I would be killed defending some poor girl's honor in a lonesome parking lot.

"That is just the way he is," she said. She thought about the prayer she and Dad used when their sons were young. It went simply: "Lord that our kids be tough but not toughs, hard but not heartless, relentless but not ruthless."

That prayer had surely been answered. Her sons were all of these things, and she thought, "My daughter will be too!"

Because I could see no reason to stay in a fraternity and could not afford their dues, I dropped from their ranks and stayed in the campus dorms. I wrote letters to my brother Joe, who, after eleven weeks of basic training, was transferred to the Marine Corps. The Marine's honored no basic training but their own and sent Joe through another eleven weeks.

Though he felt like a misfit and hated the regimentation of the military, it formed in Joe a sense of humor. Without such, survival in the Marines was against the odds. They soon discovered his skill as a drummer, and in a few short months, he was awarded stripes commensurate with his position in the Marine Band. They played for Eisenhower's Inauguration, and certain fringe benefits accrued for these elite Marines. Joe found a niche. Once Happy-Go-Lucky Tom had moved into a somber and sullen state, determined and driven, then Intense Joe had loosened up and took on more of the carefree personality he had lacked. He had been angry for so long and now, back in his element, enjoyed the tour though anxious to be home.

By virtue of Joe's Marine Band duties, he was invited into the Marine Swing Band, and they played the officers clubs throughout the country. It was a time to make a few extra dollars, and Joe took full advantage. Always a gambler and, now staked with his own purse, he free-wheeled his way through crap games, poker, and the horse track. Whenever he hit it big, the generous Joe would mail me a $20 bill and send the rest to Mom. In this way he would not gamble it back. All hardened gamblers know, it always goes back! Thus he avoided this pitfall.

Sam's band was pretty near the end of their tour now, and since Tulsa was home to Virginia and the last spot they were booked, he sought to settle there. Within a year, Virginia gave birth to the first of Mom's twelve granddaughters. Sam and Virginia named her "Toni." Sam was very proud and had Mom visit them in Tulsa. She was thrilled at the new birth but could stay only a short time; her work at the department store would not allow her longer.

Her skill in the sewing department of one of Akron's largest department stores fit her to a tee. She not only learned more about drapery making and how to hang them but also the use and repair of most of the equipment in their modern shop. All of this would be information and skill for her future employment. It was not big money for her, but she felt secure in the knowledge of her skill.

The next three years passed rather quickly. In very short order I would be graduating from Miami of Ohio and become a lieutenant in the Air Force. Joe would soon fulfill his tour of duty and be home.

At the beginning of my senior year, I was elected captain of the football team. I had a sensational junior year and was the mainstay of the Miami Sport's Department's advertising campaign. They featured me and put me on their poster. I was the "poster boy" for the 1953 season and, in several pre-season magazines, picked as an early draftee into the pros.

Mom was determined to find a way to watch me play. Providentially, Joe came home on furlough, borrowed Uncle Mike's car, and drove Mom down to see the second game of the season. It was against Xavier. I had a slight hairline fracture of a metatarsal bone on my right foot. It was very painful, and they held me out for the opener. For Xavier, I'd be ready to play.

I was exceedingly happy to see my mother and brother, and was thrilled that they were going to see me play. I only wished that my foot were better, since it still gave me pain, and I was uncertain of my abilities to cut sharply.

Here I am splitting the defenders as a Redskin.

The game was hard fought and extremely hotly contested, since the Miami-Xavier rivalry spanned many years. I was not able to be myself throughout most of the first quarter and was angry at my lack of production. Xavier sought me out and hunted me. The Miami Redskins were stymied. I was entering the huddle for our sixth possession, very much aware Mom and Joe came to see this poor showing. In one of those rare times in life, almost in disgust with myself, I said a quick mental prayer in the huddle. I said, "Please God, let me just once, show off for my Mom and brother, Joe."

On the very next play, I carried off tackle right from our own

44. Both the Xavier tackle and linebacker were awaiting me in the hole. I blasted as hard as I could and struggled momentarily. A support safety came up hard to punish me before I hit the ground.

A humbling moment after our victory over Dayton.

I saw it coming and ducked, butting him in the chest. The safety went down, the linebacker and defensive tackle who had me from the sides got wrenched away by the impact, and I was left upright in full stride for a 56-yard run and a touchdown.

Mom rose up and screamed to all around her, "What a guy! What a guy!"

Joe shook his head at the spectacular play almost in disbelief. "That was worth the trip," he yelled in Mom's ear. "I've never seen one like it!"

When I trotted to the sidelines after the score, the stadium arose as one, offering congratulations to what they perceived as a splendid display of heart. I knew I wasn't responsible.

In one brief explosive moment, I received my prayer and gratefully, humbly, jogged to the bench.

Parseghian, at game's end and in the Miami locker room, addressed our exhausted but victorious team. He told us he could not be more proud of our efforts. Walking to my locker, he bent over saying simply, "I never saw a greater run than the one you gave us today. Thanks Tommy!"

I nodded and mentally said, "Thanks, God. I know I wasn't alone. Thanks!"

On Thanksgiving Day 1953, I took part in my last collegiate game. It was against Cincinnati and was for the Mid-American Conference Championship. In the middle of the second quarter, my right thigh split a muscle, and my college career ended. We lost the game, and I returned to Akron to be married two days later.

I guess I really never knew what romance and love were all about. In high school, I did have a few dates, but mostly with my one gal classmate since the eighth grade. As much as we knew, we thought we were in love. It was a first for both of us. In an emotional rush, on the evening of my high school graduation, I got engaged to her, not ever realizing the ramifications of such a commitment. She was a lovely person and a year ahead of me. My senior year in high school, she had already joined the work force and was talking marriage.

The word "marriage" frightened me, not so much the responsibility and commitment, but that I was just seventeen going on eighteen and had nothing to look forward to but working in the factories. Football had now allowed me an avenue to go to college. I would be the first of my generation in my family and surrounding relatives to have such an opportunity. Marriage would be a big barrier to completing college, and I knew I had obligations to help our family. I tried to postpone it all until after graduation from college. I knew if I were ever to fulfill my dreams, college was a must. But it was "now or never" in *her* mind, and we parted ways. In retrospect it was best for her and me. Eventually she wed a fraternity brother of mine, moved to the West Coast, and it was over. I wasn't ready for marriage, but the loneliness of college and constantly being dead broke left me with little social life.

During my freshman year in college, along about the Christmas and New Year's break, I returned home to Akron and was invited to a high-school teammate's New Year's party. I brought a date for the evening. She too was a lovely person and one I cared for, but knew I couldn't maintain a serious relationship until graduation.

While at the party, I met one of the other guests' date. We were introduced, but somehow she already knew *my* name and had a look of familiarity shown in her expression. I had played against her high school's team, since our two schools were arch rivals. She had been a cheerleader and honor student.

Returning to Miami of Ohio, I hadn't thought much more about any of it. I had just a very few dates in college due to my self-consciousness over my lack of stylish clothes and ready cash. I didn't suffer; it was just all that much easier to focus on the classroom and football.

Nearly two years passed, and I was returning home for the summer following my completed sophomore year. For the most part, I would either work in the factory or find construction work. One summer, I did both. About the only recreation I had was playing in the summer baseball league and maybe attending a few of the stag dances, held for teens around town. It was at such a dance where I thought I recognized the girl I had met at that New Year's party a few years back. She had just graduated from high school a few weeks before. Shyly, I asked her to dance. I guess I really didn't remember what she looked like in detail until we were face-to-face dancing. She had shoulder-length hair that was naturally streaked in several shades of light brown and blonde. When she looked at me directly, I saw her luminous blue eyes and easy smile. She was fun to dance with, being very light on her feet. I felt my arm around her tiny waist and barely knew she was there. When we cut through the small talk and reaffirmed we had met a while back, our conversation became easier. She was cerebral and highly intelligent but didn't seem to flaunt it in any way.

Though she had taken heavy academic courses – Latin, algebra, geometry and trig – she was torn about going to college. She had been offered a great job with the Ohio Bell Telephone company as a draftswoman in training. Her dad was a foreman and had worked there for forty years. We had a few dates that summer, but both she and I felt great reservations about anything really serious. We had very few things in common. I was Italian, Catholic, and broke. She would soon be well on her way to financial independence and "Catholic" and "Italian" were words rarely in her vocabulary. All I knew was that I was strongly attracted to her and hoped she was to me.

Being three years older, I was getting pretty serious. At seventeen she didn't need nor want that. We had a flare up once because I felt pretty sure and possessive about her, but she was still involved with dating other people. We had not arrived at any settlement that called for exclusivity.

The flare-up proved to be a catalyst. I remember calling her for a date, but she already had one and said so. In my emotional Italian way, I mentally said, "Screw it all" and resolved never to call her again. About two weeks passed with no contact. We lived only a few blocks away from one another, and Shirley could occasionally be seen walking down my street and past my home. She had a classmate and girl friend who lived down the hill from me.

One evening I spotted her walking to her friend's house. It was an unaffected walk. She was wearing shorts and a short-sleeved blouse. Her tan body was lithe and erect. Her hair bounced easily with each step. The way she carried herself – her posture and the easy glide she seemed to own – made her so appealing that I actually hurt inside from the desire to be with her. But I knew I would never go back. It was over! She was too young and not ready to be as serious as I was. The Catholic and non-Catholic thing presented as big a problem as her uncertainty.

It was a warm summer evening and an hour earlier, I watched that easy walk descend the hill. It was not quite dark yet, and I was lying on my bed, the window screen allowing a pleasant breeze to cool the room. I was staring at the ceiling, half-praying and half-thinking. It was a conversation with God, but it was also a conversation with myself.

After one broken engagement, I didn't want to be hurt again. I didn't want to be enmeshed again. I didn't want to be playing love games with coyness and cuteness and competition. I said almost aloud, "God, if she's the right one, help me! If she's not, then let me get over her!" About that time a car pulled into the gravel drive right along side my bedroom window. I paid no attention to it until I heard a knock on the window sill. It was Shirley. She had driven her dad's Buick over. I heard her voice say, "Feel like talking?" I took it as a sign and walked out to her car.

"You were not planning on ever calling me again, were you?" Her voice was direct and sincere.

"No", I grunted sheepishly.

"Why, Tom? Why would you be so drastic? We have no string on one another? We made no promises."

"I know that," I said. "I also realize that I'm looking with seriousness, and you're not."

"You don't know that. You don't really know anything about me. I can be serious if and when the time calls for it."

We spoke of many things and slowly, inch by inch, over the summer we learned of one another. She was, in my mind, strong willed but had such clarity of thought in her reasoning that she most often was right. (I hated it when she was right!)

We enjoyed the summer and her dates with other fellows seemed less and less until there were none. Late in summer, sitting on her porch step and speaking our hearts, I confessed that I really loved her and was miserable when not with her. She had these same feelings.

By now, she knew I had obligations to my mother and family and that I could not or would not overlook these. She also knew the next few years would literally fly by. We spoke of marriage, perhaps after my senior season of football. Meanwhile she would try to save as much money as she could. We would be apart, but between vacations when I could come home, and her visits to Oxford, we could make it work. Having been in the ROTC and working to become a 2nd Lieutenant. in the Air Force ensured a reasonable job after graduation.

In truth, no woman or man has anything but an inkling of the person she or he marries or what that person will become after the marriage. With all the lack of common ground between us, with little or no similarity of background, we were deeply in love.

When I look at it in retrospect, someone or something was

looking out for me. Shirley wasn't a social person. She was a homebody who wanted a nice home, kids, and a certain security of life. These, too, were my dreams.

With Shirley in a recent picture.

Throughout all those high-pressure, emotional years of marriage, we have rarely argued and mostly when we did, it was over the children, their behavior and actions. We each brought to the marriage whatever the other seemed to lack. Where I was stern with the kids, she was the buffer. Where I was a spendthrift, never handling money well, she was frugal. Where I couldn't pound a nail or use a saw or screw driver, she sent away for craft and repair books and became as handy as any man could have dreamed. There seemed nothing she couldn't read about and finally master.

She proved to be a mother, an interior decorator, a designer. She plays the piano and reads music. She paints pictures of beautifully artistic landscapes and flowers (she paints walls as well). She is a gardener and horticulturist supreme. She keeps our books and records, writes the checks, and freely admits to being a poor speller.

It was a Friday, November 28, 1953, when Shirley and I became man and wife. My mother knew all along I would marry Shirley. She seemed very pleased, seeing in Shirley a practical and loving companion that could make me more than I was. Women know about such things with great instinct. Men seem to dawdle around and never refine this wonderful sixth sense. Mom knew she'd be losing a bread-winner of sorts, but she urged me and welcomed Shirley with open arms.

For nearly a year I had wrestled with guilt about wanting to marry. I watched Sam and Joe grind away to make the family survive. Had I the right?

"Of course you have the right!" Mom spoke forcefully. "You can't wait until everything is perfect or until you're financially secure. Life is in the living, Tom. Do what you have to do. If you love the girl, marry her. If you wait until you have the money, you'll wait a lifetime!"

She knew full well what the loss of my earning power would mean to our plan of erasing our debts. She also knew that life cannot be on hold. Upon graduation, I was commissioned as a second lieutenant in the Air Force. The ROTC training while at Miami insured my commission and four years of military obligation. With pay as an officer, Shirley and I knew we could live well for at least the next four years. Mom admired Shirley. She saw her as a homemaker and one devoted to me.

After I graduated and left Miami, the news was released that I was drafted by the Cleveland Browns. I was elated with the prospect of it all.

When I returned to Akron, Joe was discharged from the Marine Corps.

Until I reported to the Cleveland Browns training camp in late July, I would live with Shirley and her parents. Joe, Mom, and Terry (Mom's father had died) moved in with Donna Theresa.

That summer Joe and I found employment together, cutting greens and fairways at the Firestone Golf Course. When summer ended and I went to camp, Joe enrolled at Kent State University via a GED diploma in the service. He also went to Goodyear and worked on the same squadron that I worked on through college.

Joe's life revolved around taking care of Mom and Terry, college, his job at Goodyear, and, in spare evenings, playing drums with a dance band.

When I was at the Browns Camp, Shirley informed me that

she was pregnant. Things seemed to be falling into place, but the never-ending grind to pay off medical debts still haunted all of us.

I believe I showed the Browns I was worth their draft. I played the entire exhibition season and did well enough that I became hopeful I would earn a spot on their permanent roster. In those years only making the final roster validated the contract.

It was the sixth Sunday of the exhibition season. Six games were all that were allowed to be played. At midnight, all rosters had to be trimmed to thirty-three players. The Browns were returning by plane after playing the Detroit Lions in Dallas, when Paul Brown summoned me to his seat.

"Tom," he began, "you're a fine halfback, and I really planned on keeping you with the Browns, but tonight after the game, "Dub" Jones came out of retirement. I've got to make room for him on the roster, so I've made this decision. I'll keep you on our taxi squad and pay you half salary or," he paused, "I can trade you to Green Bay. Lisle Blackbourn of the Packers remembers you well from college and needs a halfback."

I was stunned. The thirty-three count had been named and I was part of it. The "Dub" Jones thing, I never figured on. Dub had been a great player and an all-pro several times. My contract was not great in terms of money, but $5,500 in those day and age seemed a lot.

In my heart I wanted badly to play for the Cleveland Browns, but half of $5,500 was not enough now that Shirley was pregnant, and I'd only have the one season before I faced active duty.

"Can I play in this league, Coach Brown?" I asked.

"Yes, you're a player."

"As badly as I want to be a Cleveland Brown, Coach, my wife is pregnant and I really do need the income. So I'd like to try for the full salary."

"I understand, Tom."

It was settled, and I flew to Green Bay while Shirley stayed with her parents. What I did not realize at the time of this disappointment was that in order to meet the roster, Brown put me on waivers. Green Bay agreed to pick me up on waivers, but the rule of the league stated that a player could not be added to the active roster for thirty days once the waived player was added.

It seemed a long time to wait out for me, but I was thrilled that I would receive full contract throughout that period, plus have ample opportunity to learn and fit into the new system.

When I received my first payment of $600, I was exuberant. Never had I lumped that much money together in one sum at one time. I was being paid for something I dearly loved and never once doubted my ultimate success. After two weeks of work with the Packers, where I filled in as the upcoming opponents quarterback or halfback, I knew my skills were equal to the task.

One day Lisle Blackbourn called me and another five or so players into his office.

"I have this friend," he stated boldly, "who runs a semi-pro team up in Wausau. If he wins two more games, he's into the playoffs. I want you fellas, under assumed names, of course, to play a few games for him. You're all on the taxi squad here. You'll be paid by the Packers and also by my friend."

The other players, hearing of the extra money, were eager. I was not. "What about injury?" I asked.

"It'll be as though you are part of us," Blackbourn answered. "No difference."

It was all arranged. The Packers flew to Baltimore, and I and my teammates drove to Wausau. The coach there explained we'd each receive $150 per man to win and $100 if we lost. They also paid $25 per touchdown, $5 per pass reception, etc.

Once on the field, with just the simplest of offenses, I surveyed my new teammates. They were ex-service men, high-school kids, taxi drivers, and bartenders. All had played some, and all thought themselves better than they were. Strange company, I thought.

It seemed to me that I was once again back in high school. The quick, alert, smooth play of a well-oiled team was not present. I romped easily for four quick touchdowns, and they pulled me out. My day was over.

Coming back to Green Bay, our group was jovial. Each had received their cash and was rather proud of their own contribution. I was relieved that it had been so easy and vowed that I wouldn't run the risk again.

In Wausau, the paper ran my picture with an assumed name. It said how I had sparkled in the game and pointed the Panthers towards the playoffs. At the end of the week, Blackbourn once again sent for the six men. "One more game, I need from you, fellas."

"Mr. Blackbourn, I'm a week away from being activated," I said. "The injury factor concerns me in such a league."

"You'll be fine, fine. Didn't last week go well enough?"

"Yes," I said cautiously, "but I'm so close to my active date. I hate to risk playing in such a disorganized league."

Blackbourn appreciated my concern and knew that he planned on activating me as soon as possible.

"Bear with me, Tom. One more game, and you'll have a place with us. Do it as a personal favor to me." I agreed.

While the Pack was playing that Sunday, their key halfback, Al Carmichael was injured. While that game was going on, the Wausau team lined up for the kick off to receive.

Though I had no way of knowing it, I was a marked man. I fielded the kickoff easily at the goal line and glided up field. At the 20, I sliced to my right. A defensive man got one of my legs, and I was going down. Somehow, the point of the ball jarred the ground as I fell, and seemingly drove the other point into my ribs. Another six or eight bodies piled on me. I felt a sharp pain in my chest. It was a searing, burning pain, and, though I scrambled up, I knew from my labored breathing that I was hurt badly. I took myself out. The coach was screaming, "Get him back in there!"

The trainer yelled back, "I don't think we should."

The coach came to face me nose to nose. "Get in there!"

"No," I spoke with pain. "I don't fake injuries, but I know when I'm hurt, and I'm hurt."

We lost the game by a considerable margin. The opening play cost me my chance to be activated. The season consisted of a twelve games only. I had already missed nearly half of it by awaiting activation, and the doctor said the X-rays showed four of the five broken ribs thrust inward toward my lung. It would take six to eight weeks to repair. My season was over.

When I appeared before Coach Blackbourn in the morning, the coach said simply, "You know we were going to activate you. Al Carmichael is hurt." He said it as though he blamed me for getting myself hurt.

"Well," I said, "I'm really sorry this all happened. What happens now?"

"Your season is over for now, so we'll just sign you to a contract for when you leave the Air Force."

"What about payment of the current contract? You said it would be the same as though I were a Packer."

"Well, yes, I did . . ," he hemmed and hawed, "but you see, the board and GM would not approve your full contract, so we'll just pay you up till today."

My eyes narrowed. Never had I experienced the guile and two-facedness of the real world. I knew in that instant that there was no intent to pay in case of injury for the season.

"You gave me your word," I said, staring at the coach.

"Yes, yes, I did, but I'm not the final word here. Look, you're paid up till for now, and we'll sign a new contract with a several-thousand-dollar raise for when you return here. You'll be a Green Bay Packer."

Disconsolately, I remained quiet. I left there to pack and catch the nearest train out for Chicago and, eventually, Akron. Within two weeks of being home, I started in again on the Goodyear Squadron.

Mom lived a few miles from Shirley's parents, so on weekends I visited with her over coffee.

"I hate like hell to see you so down, Tom," she said, frankly. "You have it all in front of you. Life doesn't end when football does."

"I know, Mom," I was disconsolate. "But I came so damned close, and I failed."

"You didn't fail, dammit. Don't say that! You got a bad break, and the guy lied to you. Where the hell is the failure?"

"Mom . . . I wanted the money. I wanted . . ."

She interrupted "To hell with the money, Tom! Money is nothing! Maybe the pros would have crippled you up for the rest of your life. There are a lot of ways to earn money."

"I wanted it for you, Mom."

"Well, that's a comforting thought," she said disgustedly. "I wanted it for you and a house and that new baby. I always thought you'd be the one that never gave up," her voice was accusing.

"I'm not giving up," I yelled. "I've just begun my life. I'll pull a 'Rosie' and spit in their eye, eventually."

She laughed.

"I'll tell you a little secret," she said, as she put her arm around my waist. "I'd bet my life you wouldn't give up."

"Thanks, Mom," I gathered my feelings, "I'm a little lost right now, but I'll find my way."

She kissed me on the cheek, "My mother used to say, 'God writes straight with crooked lines,' Tom, and surely He does!"

And he surely does. Here's a perfect example. When Shirley and I went to arrange our first home mortgage and loan, we sat waiting patiently for the loan officer in near silence. The receptionist was walking toward us now and said pleasantly, "Mr. Shanafelt will see you now."

"Oh, my God," I groaned in a half whisper, "of all the banks we could have picked, we pick one where Dave Shanafelt is loan manager. He was the counselor in my dorm whom I knocked down a flight of stairs."

"Tommy," a smiling Dave Shanafelt shook my hand and gestured for the two of us to sit.

"I hope you don't hold grudges," I smiled.

"Aw, hell no. That's long forgotten, and I chuckle to think about it now."

We got the loan and our first home, a few blocks from Shirley's parents.

I reported to San Antonio for processing and was assigned shortly thereafter to Tech school in Cheyenne, Wyoming. It would be twelve weeks there and then a permanent assignment. All the while, Shirley gave birth to our first daughter, Sandy. Shortly after Tech school, word got out that an ex-pro halfback was available. The Air Force made full use of athletic talent and assigned me to a base in New York.

It was my first real assignment, and it was in upstate New York, at the training base of Sampson Air Force Base, outside Geneva. We put in two long cold winters with our new baby, Sandy. The Finger Lakes, or in this instance Lake Seneca and Lake Geneva, were gorgeous in the summer but very tough to winter. I coached one of the many base teams and played as well. Seeking to remain in good physical shape, I also played basketball. When the base closed, various inquiries were made about the football talent. Air Force bases loved to sport great teams. It was announced that my next assignment would be at Mitchell Air Force Base in Hempstead, New York. It was Continental Air Command and 1st Air Force Headquarters. The base commander wanted a good team. After those two years at Sampson, Shirley took Sandy back to Akron, and I went on to Mitchell Air Force Base.

I would again coach and play for the base team, which had a major schedule. It was a grueling season for me. I was forced to coach and play both offense and defense. The base was lacking in major talent. Most of the elite names of college football were assigned to Bolling Air Force Base in Washington, D.C. They had a powerhouse of great college and pro players. Still, I worked very hard and garnered good coaching experience.

Military football was an enigma. Players ranked anywhere from high school talent to ex-pros. Many of the games played were against opponents easily on a par with some professional teams. At the season's end, the base commander was pleased with my performance. Since we both would shortly leave the base, he asked me what he could do to help me. I had several broken noses in college and two more this past season.

"I'd really like to get my nose straightened out, if I could."

"Consider it done," the colonel was empathetic. "We'll send you to the best hospital in the military, St. Alban's Naval hospital in New York.

It was to be a rather perfunctory and simple operation. They would re-break my nose, scrape the bone plus straighten the cartilage. Normally speaking, the patient would exit in about three days. My eyes would be bloodshot and my face would bear two black eyes and some swelling, but in a months time all would be well.

All seemed well until the third day after the surgery. I hemorrhaged badly and the flow of blood soaked through the nasal packing so badly that it hardly allowed me breathing air. I could not lay down because the flow of blood went down into my throat. Several times the doctors brought me into the surgical room to cauterize the bleeding. I could not eat, bathe, shave, or sleep. It was going on the fourth week when Joe got through on the phone.

"Tom," the familiar voice rang out, "How're you doing?"

"I'm . . . dying, Joe," I said softly through gasps, convinced the blood flow, like my father's, would not stop.

"I'll be there. Hang on."

When Joe walked the hallway of the hospital, gazing at each patient in each room, we stared directly at each other, but he continued down the hallway. I saw him, but remained motionless and silent. There was a shuffling in the hallway, a turn around, and a voice that asked, "Tom?"

"Yes," I groaned.

Joe looked at me a long time. He was almost in disbelief of what he saw. Small wonder he had not recognized me from the hallway. My eyes were of one solid color, blood red. My face was distorted greatly from the swelling and pressed outwardly so forcibly one could not see my ears when looking at me directly. It had been a month since I shaved, and blue, green, and purple masses of bruises lined my face under the eyes. I looked horrible and had lost 25 pounds in that month. Not once did Joe show his true feelings. Never did he act disdainful of the sight or odor of his kid brother.

My roommate, a much older and nearly retired commander, observed the love we brothers displayed with small subtleties. Joe brought me ice water with a straw and then bathed my face gently. On the second day he got me into the shower and toweled me down with soap. Near exhaustion, I sat in a chair, and Joe shaved me, trimmed my toenails and fingernails, then he washed my mop of hair that contained clots of blood, accumulated from my pillow where it seeped when I slept.

"You're gonna be okay," he said.

"I don't know, Joe, I don't know."

"Hey, you've had tougher times. Why, hell in two more years, you'll be playing in the Green Bay Packers backfield."

"No," I said softly, "I know when I've had it. I'll never play again."

Slowly, Joe fed me fresh grapes one at a time. I was convinced that my brother willed me back to health. He sat on the bed's edge and hugged me a long, long while. No brothers were ever closer.

Joe spent nights sleeping in the chair next to me. Only one more night did they have to cauterize. Then I began to heal. His presence affected me.

"Pray," Joe said softly, "and I'll pray."

Before Joe left the room for good, the commander roommate beckoned him to his own bedside.

"When he feels good enough to read, he might enjoy this." He gave Joe a book to give to me. It was *Away All Boats*. "That book," he told Joe, "is the only other time I've seen such brotherly love."

"Our family is kinda like that," Joe responded as he thanked the commander.

In the days that followed, I was able to begin to eat a few solids. I could now shower and shave by myself and do a little reading. The blood from the packing was slowly being dissolved and slowly I was becoming more myself.

It was late afternoon, and the commander was in a deep slumber with a light snoring sound. I was deep *into Away All Boats*. I was at the spot in the book when the *U.S.S. Belinda* was being bombarded with kamikaze pilots. There was a scene where the young U.S. sailors, burned almost beyond recognition, were being transferred off the ship to life boats. One was screaming to be killed, such was his agony. The story settled on a young chaplain on board, feeling helpless with what to say or do in such a pitiful circumstances. Overwhelmed, with the grief and sorrow of so many scorched young men, he could only think of one thing to say to each man as they were moved.

"God promises, 'I shall never leave thee or forsake thee,' this the chaplain wept with a sense of helplessness."

So too would the tears fill my eyes as I read that scene. I didn't know that my tear ducts were clogged with blood and that the streaming tears down my face were rivulets of blood as red as wine.

It was at this point when the commander awoke. He saw across the room, the red streaks staining my face. He could not

In 1958, at Youngstown AFB, before my discharge.

know that though the scene filled me with compassion and mercy. It was the unknowingly accurate recall of the chaplain's that moved me to inspiration.

"I shall never leave thee or forsake thee," I repeated it. "If God is God," I reasoned. "He cannot break a promise. He'll always be with us and it's up to us to know and learn that."

Shortly I would recover, but forever, until death, will I carry this ineffable wisdom. The commander spoke to me, "A great book, huh?"

"A great book," I assured him.

"May I tell you a sidelight?", he asked.

"Sure."

"That is a true story, you know?"

"No . . . I didn't know."

"I was on the *U.S.S. Belinda*. She was my ship."

Nearly three and one-half years had transpired for Shirley and me, and we were anxious for my discharge. The Green Bay Packers asked me not to take any leave, and in so doing, requested an early out by virtue of the accrued leave. In this fashion, I could join them at the season's beginning. The Air Force granted the release. It was late September 1958 when I stood before Lisle Blackbourn, having been on a train all day and night.

"Well," Blackbourn addressed me, "we've decided that since you've missed the exhibition season, that we'll go with some of our rookies and release you."

I was dumbfounded, and stared at him in disbelief.

"You've taught me a great lesson," my voice seethed with anger. "I plan to coach, but I will coach and deal with players with honesty and integrity. I will be going up when you're on your way down." I stormed out.

Many years later, while I was a young coach at Notre Dame, Lisle Blackbourn visited practices as a scout. He was fired as coach after only his second year but was retained to scout. I made sure he had a stool to sit on, got him a cold drink, and spent many gracious moments answering questions about Notre Dame Players.

"Screw him," Parseghian scolded me. "After the treatment you got, why bother?"

"Because," I answered, "it is to satisfy me, not him, that I do it."

"Damned dummy," Ara chuckled at me. "I'll never understand you."

Chapter 11
The Summer of Our Rose

Upon discharge from the Marine Corps, Joe moved into Donna Theresa's home with Mom and Terry. It would not take long for him to realize the utter urgency of his presence. Mom and Terry were living meagerly in the bottom half of Donna Theresa's home, while she occupied the upstairs. Joe was grateful and treated her with great respect. Donna Theresa dearly loved Tony's children and often showed favoritism. She was widowed again and was alone for some time.

While Mom, Joe, and Terry lived with my grandmother, they made plans to purchase their own home. It was forced upon them sooner than they thought, since Donna Theresa, nearly eighty now, died the first winter after Joe's discharge. The house would be sold to settle the courageous woman's estate. Mom was left a small portion, as were each of Donna Theresa's other children. Joe and Mom used the money along with Joe's mustering pay to place a small down payment on a nearby bungalow.

With the need for greater income, Mom left the department store; their pay scale was ridiculously low. She found employment in a small factory, where they placed their seamstresses on piece work. Mom had full faith in her speedy and accurate sewing talent and made the move out of practicality.

For nearly three years, Mom, Joe, and Terry struggled to get on a plateau where their lives would level out. Joe worked at a loan office and played in a dance band several nights a week. In many ways, because of his age and the responsibility he felt, he became the man of the house and the father figure for Terry. He gave up his job at Goodyear and the pursuit of college, once he caught on well with the finance company. Slowly he climbed the corporate ladder, starting at the lowest rung, as a collector. His shrewd evaluation of people and business acumen soon brought him a promotion to assistant manager. The most difficult task for Joe was to remain a brother to Terry, while still being an acting father. Trying to raise his own sister as a daughter, while at the same time trying to curb the spending impulses of Mom, caused him to vent emotion frequently, causing strained family relations.

"I wish," Terry, by now a sophomore cheerleader, screamed

at her brother's domination. "One of my other brothers were raising me!"

"Well, by God," he shouted back. "I didn't ask for the job!"

If ever he had to smack her, it was as his dad had done to the boys, always restrained and on the butt with the flat of his hand. He hated having the "yes and no" command over her actions, but it had to be done. Joe saw too early in life the ways of the world. At sixteen he had known more about women, booze, gambling, and life than most men at forty. The musician's life, especially a single musician, was exposed to all of it. He became wary of Terry's growing attractiveness, her high-school popularity, and the pimply-faced kids who arrived at their doorstep. Dad's quote by the philosopher Nietzsche, haunted Joe, "Youthful sinners make senile saints." He remembered the line and felt the guilt his own escapades brought him.

"What are you afraid of?" Terry asked him. "What in the world do you think I'm going to do that is so bad? Don't you trust me?"

Joe was shook with the responsibility of it all. He loved his sister dearly, and nightly he recalled the three brothers promising their father that they would take care of their mother and sister. It burdened him heavily, and he sorely wished there were a manual to read. He was certain a book entitled, *How To Raise a Daughter* could easily be a bestseller.

After a particularly heated argument, after Joe had swatted Terry for sassing him, he sent her to her room. Shortly he went to his own room and threw himself across the bed. He was face down, his arms covering his head. When Mom entered, she sat on the bed and lightly placed her hand on his back. She had done the same to Terry only minutes before.

"Joe," she said softly, "She's a young girl. You've got to let her grow up. She doesn't even know what it is you're so worried about. I never really had a childhood, Joe. I want Terry to have one, enjoy school, her friends, her home."

There was a brief pause, and Joe turned to face her.

"Mom," he wiped his eyes, "I love you and her more than life, but I really don't know what is right and wrong to do. I do know," He was emphatic now, "she sure as hell hasn't got a clue. She has no idea of what is out there!"

"I know, Joe, but you can't mistrust everything and everybody. You can't over-protect to the point she'll do things to spite you. Show her you love her and trust her and pray to God she's doing the right things. That's all you can do."

Joe nodded agreement and said half kidding, "She'll probably hate me until she's thirty!"

"No, she won't. Not if you are fair, and she knows you love her."

Joe arose, straightened out his shirt, and walked down the hallway to his sister's room. He knocked gently on the half-open door and said in an apologetic voice, "Can I come in?"

Terry was also lying across her bed face down. It was obvious she was crying.

"Stand up," Joe said softly in a mock order, "Kiss your brother," then, "hug your brother."

Terry knew the game well enough and as she hugged him said, "I love my brother." It was all well again and would last until the next explosion. Mom heard and saw all of it. She marveled at the ability of her children to be resilient, to let go, to love.

Not only did she have her own arguments with Terry, she had them with Joe too. While Terry's needs in high school were acceptance, clothes, spending money, transportation, and home support, Joe's were not as clear-cut. Mom wondered if he would ever date or meet anyone he could love. Not only did she hold the concern, but sometimes she'd echo it and wind up in a huff with Joe.

"Find a nice girl," she'd say.

"Mom, I like living at home, and there are very few nice girls."

"You're worried about Terry and me and can't leave. Is that it?"

"Yeah, Mom, I worry, but that's not the reason. If it happens, it happens."

Mom wouldn't let go of it and offered a sarcastic, "We can manage, you know."

"Who the hell are you fooling, Mom? You like nice things, a nice home. You and Terry need clothes, food, insurance, and transportation. We're up to our ass in debt."

"I'll manage," Mom retorted.

"Sure, Mom," Joe exploded, "I get married to a nice girl and leave and for the rest of my life feel guilty!"

"Why the guilt? Hell, You're not my husband, you're my son. I told your brothers the same thing, and I..."

Joe cut her off, tired of covering the same ground over and over. "Mom, please, I don't want to hear it all again. We're a family . . . you, Terry, and me. Like Tom and Sam, if the right one comes along, I'll tell you, but let's not argue about it."

Through these tough years, Joe saw Terry through high school, saw to it that she had the gowns and formals for dances, class ring, graduation pictures, the prom, her own car, and spending money. It took some doing, but he saw to it that "she had a childhood," as his mother had wanted.

Joe was thrilled that soon I would be back in Akron. The two of us, now adults, would chum together. He enjoyed visiting me and Shirley, along with his niece, Sandy.

About the only job I could find during this recession time was as a substitute teacher. It paid only about $18 per day and was sometimes only a few days a week. With the school year half over, I had to wait for the new school year to catch on full time. At Joe's insistence, he brought me to the bass player of the band he played in. The fellow was a professor of music at Akron University.

"He's got rhythm, Doc," Joe told his friend. "See if you can teach him a few chords to get by with." I took well to the bass fiddle. My hands were strong, though a bit clumsy, but I managed about four different beats – a waltz, polka, fox trot, and rhumba.

I knew just enough and joined the musicians union for $16 per year. Joe had me invest $6 per lesson, and I took just four lessons.

All in all, the investment of $40, some time, and raw fingers brought me another income. Whenever Joe got a call to play drums, he asked if there would be a bass. If the answer were "No," he suggested his brother at scale. Scale was $11 per hour, and most jobs were a minimum of three hours. Whenever we could, we played together.

After the half year of substitute teaching, mostly grammar and literature, I realized my great luck. Though I read much in the past, my command of authors and the spoken word became greatly enhanced by my teaching. I felt as though I were taking remedial English, though, sometimes being only a page or two ahead of my students.

During the summer, Mom, Terry, and Joe moved again, into a bigger and better house. They moved at least four more times before Joe turned thirty. The longest they stayed anywhere was the four years when Terry attended high school. In her lifetime, Mom moved an incredible twenty-four times. Each time, she remodeled and sold for a profit.

In the fall, I applied and was accepted at North High School in Akron proper. I was hired as a teacher and head football coach. From the music room, I could borrow a bass for weekends to play in the trio Joe formed. Joe booked three nights a week at a supper club. We thoroughly enjoyed the diversion.

Sometimes, when my exuberance got carried away with the moment, I'd stick in a run of ad-lib notes. Joe understood but, knowing all the notes weren't the right ones, would hiss at me, "Soft . . . dammit . . . play soft."

The nearly $100 per week income was more than I could make at a full teacher's salary of $3,400. My new job would allow me an additional $800 for coaching, but I spent the money for two of my ex-Miami teammates to help as assistants.

Shirley was pregnant with our second child, and the climb got a little steeper.

On holidays, Mom now had two of her sons, her daughter, and a grandchild to enjoy. On weekends, she called for Joe and me to help her with a chore or two where she needed our strength.

The three of us would sit at her kitchen table and talk about all kinds of things. Mentally, she had grown very strong. She attributed it to our stay in Colorado.

Once, when Joe was telling of the inequities there were at his office, she fumed, "By God, if I were a man, I'd uproot telephone poles if they were in my way." We roared with laughter. We knew she not only could but would.

As close as we were to her, she kept one guarded secret she

never shared. No one knew or guessed that she was not a U.S. citizen. The one confidant she had was my wife, Shirley. Since Mom didn't drive, and didn't want anyone to know her business, she'd prevail upon Shirley, once a year, to take her to the courthouse to register. But now, in 1959, she was late, and Shirley, ready to give birth, was not available.

Fearful of not passing her naturalization test, Mom had never taken it. She reasoned that by arriving in America, at only six months old, marrying, raising her children, paying taxes and Social Security, she was as good as any citizen.

Without divulging why, she ordered me to drive her to the courthouse. It was the last day she could possibly register without penalty, and she insisted that I hurry, since it was close to the 5:00 PM closing time of the federal office. There was a virtual flood of water falling around the block!

"But Mom," I started to object. "It's pouring rain. You'll get soaked!"

"Never mind," she said, obviously in a great hurry.

The federal building had nearly one hundred steps of approach to the main entrance. Obediently, I pulled the car into double park. The rain was slashing down in torrents. Mom opened the car door, and the rain immediately halted. She climbed the steps hurriedly and entered the federal building. The instant she entered, the rain commenced again, accompanied by lightning.

A traffic cop forced me to move on, so I circled the block several times. After about my fourth trip, Mom appeared at the glass revolving doors, but the lightning and rain were too strong. Almost defiantly, she pushed through the revolving doors to the outside. The rain, within an instant, halted again. Not even a drop fell as she descended the long open cement staircase. Halfway down, the sun actually shown for a moment and a quick glimpse of a rainbow appeared. When she entered the car, the storm resumed at an even greater force than before. My windshield wipers could hardly clear away the water fast enough for me to see.

I pulled along at a cautious pace and started to laugh.

"What's the matter?" Mom eased into her own chuckle at my laughter.

"Mom," I looked at her, completely dry, "I think Joe was right, you're a witch. You didn't even have an umbrella."

We both had a good laugh at her timing and nature's cooperation.

Secure now in the car, registered as an alien for another year and her secret intact, she said simply, "Let's go home, I've got dinner to fix."

"She wasn't a witch, but if she were, she was a good one," I thought to myself.

In many ways, Mom was psychic. She seemed to have a sense for the safety and whereabouts of her family. There was a wisdom to her far deeper than any formal education could have produced. She lived on intuition and what her gut felt. It seemed never to fail her. I believe the secret was that she never doubted it, and learned to trust in it implicitly.

I recall times when Sam, away at college, would be on Mom's mind and suddenly she'd utter, "I feel the presence of Sammy." Shortly after, you could hear tires across our gravel drive. Sam, trying to surprise, had got away for a weekend home.

"I'll be damned," my Dad said a thousand times. "How did you know?"

"I just know," would be her answer.

Our family's love and closeness never wore thin or left any of us. The normal young adult grows up and wants to leave and try his own wings. We were always trying to get back home.

My Dad was far more demonstrative than Mom. He would hug you and say some gentle Italian phrase that would let you know. Mom just did. She hardly received any display of love, after her mother's death. She was always too busy raising a brother and sisters and then all of us.

Mom's pace was that of a dynamo. Until seeing our mother in the hospital late in her life, we could never recall ever seeing her in bed. She was always up before us and in bed after us. She had tireless energy, and, though she loved each of us deeply, only Terry received the praise and embraces due the very young. Mom thought we boys had to accept that we were loved. Demonstrations took time.

One evening, when Joe arrived to pick Mom up at the sewing factory, she entered his car with tears in her eyes, not a frequent occurrence.

"What, Mom, what?" Joe's voice was loud and excited.

"Don't yell at me, Joe. Dammit, sometimes you act like my father."

None of us could stand to see our mother cry.

"Aw, Mom, I'm sorry, but I wanna know what's wrong."

She explained how the factory offered her piece work. She was so good – never taking a smoke or coffee break – that her rapid pace set a higher level than any of the other girls wanted to produce. They ridiculed and isolated her.

"I wanted the piece work," she said calmly, "because I thought if I only depended on myself, I could make more money. Was that so wrong?"

Joe ran it by his creative mind as they drove home.

"Mom," he said, "to hell with that job, quit this Friday!"

"I can't quit!" She was angry.

"Listen to me Mom. Before you quit, let me take a peek at their operation. Before you leave Friday, I'll come in and walk around the shop." Joe was enthused. "Is there anything we can't do in our own basement?"

She looked hard at Joe while he was driving. Her mind grasped his thought.

"Hell, no," she said defiantly. "We don't have the machines to mass produce, but I know every operation."

It was settled. Joe got to the cushion factory Friday at 4:00 PM. He said he would wait for her and meanwhile asked if he could look around. The supervisor was glad to have him do it, frightened he might lose one of his best workers.

With the eye of a thief and the mind of a genius, Joe observed each operator and their skill. He chuckled as he recalled our father saying so often, "Necessity may be the mother of invention, but it is also the father of crime."

It would not be a crime, Joe thought, but we can make this same tractor seat cushion of vinyl panels, a steel grommet, a draw string, and air foam rubber fill.

"We can make it better and cheaper," he thought, "but maybe not as fast and not as many."

Before they headed home that evening, Mom served her two-week notice. In the next two weeks, Joe put together all the patterns for panels that they would need. Two weeks later Joe and Mom went to their basement for a try at their first cushion.

"Who's their biggest customer, Mom?"

"I guess it would be Standard Oil Company," she answered.

"Okay, then we'll have to make samples for Standard Oil."

Mom too was excited now as they set about to alter the design and improve the product. After several evenings, with her own sewing machine and only scraps of material, she produced a half-dozen cushions. They had just enough grommets to make an even dozen.

Mom called Uncle Mike.

"Mike," she said sternly with Joe at her side. "You're always playing like a big shot. Get your best suit, wear your fake diamond ring, and look like a prosperous salesman. You're calling on Standard Oil with cushions that they buy to give away as premiums to farmers who buy their fuel. Standard's been paying $7.50 per cushion. We'll ask $5.50. Think you can do it?"

Uncle Mike took the challenge, "I've been a bull slinger all my life. Why not once for the family," he laughed.

When Mike called on the purchasing agent, presented the goods and the new price, the man calculated the $2.00 per cushion savings and swiftly multiplied their volume.

When he looked up, he said, "you've got a deal Mr. Crimaldi, when can I see the factory?"

Uncle Mike mumbled something about allowing him to call the office and set it up. The man insisted that he use the desk phone right there and then. Sheepishly, he called his sister Rose.

"Rose," he said somewhat nervously. "This is salesman Mike Crimaldi, and I'm sitting in the office of Mr. J. L. Adams of Standard Oil. He wants to know when he can see the factory . . . and, oh yes, he likes our product and price."

Mom at the other end surmised the dilemma. She told Mike, "Be calm, tell him in two weeks. We'll call him back. Tell him we are down for a two-week vacation and I'd like him to visit when we are in full swing."

It was done. Mom had two weeks to find a shack, pay a one-month deposit in advance, and have her carpenter friends repair the walls, put in work bins and shelves. No sooner had that been started when she called her friend at the bank.

"Mr. Matthews," she said earnestly, "I need a helluva favor."

Mom made draperies for Mr. Matthews and his wife, outfitting their entire home.

"For you, Rose," he chuckled, "anything." She requested a $2,000 loan on signature for only 90 days.

Matthews thought a moment and said, "Okay, Rose, when do you want it?"

"Today," she replied.

With cash in hand Mom bought enough vinyl to fill the shelves. She bought graded air foam and filled the bins. Next, she called the Singer Sewing Machine Company.

Mom at the sewing machine.

She wished to buy an industrial machine, a cutter and an edger for fabric. She also wanted to rent five more, but they had to be there within 48 hours. And so they were.

With this done, she called her sisters and friends. She taught each of them to sew in straight lines, stuff the air foam, insert the metal grommets, and wrap the finished product. All the actual work was done by Mom, Joe, and me in the basement at night. Whatever finished product we had went onto the shelves in the renovated shack.

When Mom called Mr. Adams at Standard Oil to set the time of the visit, Mr. Adams added, "Of course, Rose, you'll have to box the cushions in cardboard cartons, six to the box, because we will ship them all over the country."

"Sure, of course, Mr. Adams," she replied, precariously. When she shopped for the last item, the cardboard containers, her heart sank. The price of the containers with the company logo and name printed would cut way into the quoted price per cushion. All the profit margin would be eaten away.

The salesman then said, "Then too, Rose, I could let you have this old stock that's unclaimed for about one-fourth of the other, but they're all marked C.C.C."

Mom nearly screamed with delight, "Deal, I'll take them!" It was with that incident and at that instant that she named her newly formed company the Cramer Cushion Company.

"God provides," she spoke aloud, "but He sure doesn't make it easy!"

When Mr. Adams entered the store house. He saw the busy hands of six ladies sewing and stuffing cushions. Another was wrapping the, in cellophane and arranging six to the box. Coffee was brewing on a hot plate, and Mom offered him a cup. Mr. Adams saw the workforce, the machines, the stock, and her raw energy. He liked what he saw.

"Rose," he said with a genuine smile. "You've got a deal. How about we start off with 5,000 cushions a year for five years. If we need to increase that amount, could you handle it?"

Mom shook his hand. "Get me the orders, Mr. Adams. We'll turn them out."

Though she kept the workroom for a storage area, all the demonstration sewing machines went back to the store the next day. The sisters and aunts went back to their homes, while Mom, Joe, and anyone who ventured home turned out cushions. The Cramer Cushion Company served Standard Oil Company for at least those next five years before Standard Oil changed their premium gift.

"Thank you, God," Mom always said, "for Standard Oil."

When Joe neared his thirtieth birthday, Terry was well raised and all the old debts and medical bills plus credit card balances were zeroed out. We held a celebration. We were free of debt and flat broke. I know now that we were never poor . . . broke, yes, but never poor. Poor is of the spirit; broke is of the pocketbook.

Terry knew Joe as a brother and as a father. Mom knew him as son, friend, and confidant. They struggled the same economic struggle we all fight daily, but beyond existing, they had cleared old debts. Even with a rising cost of everyday living, they still moved upward. Shortly there after, Joe married.

Mom never thought Joe would marry or settle down. He was

moody, skeptical, and mistrustful, but through it all had a vision that saw through things others never could. Marriage helped him become himself. His wife, Angie Vardon, also of Italian heritage and ten years Joe's junior, accepted all of this and became close friends with Terry.

Two years out of high school, at the age of twenty, Terry announced that she was to be married. Sam flew in from Oklahoma. He and Virginia, now divorced, had only one daughter, Toni, and she lived with Virginia.

It was Joe who gave Terry away. He had surely raised her, supported her, and saw to it that the wedding was first class. As he walked down the aisle, escorting our sister to the young groom, Sam Scaduto, tears welled up in his eyes. Both Sam and I, as ushers, understood our brother's response. For nearly the last ten years, he was Terry's father.

The wedding was a tasteful, modern event, beautiful in every way. At the reception, we brothers took the stage. Sam played the piano, Joe on drums, and I on bass. It was a moment we would all remember as we played the Anniversary Waltz to our sister's bridal dance.

"Take care of her," Joe told Sam Scaduto, and then half kidding and half sincere gave the old warning Italian fathers always give, "or I'll break both your legs."

What it really implied was, "never strike her or you'll answer to me." That "old fashioned Italian trait" never left our personalities where Terry or our own daughters were concerned. We need not have worried. Sam Scaduto was a well-bred and educated young man who dearly loved our sister.

Shortly after the wedding, the good news of our second child was announced. She was another daughter. We named her Susan.

Good news unfortunately was followed by bad. With too much to drink, Uncle Mike was driving back to Cleveland late one night. The food and drink caused him to doze off, and he ran off the road and totaled his new Oldsmobile, crashing into a roadside barrier and a light pole. He was hospitalized for months, and Mom made many trips to the Cleveland Hospital.

Uncle Mike would be crippled from the waist down for the rest of his life. He could walk with crutches, he had feeling in his legs, but the legs could not sustain his weight. On rare occasions, he could take maybe two or three steps without the crutches. He would need care, and for a long while before he died, moved in with his sister Rose.

Before coaching at North High School, I didn't realize that North had not won a game in the previous three years. Prior to my coming there, a player had become a quadriplegic as a result of a neck injury. The school had soured on football. The tough Italian, Polish, and black athletes went to other schools, either trade or parochial. It was a tough first coaching assignment.

Only fourteen players reported for my first practice. I roamed the halls, where it seemed that even the girls were larger than the boys that remained. I talked to another fifty or so of the students and enticed at least twenty or so to come out again. It was an experience I would never forget. Afraid they would give it up, I was determined to make it fun. Though they had high morale, we took our consistent losses. After each one, I would persuade them to return the next Monday for practice. I plumbed the depths of human psychology and persuasion and just barely kept them together.

Joe sympathized with me and saw the many long hours I put into the season. In the second season, we saw improvement, a tie and a win, but I became depressed. I knew I had the knowledge, the temperament, and the makings to be a great coach. Losing embittered me, and the apathy of those around me made me question my goals.

"Get depressed, get angry, do all of that, but damn you," Mom scolded me, "don't you ever despair!" We had spoken often of that one sin God would not forgive. Despair was denial that God existed and that anything could change. I tried never to despair, but I was taking a long hard look at returning to Akron U. or Kent State and night law school. I would even consider going back to the factories.

Just as I was about to choose the factories, I received a call from Ara Parseghian. Ara for the last three years was the head coach at Northwestern University in Evanston, Illinois. He offered me the head freshman coaching job. It was the Big Ten, and I was elated.

Northwestern was a grind. Living in a high cost of living area, Shirley, Susan, Sandy, and I rented what we could find. Being the frosh coach, I was at the lowest rung of the staff. I caught all the duties and assignments the others had already worked their way through. Each summer I gave up my vacation time and entered graduate school, working toward my masters in education.

Joe and Mom drove up for a few games each year and always caught Northwestern when we played Ohio State at home.

Mom and two of her sisters, Dixie and Mary, were once again together. Dixie saw Donna married and gone. Mary, now widowed a second time and lonesome for her family, returned from the West Coast. The three sisters lived in a very fashionable home in Cuyahoga Falls. It was a new, warm, and cozy arrangement.

Aunt Flora and Uncle Nate Weiss had lived in Puerto Rico for nearly eight years. It was a business venture Nate entered into after Uncle Mike and his bingo business went under. With the Weisses again back in the Akron area, the sisters were happy with the reunion.

After a short time, Aunt Flora died of lung cancer. She was in her early fifties. As a result Mom forbade smoking in her home, but Dixie could not break the habit, so Mom relented. Within two years, Dixie too fell prey to lung cancer, and this time Mom enforced her rule.

On a trip back from a Northwestern game, Joe and Mom were driving the Indiana Toll Road, and Mom saw the green and white sign for the upcoming exit, Notre Dame. It was early Sunday morning, and she said to Joe, "I've always wanted to see it." They pulled off at the exit and found their way to the campus. Soon, they entered Sacred Heart Church. Mom remembered the Sicilian belief that each time you entered a church for the first time, your prayer would be granted. She prayed that I would someday coach at Notre Dame. There was no question in her mind that I would.

Now that Terry was married and settled in a home near Mom, and Mom was comfortable living with her sister Mary, Joe

The Crimaldi family: Betty, Dixie, Flora, Mike, stepmom, Joe Crimaldi, Rose, Mary, and Ann.

felt he could at last entertain the idea of a promotion and a possible move out of the area. His company asked him to relinquish his drumming now that he was a manager. Reluctantly, Joe held a ceremony and burned his set of drums.

"They've worked long and hard. Goodbye, old friends," he said casually, as he watched the blaze in Mom's backyard.

Shortly thereafter, he accepted a company move to Pittsburgh. It was a quantum leap in salary and position. Joe and Angie would live the next thirty years of their lives in the Pittsburgh area. There were many offers for Joe to move on to bigger and better things with the company, but each opportunity required a physical move from Pennsylvania. By now Angie had the second of what would be four daughters, and they liked their roots. Joe declined. He had full knowledge that declining meant he could rise no higher. For his family, he accepted this.

Each year, as a regional manager, Joe's offices loaned out more money with less delinquencies than most of the other regions. Joe was known as somewhat of a rebel at the corporate headquarters, and while reviewing his records, the president of the company was known to have remarked, "We're always trying to get Joe Pagna to conform to our ways and listen to our theories, and every year he leads our sales and collections. Maybe we ought to conform and listen to Joe Pagna!" It was a high compliment, and through the years, Joe would be responsible for training at least a half dozen young managers who would eventually spiral upwards to vice presidencies. He never looked back, however, nor did he feel regret or remorse about his choices. He helped raise four beautiful daughters – Michelle, Sherri, Lisa, and Judy – in the Quaker State. Pittsburgh was only a two-hour drive from Akron and both Joe's and Angie's mothers, and that made them comfortable in Pennsylvania.

Soon after Joe had made the initial move to the Pittsburgh area, Terry and Sam Scaduto started their own family.

Terry also would have three daughters – Toni, Vicki, and Lori. Sam remarried after a five-year hiatus, to Pat McCormack, and Sam and Pat had two daughters of their own (Keri and Kristi), plus Toni from his first marriage.

Mom reflected on the dozen granddaughters she had. "You'd think someone would have had a boy," she said to Terry wistfully, "to keep the Pagna name in circulation."

"Mom," Terry said proudly, thinking of the three brothers, "The boys broke the mold."

"Maybe you're right," Mom agreed.

Truly, we tried to be excellent sons. Mom understood that we were each different and yet so very similar. We were men and somehow never lost our sensitivity. We were workers and warm and friendly people with no facade.

In my third year at Northwestern, Ara Parseghian promoted me to offensive backfield coach. In the next two years Northwestern became a Big 10 contender. I coached a sophomore at quarterback in the first varsity try for both of us. The young QB, Tom Meyers, became an All-American. We fell one game short of the Big 10 Championship and an invitation to the Rose Bowl. During the season, Northwestern posted wins over such teams as Notre Dame, Ohio State, Minnesota, and Wisconsin. Ara Parseghian's stock was high, and there was a vacancy in the head coaching position at Notre Dame. In the four previous years, Northwestern upset Notre Dame four straight times.

Mom heard the news flash on the radio. In Akron (Ara's hometown also) it was big news. "Ara Parseghian named the new head football coach at Notre Dame."

"My God," Mom called Terry. "I wonder if he'll ask Tommy?"

When the news broke that Ara was offered and had accepted the head coaching position at Notre Dame, everyone in my family was thrilled at the possibilities. Only two days later, however, the media reported that Ara had walked out of a scheduled press conference.

This caused a great deal of speculation. Rumors floated over what caused the walk-out – was it over salary, or religion, or the number of assistant coaches he'd be allowed to bring with him from Northwestern? Whatever the real reason, Notre Dame and Ara never made it public. I've always thought it was a deeply personal reason, and though Ara and I are great friends, I've never asked, and he's never volunteered.

There was a particular story, though, that over the years has gained more and more credence. It seems that when Joe Kuharich was released from Notre Dame, Fr. Joyce pursued the possibility of hiring Dan Devine. He was then under contract with the University of Missouri, and breaking that contract was not really acceptable. The rumor has persisted that Fr. Joyce had promised Devine the position in the future.

Whatever Ara's or Notre Dame's misgivings were, they were resolved because a week later Ara was officially named head football coach, the choice of Fathers Hesburgh and Joyce. So Ara got the job, and maybe Devine got a promise for the next time around. The truth about these rumors have never surfaced, but when Ara resigned eleven years later and Dan Devine was expected to be fired at Green Bay, the press broke the story that he was leaving Green Bay to go to Notre Dame. If indeed it all happened that way, it would certainly explain why Devine was ushered in so rapidly.

At the time of Ara's hiring in late 1963, I was one of his three assistants brought in from Northwestern. The next twelve years would be the highlight of my life, and I had Notre Dame, Ara, and my mother's prayers to thank.

In more of a comfort zone than she had ever had for years, Mom was busy training young seamstresses for her own drapery shop. It afforded her more and more time for herself. She used it to visit each of her sons. When home alone, she'd play her Mario Lanza records and watch television. In her quiet moments of the weekends, she read her Bible.

"God, that I could understand," was her constant prayer. It was a reflecting time in her life. She had outlived her mother and father, her husband, her younger sisters Flora and Dixie, and her younger brother, Mike. She prayed for all their souls just as she had learned as a child. Everyone needed prayers.

She especially worried about Flora. Flora had been a dark-haired beauty, a soft sensitive lovely woman who, by sheer determination, refined herself and her life. Flora had Carl, her son, out of wedlock and then married Nate Weiss, with whom she had two daughters, Dana and Joni. Flora dared to break the biggest taboo, marrying into the Jewish faith. Later of course, Mom's youngest sister Betty did the same by marrying Nate's brother, Herb.

"Where was her soul now?" Mom was worried and concerned. But more than even Flora or Dixie, she fretted about Mike. She knew he had not lived an exemplary life. These things troubled her deeply, especially when she was alone and in thoughtful prayer.

Her own children and her twelve granddaughters brought her much joy. Since Terry lived nearby, they were often at each other's homes. They became great friends. It is a special thrill for a parent to realize that she is a friend to her own children. Many are not, regardless of age.

It was Terry now who organized homecomings for her brothers and our families. She took the pressure of entertaining off Mom, who consequently had the time to travel. On occasion, she, Mary, and Ann (now also widowed) would drive to visit one or the other of her sons.

It was nearly Christmas 1963, and I was to join Ara Parseghian at Notre Dame after the holiday, when Terry concocted her idea to Mom's surprise. Never one to write her brothers, Terry called each long distance.

"Remember the Grandfather Clock?" she asked each of us. "Well, I want to have one made for Mom, and I want to know if you'll put up one-fourth of the money."

"Hell, yes," we all were agreed. "It's a great idea!"

On Christmas Day, Mom called each of us and Terry to thank us. It was a long-lost treasure that symbolized we had made it all the way back. It had taken twenty-five tough years, but the clock served as her special reminder.

With the success young Ara Parseghian realized at Northwestern University, the demands on his time became greater and greater. In many requests for him to speak at a banquet, he became weary and inundated with dates. He relayed some of these to his staff. In this way, each staff member became a surrogate speaker for him. During the Miami years when I played for Ara and was one of the Miami star players, Ara invited me along to say a few words. It helped an inexperienced speaker like Ara to fill the program, and it gave me confidence.

Ara discovered the show-biz presence I had in front of an audience. He marveled at my mimicry, as I had the ear for replicating the voices and words of current movie actors. It was this and my ability to tell a humorous story that led Ara to send me out often.

I really never thought much about it except that it became a way to supplement my income. At our family get-togethers, we were all storytellers. From those long days of lying flat on my back and reading the classics, to the nights I watched Sam's orchestra rehearse their acts, I became a human recorder. Sam's vocalist did singing impersonations. I copied many of them, though my own singing voice was poor in comparison. With the rudiments of speaking, impersonations for humor, and spellbinding stories of Dad's wisdom, plus the grammatical training from having taught in the classroom and coaching, I felt well fortified.

Every time I stood before a podium, I was challenged to make the audience laugh, respond, be inspired. It became something I took great pride in, and I developed a strong presence as a public speaker.

Whenever I spoke at a banquet near Akron, I invited Mom to go with me. Always, I acknowledged her to the audience as "the most precious Rose I'll ever know." She was embarrassed but proud, and would stand and accept the applause.

For the next thirty-five years, I would be an invited, reasonably priced speaker throughout the United States. Never would I know or realize where the talent or the thoughts came from. In Mom's mind, she saw it as one of the many blessings her children had been given. Though none of us would become independently wealthy, we, like she, had been given a gift to survive. This was mine. Mom saw these gifts as her answered prayers, and privately thanked God.

In the spring of 1964, Shirley and I and our daughters Sandy and Susan moved to South Bend, Indiana. In the previous five years, Notre Dame had not had a winning season. There was energy and expectancy in the air as Ara Parseghian formed his new staff. It did not surprise Mom that we were together again at Notre Dame. She seemed at ease with it and saw it as another prayer she had held sacred that came to pass.

"None of them come quickly," she told Terry, "but they do come!"

"Notre Dame," Terry was fond of the thought. "Tom is at Notre Dame!"

When I was a boy in Colorado, I had a strange recurring dream. It was a familiar place in my dream. It seemed I was approaching, through high grass, a rather large pond of water. I was walking cautiously so as not to frighten any fish I might spot. At the lake's edge, I spotted several fish undulating. I got down on all fours and peered closer and more intensely. Then I saw not several but thousands of fish.

Through the course of Colorado, college, and early marriage, this same dream must have occurred at least a dozen times. When I relayed it to Shirley, she always supposed it was my boyhood at the home with the lake, or some scene in Colorado. Shirley was not Catholic and failed to feel or absorb the mystique I felt present at Notre Dame. "It is another place, that's all." She was busy with arranging our newly rented home. I was at work and it was late March of the new year.

That spring of '64 as the snow melted and the new grass arose, I walked out of the Rockne Memorial building, where our offices were located. It was just a lunch-time walk, and I headed for the two lakes at Notre Dame. When I approached the water just past the pavement, there was a knoll of high grass. As I peered through the grass, I was totally astonished at the thousands of fish swimming in the shallow water. Until that moment, I had never been near the lakes on the Notre Dame campus. I knew then that I belonged here and it was in the making for a long time.

It was in Colorado that the dreams began. It was there that I'd lie in bed with closed eyes and see live pictures of this place that really existed. It was also in Colorado, shortly after my father died and my mother was in a deep depression, that I placed my hands on her while she asked, "What will we do?" I said, almost trance-like, a long rehearsed thought. "Mom, my hands will wait upon you." It was a vow, a prayer, and a promise.

Swiftly I ran to my car. I drove home and cajoled Shirley into coming with me. She was in the middle of cleaning and didn't want to leave. I insisted, "If you don't see it, it will have no meaning."

I drove her to the very spot where the tall grass edged toward the lake. Cautiously I parted the grass and made Shirley shade her eyes.

"Oh, my God," she whispered, so as not to frighten the fish.

"Do you see them?" I asked in a hushed voice.

"Yes . . . yes," she too was excited.

"And," she said as we walked back to the car, "if I hadn't, I'd swear you were lying and the dream was your imagination."

"Good," I said, as though it was now all confirmed. "I didn't imagine it, and it was a place I had never been."

When I told Mom the story, she smiled a knowing smile. No matter how many times I would return to that spot, and I did often, I would never again see the cluster of fish and never again have that dream.

In 1964 Notre Dame had a Cinderella season. We won handily against eight straight opponents and ventured to the West Coast to play our final game against Southern Cal. To win would mean an undisputed National Championship in our first year. Throughout the season, Mom arranged her priorities and, through Joe or Terry or friends she knew through work, managed to get a ride up to South Bend to see the Fighting Irish play. More than ever before in her lifetime, she became caught up in football and Notre Dame.

Since Notre Dame commanded national respect and press, we were always in the news. After the home games, Mom delighted in bringing her friends to stop at my home for a drink and a sandwich before heading home.

She didn't travel to Southern Cal but listened to the game over the radio. In the last ninety seconds of the game, Southern Cal came from behind to edge out the Irish 21 to 17. It was only a game, but Notre Dame fans looked upon it as a tragedy. Late that year, we were still crowned mythical National Champions (at this time, there was no crowning of a national champion other than the symbolic one of the presentation of the MacArthur Bowl.

I coached Notre Dame's unknown and unheralded quarterback into position as a Heisman Trophy contender. Ara allowed me to represent the staff in accompanying John Huarte to New York City, where he won the award.

Shortly thereafter, I began traveling the country as a speaker for "Universal Notre Dame Nights." This was the annual dinner set aside for every alumni club, with different dates in different cities. It would take me to every major city, and I would mingle with the family and extended family of the Notre Dame powers. Mom felt I had arrived, and the next decade of success brought her many thrills and delights, much travel, and a satisfaction that things were unfolding well for her family.

In her home, she arranged a picture collage over her piano in the living room. Centered was a teenaged-bride, Rose, with Tony in their wedding garb. In each of the four corners surrounding that picture were the wedding pictures of her four children. On top of her piano was a small tree, entitled Grandma's Peaches. There were twelve peaches hanging there, each with the name of one of her twelve granddaughters. These were the symbols of her life.

Mom's drapery shop, Rosalia's Draperies, was a big hit. Not only had she turned out impeccable work, she was reasonably priced. She had more business than she herself could handle. She hired and trained young willing women to produce more of the same work. Each job they completed produced referral after referral. Work was work, and she never dawdled there. The rapport of the girls working for her was unique and relaxed. They were thrilled at the opportunity to learn such a skill in a climate of high morale, plus Mom paid them well.

The rewards allowed her much free time, extra spending money, and a chance to make plans to travel. She flew to South Bend, Tulsa, and Pittsburgh to visit her grandchildren, see their homes, and measure our rooms for draperies, her own personal gift.

As it does with everyone approaching the autumn of their years, her mind turned to deeper reflections. She had lived and worked all of her life. She had done it without asking anyone for something without paying for it. Through those years of work she managed a slight savings and cleared a lovely home for herself and any one of her sisters who might need a dwelling.

Her days were less busy now, and when her visiting was over she cherished the privacy of her own home. Her silent hours were again spent reading the Bible. She always had great belief in prayer. She saw clearly that with God, all things were possible.

Though many of her prayers had been answered, she still felt inadequate because of her limited education. How, she wished, could she decipher the hidden Biblical meanings she so deeply loved to read.

"I'm not asking for a sign," she'd say. "You've answered so many prayers, but . . . you know."

As she dwelled more on her own life, she was never one to look backwards but rather forward. Her thoughts of the future triggered long held desires.

"I want," she phoned Terry, "to move your Dad's grave."

Terry phoned me as she had all the brothers. She was frankly upset. It had been too many years.

"She wants to move Dad to a plot alongside Uncle Mike and Aunt Dixie, and buy two empty plots for her and Aunt Mary," Terry said over the phone, distress in her voice.

"Why does that upset you, Terry?"

"My God, Tom, it's been years. It's hard to know what they may find. I can't bear the thought!"

"What does Joe say?" I asked.

"Joe says, she'll do whatever the hell she wants to, she always has, and to go with it!"

"That's true," I agreed.

Joe was present with Mom, as he always was when someone in the family needed a lift or strength. Joe was always where you needed him. Later he explained how he and Mom watched the crane lift the heavy outer vault out of the grave and motor it down to the site she recently purchased.

When it was over, she told Joe, "There, now I'll rest easier." Joe was visibly shook at the actual move.

"The dead sleep, they know nothing," Mom paraphrased Isaiah.

It was kind of frightening for Joe, but the strength of Mom's will seemed to overcome all objections and barriers. As with all things she set her mind to, it worked out well.

Later, when I saw Joe at Terry's house and we were sitting at the dinner table discussing it, he shrugged and showed two palms up saying, "Hey, that's our mother, and she can do whatever the hell she pleases." We all agreed as we laughed at her imagination and indomitable will.

Chapter 12
A Special Favor

By late fall 1968, though Notre Dame was the 1966 National Champion, we could only manage the next two seasons with mediocre success. The late sixties were a time of great national discontent, and historians would write about it as the time of America's lost innocence. The Vietnam War prodded actions by groups that demonstrated, and sometimes such demonstrations turned ugly.

The war, the economy, and the times caused a great upsurge in radical protest. Music and the media were changing drastically, and views on morality changed with it. Crime seemed on the increase, and constant tension was apparent over racial and religious differences. It became difficult to hang onto older values. Even the Catholic Church allowed many changes. The Latin Mass was replaced with English, and the altar was turned around to face the people. A barefoot, pimply-faced hippie type clasped your hand at Mass and uttered, "Peace." It was bewildering for Mom. Gays were coming out of their closets, nakedness and sexuality highlighted the television screen. From a society that had prospered with a strong moral code, we could now be defined in two words: *No rules!*

Many baby boomers (those born between 1946 and 1964) were slowly dissolving their faith in God. Mom was deeply troubled with this. Nearly all of her twelve granddaughters were born during this period. Only time would tell whether they survived the pendulum shift in mores.

The winter was passing slowly, as winters do, but her children would be coming home for Christmas and, of course, she'd see each of her grandchildren. She was now the "Nana" and felt herself still a young woman, though she had just brushed near sixty.

It wasn't always easy for us. Sam's orchestra was in their greatest demand during the holiday season, and I might or might not be involved with a post season game. This time, we all made it home for Christmas.

It was an exquisite time. Sure we missed Uncle Mike and Aunts Dixie and Flora, but that was life, and life surely must go on. The holidays recharged our ties, and all, except for Terry, who lived close by, trekked back to our own homes after Christmas.

It was New Year's Eve, and Mom was especially tired. Though she was invited to Terry's or her sister Betty's, she chose to remain at home. As was her custom, at 12 midnight, she'd watch Guy Lombardo play "Auld Lang Syne," and then she'd retire. It was about 10:30 PM when she turned off the TV and picked up the Bible. She sat in her favorite recliner and opened to a passage of St. Paul's Second Letter to Timothy: "I have fought a good fight, I have finished my course, I have kept the faith." She stopped there, looking up to ponder a moment and examine whether or not she could say that. In the instant she looked upward, she viewed a young woman; her hair was pitch black, her face crystal clear and wearing a warm smile. Her eyes sparkled with love. She was dressed in a regular dress, fashionable for the day; it was pale blue.

Mom was not surprised but not stunned or afraid. With a vague recall she said to the stranger almost as a question, "Flora?"

"Yes, it's me, Rose."

The two sisters hugged one another, tears of joy streaming down their faces. Mom was certain she was dreaming and pinched her arms and patted her own face.

"It's not a dream, Rose," Flora said to her, exhilarated with the reunion. "I really am here . . . with you."

"But," Mom stammered, "how did you get here? How is this possible? It must all be a dream."

Flora hugged her again, and the two of them began to laugh together out of happiness and their reunion.

"I cannot explain it, Rose, and I cannot stay long," she said, "but this one time I am permitted to be with you."

"Your hair." Mom touched it. "It's black like you were a young girl . . . and when you were in the hospital it was all white like mine." Mom pointed to her own all white head. "Well . . . where are you, or where have you been?"

"These things, Rose, I cannot speak of, but I will tell you that I have seen Mike and Dixie and Tony and our mother and father. They are all well. Mike does not need crutches anymore."

Mom sat down on the couch and held both her hands out to Flora. Flora sat next to her and extended her own hands.

"But your hands are warm. You're alive!"

"Of course, I'm alive, Rose, but yet it is different from what you think of as alive."

The sisters talked of all their sisters and their brother Mike. They spoke of Nate, Flora's widowed husband, and of Flora's children, Carl, Dana, and Joni.

"How long can you stay?"

"I really don't know, Rose, but I was told that it would not be long and that I would not return."

Mom was mystified but resolved not to examine it, but rather to savor every moment. As the sisters sat face to face on the couch, Flora reached to the corner of the couch and pulled toward her lap a silken blue pillow. It was the counterpart of a pair Mom had made for the corners of her couch. Flora held the tiny pillow on her lap as she spoke to Mom and excitedly patted it.

Their conversation seemed to have lasted a long while, for they had spoken of many things, shared much laughter and more than a few hugs. Flora stood then, and Mom followed her lead. Flora reached out for one last hug. "I must go, Rose. I love you!"

Mom barely said, "love you too, Flora," and Flora was gone.

As Mom stood in the room, fully awake, she was startled to see her clock. It was only 11:00 PM. It seemed Flora had visited for several hours. Mom was not sure whether she had dozed off and dreamed it all, but she surely was awake now. It was then that she saw the crumpled blue pillow in the middle of her couch. Mom's home was kept immaculately. There was no way she could have sat in her recliner chair and observed such an out-of-place pillow. She knew in a flash that Flora had really been there. God had granted her a "special favor."

She picked up the pillow and hugged it to her face. For her, that moment confirmed all she believed in and erased every doubt about after-life, God, and immortality. Quietly she turned out the lights and went to her bedroom for the sweetest rest she had known. Before she fell to slumber, she mouthed a heartfelt, "Thank you, God."

It would be weeks and months and, in some cases, years before Mom could know the true peace Flora's visit had brought to her. It was not something she could openly talk about and though it was very real to her, no one else could appreciate what she had undergone. Rarely, in one's lifetime does one receive such a special favor. Whether or not it was a dream, her vivid imagination, or a "special favor," no one can know, but the peace it brought her was real.

In 1970, Terry again culled her resourceful mind to present our mother with a special gift. Sam and Pat were giving their daughters Keri and Kristi a graduation gift of a trip to Italy. Keri was graduating from high school and Kristi from grade school. Terry asked the three brothers to chip in once again to sponsor our mother on the trip. All of us, of course, agreed. They would leave in late April of 1971.

At the end of the 1970 year, Notre Dame, for the first time since 1935, elected to drop its objection to going to a bowl game. With a 10-and-1 season, we were selected by the Cotton Bowl to oppose undefeated Texas University. Texas had a long winning streak that spanned nearly three seasons.

It was a gala affair, and the Irish arrived in Dallas nearly nine days prior to the bowl game. Mom set aside her savings and ventured to Tulsa to be with Sam and his wife Pat. Sam would drive in with Mom a few days before the game to visit with me.

The bowl games provide nightly entertainment and exquisite dinners. I got tickets for Mom, and she thoroughly enjoyed the holiday and excitement brought about by the history-making spectacle.

Notre Dame played nearly flawlessly, and though we led throughout the game, we were beaten on a last drive by Texas. There was no reason for shame or sadness; it had been a great game. The Texans had lost a stellar player by virtue of a leg amputation because of cancer. Their emotions overrode our Irish furor. In the years that followed, I penned a book called *The Era of Era*. That chapter I entitled "Someone Else's Gipper."

With many fond memories, and a feeling she had shared in the pageantry and tradition that was Notre Dame, Mom returned home.

On the sidelines at the 1964 Southern Cal game with Heisman Trophy winner John Huarte, Doc Urich, and Ara.

After the loss-ending the season melted away and things settled down to a more normal course, I began my recruiting responsibilities with a few speaking engagements squeezed in between. In those Notre Dame years I met many prestigious people and became friends with them. At the previous Notre Dame Football Banquets, I was seated next to another South Bend resident, John Brademas, the Democrat Congressman and the House Minority Whip. Our dinner discussion that evening revealed many of our commonalities. A friendship was struck on the chords of such similar background. John Brademas was more the scholar than I, but we found to our amusement that we were both first-generation offspring and in many ways grounded in the values of our mothers and fathers. This meeting proved to me that there are no coincidences in life, only a string of events pointing one toward the next one.

When I spoke in the Akron area, I, of course, stayed at my Mother's home. Like Joe or Sam before me, I usually took her out to dinner if she were willing. On just such an occasion I spoke to her. "Pick your favorite place to eat, Mom, and we'll go out to dinner."

We drove leisurely to the restaurant. For me, it was always one of my favorite times. It provided a rare chance to slow down and inquire of my mother's life, her concerns and plans.

"I'll bet you can hardly wait for the trip to Italy . . . eh, Mom?"

"Yes," she spoke abbreviated and rather coldly. That wasn't the response I expected.

"Uh-oh," I thought, "I sense a fly in the ointment."

She was hesitant and was not planning on volunteering further information.

"I really thought you'd be excited as hell about this, Mom."

She relented, "I was in the beginning, Tom."

"What changed? Don't you want to travel with Sam and Pat and their daughters?"

"It isn't that."

"Then what?"

There was a pause. She dabbed her lips with her napkin and sipped her ice water.

"There is something you don't know. Nobody knows . . . well," she corrected herself. "Your wife knows."

"For God's sake, Mom. You're making this into a dark mystery!" With this, she said the next line in a single breath.

"I'm not a citizen, Tom!"

"You're not?"

"That's right, I'm not."

"But," I blurted out, "you've lived your whole life here Mom. You must be one."

"I'm not, believe me. I was six months old and a baby in my mother's arms when we arrived here. I've never done anything to change my status."

"Mom, it's a simple thing. Hell, you can answer five questions or fifty and be a citizen overnight!"

"Well, that always frightened me, and I saw no reason to do it."

"Dad was one, wasn't he?"

"Sure he was. He became a citizen six months after he arrived here."

"How come you told only Shirley?"

"Because I needed someone to drive me to the Federal Building and register, someone who wouldn't ask a lot of questions." I laughed easily and suddenly remembered our trip in the pouring rain.

"So when Shirley was pregnant, and you asked me and wouldn't let me park and come in with you, that was the reason?"

She nodded.

"And Joe, Sam and Terry don't know either?"

"They don't know."

"Well, I'll be damned," I was flabbergasted about my mother's secrecy. "So now it comes time to get a passport and Rose gets concerned. So that's what's been bothering you."

I thought a moment, and an idea struck me.

"Mom, this shouldn't be that big of a problem. I met a great guy at Notre Dame. He's a Congressman and a native of South Bend. Let me call him and see what we can do."

Now that Mom had revealed her long-held secret, she relaxed and finished her meal. Shortly, I would be heading back to South Bend . . . and an answer.

Immediately upon reaching my office, I called Brademas. Like so few people in high places, John Brademas always returned his calls and letters. For him it was common courtesy to reply and a gesture he felt obliged to make. I told my story to him and how long and well my mother had guarded her secret. He laughed heartily.

"Believe me, Tom," he said, "I understand! You know that I'm of Greek extraction, and we all wanted to give my Mom a gift of visiting Greece. It was exactly the same with her, and none of us ever knew."

Then he instructed me to have my mother send all the particulars to him and to get all her shots and photos and not worry. "We'll get it done."

In the end, Mom never did become a citizen.

Poor Sam had no idea of what he had bitten off . . . touring Europe and carrying the major load of luggage for four women and himself was a task he had not imagined. Later he would caution his brothers.

"If you go, go alone and don't pack a damned thing but money!"

Keri and Kristi, like all tourists, wanted to sample the food, the sights and sounds, and the culture of as many places as they could. Mom, however, was sick at the thousands of pigeons everywhere they walked in Rome. Refusing to climb yet another set of steps to visit yet another museum, she stated succinctly, "I'll be right here on this park bench when you come out . . . just scrape away the pigeon crap and carry me back to the hotel when you're ready!" She was leg weary and really didn't have the interest in sculpture and painting that the others did.

That evening, in the hotel dining room, Sam asked Mom what she would really like to do. They finished dinner and were just sipping their coffee. She explained simply, "Sam, I don't even understand the language in Rome. And though I appreciate art and museums, I'm up to here with all that." She held an open palm face down at her neck's level.

"I want very much," she continued, "to visit Sicily, Messina, and the nearby localities, where your father grew up. I speak their tongue, and I have a few distant relatives there."

Taking an address from Mom, Sam wired the relatives the time of her arrival. From the boot of Italy and the edge of Calabria, Mom would take a ferry boat over to the Isle of Sicily. The train ran as far south as Reggio Calabria, but ended there. Though Sam worried about his mother's safety and well being, he followed her wishes. They would meet in Rome two weeks from the day she left.

When Mom set foot on the small deck in the remote southern tip of Italy to board a ferry to San Marco, outside of Messina, her heart felt a pull she couldn't explain.

Her mother had two sisters that were still alive. Their offspring met her at the docking of the ferry boat.

"Signora Pagna," the sign said, as a good-looking, tall and dark great nephew weaved his way toward her. He asked "Zia Pagna? Zia Rose Pagna?" He spoke excellent English.

"Yes," she said, excited to have arrived.

In the two weeks' time she had to visit there, Mom clearly understood Dad's recollection of the place. How the stingy mountainside grew very little, but somehow the stony rubble slanting toward the sea allowed a density of orange, lemon, and olive trees. She walked up a steep marble staircase. It was a tough, long climb to the top of this small flat-top mountain, where she would enter a small and beautiful church, the one where Dad had been an altar boy.

She stopped at each broad marble step to read the family names carved there. She saw Ferranti, Crimaldi, Lombardo, Pacelli, Patrino, and Pagna. Some were relatives, but they were all familiar names back in America.

Her aunts made Mom feel very welcome, though they had little of anything. A few small rooms housed as many as three generations. There were no screens and few refrigerators. No one minded. They sat on their porches and balconies and ate fruit and drank wine. Strolling musicians stopped and sung to them; sometimes the listeners would join in the song.

Mom observed how little they all had but how wonderfully happy they all seemed. They shared their wine, their conversation. No one had false airs or fancy clothes; they were merely living their lives. The young took jobs in the nearby cities, but this would remain their home.

Mom was overwhelmed at the respect they showed her. She thought that maybe her new luggage or her new clothes made them think that she was rich. They treated her as a royal guest. When the time came for her to leave her aunts and all their children and their children's children, Mom asked whether she could pay for a small celebration.

Somehow the word spread, and Mom began to worry whether she had enough money to pay for the entire neighborhood of nearly 100 people who appeared out of nowhere. They brought pasta dishes and fruit and wine. The musicians played. The world, as they knew it, danced and sang. Mom would always remember "the party." Later, she explained that it cost her but $75 in American money.

Just before she was to board the return ferry, she asked her mother's youngest sister why everyone had been so receptive and respectful. Her aunt told her a story that Mom had never heard before.

"Your husband, Anthony, was raised by the widow Theresa Pagna. Her husband died in America. When Donna Theresa would go to the city, she would drop her baby Tony off at San Marco's parish. The old priest loved the boy as his own. Not only did he teach Tony to serve Mass, but he taught him languages and music. It was there he learned the guitar. As he grew older and finished his schooling, the nuns at San Marco sent him to trade school. Tony never forgot the love and care.

"When Mussolini was drafting young men for his Black Shirt Army, the San Marco priest who had so loved Tony begged Donna Theresa to go to America. He loaned her the money. She paid it back from Tony's paycheck years later. Much of the property surrounding the church belonged to the church, but during the war years, all was crumbling. In distress, the priest deeded nearly twenty pieces of land over to Tony. He knew his time was short there, and Tony was the only one he felt deserving enough to inherit the land and that someday the deeds would be honored.

"Years passed, the war ended, and the Italian consulate representatives called on Tony in America, presenting him with deeds of properties surrounding the church."

Mom vaguely recalled the breakfast meeting and the gentlemen speaking with Dad in her living room. Dad had never really explained to her anything about this. He merely said to the consulate representatives, "Whoever lives there owns them."

"The people who lived there," Mom's aunt continued, "looked upon the gesture as one of great generosity. They would never forget that Anthony Pagna made them landowners. And so the name became revered. You are the wife of a well-remembered and -loved man. He gave in a land where no one gives freely."

Mom felt an ineffable warmth in her heart. "Tony," she thought to herself, "you died too young, but you've never really been gone."

When Mom arrived back at her own home in Akron, she picked up the blue pillow her sister Flora had held in her lap. She carried it with her to her reclining chair and gently pushed off her shoes, leaning the chair back and hugging the pillow tightly as she closed her eyes. It had all worked out. She was very tired from the trip, but a peace fell upon her, and she slept very well.

In the morning, Joe called her. Shortly thereafter Terry called, and in the evening, I called. "How was the trip?" We all wanted to know. "Did you have a nice time?"

She had a great time when she arrived in Sicily, but she was glad to be back home now. In the retelling of her adventures to her granddaughters she would explain about Rome and the pigeons and the statues and "Peter and Balls."

One of the more scholarly of the granddaughters interjected, "Nana, you mean the statues of Peter and Paul."

"No," Mom was emphatic, "I mean their damned statues with their peter and balls sticking out everywhere!" The granddaughters roared with laughter. They loved their "Nana Rosie" and knew well that she never minced words. She could be saintly, but she thought even the saints should call things the way they were and, "for God's sake, wear clothes!"

Chapter 13
Petals and a Rose in Autumn

Whenever I was a guest speaker and my mother was in attendance, she secretly marveled at her clumsy little cherub "that used to be." It made her think back to a day in Parma, when she carried me to my bed and we both reclined for my daily nap. Her stomach growled a quiet rumble.

Ever alert, I told her, "It's gonna rain."

"How do you know?" she asked quizzically of her four year old.

"Cause I heard thunder."

We had come such a long way. She was watching me now while I was at the podium. She saw that my eyes were alert and shiny with the humor I seemed to see in everything.

I guess humor highlighted my speeches. My gestures always brought forth two rather large hands. I used my finger or fingers, sometimes a fist, most often an open palm. I tried always to be honest, open, and articulate, thinking to weave a spell for the audience. People reacted, saying I had a sage kind of wisdom that belied my years.

Mom was very proud of all her children and thankful she had the opportunity to know our lives and families. Though much closer to Terry, she always enjoyed the presence of her sons.

It was 1973. The Notre Dame football team was crushed at the end of 1972 to the tune of 40-6. Nebraska had mauled us. I was the offensive coordinator for Ara and in my tenth year at Notre Dame. As she had all my days at Notre Dame, Mom made every home game in South Bend and, if we went to one, a bowl game.

Sandy, my oldest daughter, enrolled at Notre Dame, as a freshman and was thrilled by the games as much as the other students, maybe more than others because of my position.

In the autumn of 1973, Notre Dame fielded one of its best teams in the era of Ara. We won every game and were undefeated and untied going into the Sugar Bowl for a game against Bear Bryant's undefeated and untied Crimson Tide. The winner would emerge as the National Champion. The match-up grew larger in size and importance as the regular season wore down. There would be the month of December for a slight vacation, workouts, travel to New Orleans, and more workouts.

Mom flew into New Orleans two days before the game. She never was afraid to travel alone and seemed to manage well wherever she went. When Notre Dame people heard her last name and recognized that I was her son, they rolled open many doors. Mom looked for no favors but was impressed that our name held such recognition.

The New Orleans skies poured rain all day long, and the field that evening was puddled in several places including the end zones. A huge capacity crowd withstood the rain and at the game's start, the rain finally stopped.

The crowd was electric and literally millions

With daughter Susan.

of TV watchers were tuned into the classic of the season's end – two undefeated powers vying for the National Championship.

The game produced every facet of a classic. The squads were so evenly matched, the slightest break one way or the other would create the winner. Our break came an instant after Alabama's, late in the fourth quarter. Bear Bryant's punting team downed the ball at Notre Dame's 2-yard line. We ran a series of two plays and a penalty called for yet another third and 4 try. Ara called a run action pass from a tight formation. It caught Alabama thinking of a more conservative call. Tom Clements, the ND quarterback, lifted a 30-yard plus strike to Robin Weber for the winning blow, as Notre Dame squeezed out a victory 24-23. For the third time in a decade, we were National Champions.

Back in the hotel several suites were set aside for the Notre Dame traveling family, the coaching staff, and our immediate families. Mom found her way back to the hotel from the game and into our suite. I brought her to a huge ice dish full of champagne magnums. "There's one of these babies that's got our name on it," I said pridefully.

There was a warm nostalgia that crept over us. Shirley and I, Mom and our two daughters, Sandy and Susan, toasted the New Year.

"Part of the dream?" Mom asked me.

"Yeah, Mom, part of the dream!"

Though 1974 started on a very high note, it witnessed staggering changes for Mom, me, and many others. Ara Parseghian was showing the wear of intensity, and his health took a poor turn. There were personal heartbreaks for Ara as three of his close friends had passed on through heart ailments. Mounted on top of his demanding schedule as head coach were fund raising chores for the Multiple Sclerosis Society. He was their National Chairman and reacted to it with full energy, since his oldest daughter Karan had been diagnosed positive. During the spring of 1974, six athletes were charged with a dormitory rape incident. Though each made major contributions to our National Champion year the University expelled them for the next year. In 1974, the Irish lost two games, the last one a sound beating from Southern Cal. Many rumors spoke of dissension. The bitter end of the season, Ara's dwindling health, and many hidden factors prompted him to resign from coaching. He announced it as we were preparing for a rematch with Alabama in the Orange Bowl.

"I don't want to be maudlin about this," he spoke to his staff, "but I tendered my resignation. The University has already named my successor!" It was obvious that he was disappointed that not one of his own staff had been considered. "They've gone outside!"

The football world knew that Dan Devine would be fired as the Green Bay Coach by the week's end. To avoid the stigma of hiring a newly fired coach, word of his hiring at Notre Dame was leaked to the press. No one ever knew the source of the leak.

Each of the assistants were told that we could have an interview to maintain our position. I was so thoroughly shocked and felt such hurt, I refused. I was in disbelief over the entire scenario. Over the years, I had declined moves, knowing this day would come. I was certain I would at least be considered, interviewed, and well received. It never dawned on me to leave Notre Dame, though the offers were real and good ones. I also vowed never to be an assistant to anyone in college football again. I was more than ready to assume a head coaching status. My loyalty and energy, plus my youth, had been spent in the Notre Dame dream. Had Ara stayed, I would have been perfectly happy to remain an assistant coach.

Having heard Devine speak at various coaching clinics, I did not hold the man in high regard. Sure that I would not place myself in the situation of being turned down by Devine, I cleaned out my desk and worked only for preparation of our last bowl game.

All of my hopes, dreams, prayers, energy, all of the hours of preparation and grooming, were now nothing. For the first time in my life, I was near despair. It was in this mental state I drove to Akron to see Mom. I pulled into her drive late in the evening, She kept a meal ready for me and warmed it as I entered.

"You look tired." She saw my glazed eyes. "Eat and get a good night's rest. We'll talk tomorrow."

In the morning, Mom rose early and had prepared coffee for me for when I emerged from the shower. I slipped into my trousers and a shirt and remained barefooted as I sat at her kitchen table. I sipped the hot coffee and was staring at nothing. She filled her cup for a second time and sat down to join me.

"And so," she began. "And now you die?"

I laughed lightly, "Naw, Mom, I don't die."

"Then what?"

"I'm not sure. I, honest to God, don't know if I've got anymore to give than I already have."

"Who called this shot, Tom?"

"I don't know, but from all indications, Father Joyce."

"Doesn't he know of your ability, your background?" She had more confidence in me than I had for myself.

"It doesn't matter, Mom. That's the tough thing to live with.

Nothing matters. It was cut and dried, and no matter who I was or what I did, it would not have mattered."

"Well then," she spoke in a concluding fashion, "it was decided long before Ara resigned!"

"Yes, there's no doubt about it."

"And this Devine, he's such a great coach?"

"That doesn't matter either, Mom. Hell, we left him enough talent that Sandy could coach a National Championship. It isn't fair!" My voice rose.

Speaking very slowly, accenting each word with great enunciation, Mom said sternly, "Who the hell told you, and where is it written, life is fair?"

There was a pause, we both stared out the window.

"Life will go on Tom. It always does."

"I know, you're right, Mom, but how can one man, not even knowledgeable about the game, make one decision and disrupt the lives of ten coaches, their wives, and twenty or so children. Hell, if I were Rockne, it wouldn't have mattered."

Mom went another direction and made it sound light. "Do you remember when you were a kid and you fantasized about Rockne dying in March of 1931 and you were born January 28 of 1932, just nine months later. You always swore you were him reincarnated. Maybe you had your chance."

"I mean it," I said again. "It wouldn't have mattered if I were Rockne. It was a done deal."

"Maybe each assistant felt it should be himself to replace Ara."

"Maybe that's true, but I thought they'd take several recommendations and a board would screen us. No way. They acted, and it is over and I want to get on with my life."

"I'm glad you said that, Tom. I didn't want to say it, but maybe it is time. Maybe getting out, you've just added ten years to your life."

"The hell of it all, Mom, is that's all I've ever done or wanted to do. I spent fifteen years playing and twenty-five coaching. I'm spent and can't bring myself to start all over again as an assistant anywhere. I don't have the time anymore." I paused, "I feel like I've wasted my life."

"Damn it!", she looked and spoke sharply at me. "I'll let you feel self-pity for a while, but don't you ever say you wasted your life! You've been places and done things most people only dream about! You've changed people's lives! Forget about it! After you hurt a while and cry if you have to, get over it! Nothing was wasted. Nothing!"

"I knew that was coming," I said sheepishly.

"Well, if you knew it," she said sarcastically, "why'd you ask for it?"

"Mom," I said calmly and thoughtfully. "I'll get through this, I know, but my motives were always good, and I can't realize that my whole life got summed up by one priest, in one day."

"What were your motives, Tom?"

I looked at her almost in disbelief, "My God, Mom, who would know them better than you?"

"No," her voice was sharp again. "I asked *you* what they were."

I was quiet as I mulled her question over in my mind.

"You mean, maybe I really didn't want it for the right reason, the reason I told myself? You mean it wasn't to secure your future and my family's future? Maybe it was to glorify myself?"

My mother let me talk through it, and when I finished said, "When we were so proud of our home on the lake," she paused, a little choked up at the mention, "I thought about the Italian saying that, 'God humbles us most in those things with which we take the greatest pride.' When your Dad died, and we lost the home . . . well, you know, everything . . . I thought that maybe we were being taught that all glory is God's. In a way, we were glorifying ourselves."

"Did I do that, Mom?"

"I don't know, Tom. I truly don't know. I wanted this for you. Whenever I heard you speak, so full of conviction, so full of Notre Dame, I thought you belonged there."

"Well," I said, resignedly, "it's all over now."

"Your brother Joe called last night. He says you'll land on your feet. Sam says the same, but Terry thinks it is all a terrible mistake."

I left my Mom's house early the next morning. Our visits always helped me see things more clearly. When I arrived back home, Shirley gave me a message to call Fr. Joyce. He wanted to speak with me for the possibility of taking over the Notre Dame Alumni job, just recently vacated. In eleven years at Notre Dame, I had spoken to nearly eighty different alumni clubs across the nation. It was completely possible more than a few grads had called the good Father by now. I always did respect and like the man; I just thought his choice of a new coach was too impulsive.

Because I was out of a job and wished not to be an assistant anymore, I accepted his offer. In the six months that followed, I spoke to ten different Notre Dame Clubs, touching both the East and West Coasts. I returned from my last one in Boston, completely exhausted. I had been subjected to questions and answers about Devine. I felt like a hypocrite as I represented the University at these outings but could not respect the man. Always, however, my public utterances came to the defense of Devine. Whenever I had spoken of Notre Dame and Ara and the tradition, I had full conviction. All of it changed for me now, as I unpacked and told Shirley, "I'm exhausted and going to bed."

That very night, I had a vivid dream. I was a young man, lying on a grassy hillside, gazing up into a blue sky. A few light and very white clouds were spaced throughout. As I gazed, the white clouds took on long vertical shapes like fibers several feet thick. Slowly they came together over me and formed a replica of a skeleton dome. I was looking up through the Golden Dome, but it had no gold, only naked structures of white cloud arcs. I could easily see that the dome was empty for me. In the morning, I resigned. I had held the job six months through 1975.

For several months I was aimless. For an interim, I joined Ara's Enterprises. It was an agency for accident and health insurance. It was boring, and the days were dull. I hated it and could not help but think my life would forever be an anti-climax. I remained there until 1978, at which time I took an interview with Marv Levy, the new head coach of the Kansas City Chiefs in the NFL. I accepted the job offered to me there. It would be the first time in many years that I would not have Ara's great supervision. He was always such a great man and friend to me, I doubted I could give such loyalty again. I had so hoped Marv Levy was of the same cut, and he was.

Mom was at her home and now enjoying the company of her

sister Mary. They decided to try to spend more time with their remaining sisters, Betty and Ann. They all got together more often now, as Ann lived in Cleveland, but drove very well and could easily join Mom and Mary for a weekend. The three – Rose, Ann, and Mary – were all widows. Only Betty, the youngest, still had her husband, Herb Weiss.

As the sisters grew older, all of their hair turned white. Being all about the same size, they closely resembled each other.

Aunt Mary still had a small financial nest egg and, being lonesome to see some of the many friends and neighbors she had known in the twenty-five years she lived in Phoenix and Los Angeles, was planning a return there.

Mom and Aunt Ann also desired to travel, and each of them had a yearning to see Italy once again. Ann was never able to travel much, and Mom, nearly seventy now, wanted her to see Italy at their own pace. Like two giddy children on their own, they visited the land of their heritage. They ate at sidewalk caf s and listened to the music of the streets. They went to St. Peter's Basilica and attended Mass. They ordered room service often and slept late when they felt like it. They shopped the surrounding shops near their hotel. After a week, they planned a train trip to Sicily, where they would stay still another week and then return to their homes in the America.

On the day before they were to leave for Sicily, the streets were crowded and the ladies had just finished their lunch on the patio of an outside *ristorante*. Ann opened her purse to look for two single dollar bills to tip their waiter. Apparently the waiter saw from where she pulled the small change purse and winked at a figure not far removed. As Mom and Ann readied themselves for a stroll down the busy thoroughfare, they did as they had been told and moved their shoulder purses to the inside of one another walking side-by-side through the crowd. It was 1:30 PM and the two tiny white-haired women were laughing at their recent conversation at lunch. It was a lovely sunny day, not too warm. Music filled the air, and the hustle and bustle of the streets filled both Mom and Ann with feelings of holiday. They ambled with the crowd, slowly examining each shop window for articles of interest. As the two moved forward slowly, they were assaulted with a heavy knifing blow between them. A large young man, running at full force, burst the crease between the two. As he did so, his hands clasped the shoulder straps of both Mom's and Ann's purses. The initial blow knocked Ann to the ground, breaking her glasses. Mom was twisted around, since her shoulder strap didn't slide off her arm. The thief pulled the purse, thereby swinging her into the curb side. She fell heavily, and her purse strap broke. She had bruised her shoulder and back and suffered a slight cut above her right eye. There was screaming and rushing, but no one broke stride or attended them. The thief sprinted and lost himself in the crowd. Within minutes the *Carboneri* gathered around the two. One spoke only a little English and conveyed to them to come with him to the *stazione*, or police station.

When they entered, there was an officer behind a desk and one standing next to him. The two officers escorting Mom and Ann spoke in Italian, and the two near the desk broke into laughter. None of the four officers realized the ladies were Italian, and both spoke and understood a little of the language. The laughter of the two officers was prompted by the news that "Luigi has been busy today!" They knew exactly who had committed the act. When Mom got the gist of the whole conspiracy, her temper exploded on them, *"Dishonorado . . . eh Carboneri,"* she screamed at them in Italian ("Dishonorable police"). Then she ripped them long and loud with a litany of more Italian negatives intermingled with *"bestia"* ("beast") and *"figlio de putana"* ("son of a bitch") as she described the thief who had done this. As a finale of her wrath, she said in her best Italian, "In America I have three sons. Any one of them would kill you for what you've allowed here today!"

The older of the *Carboneri*, and presumably the one of highest rank, began apologetically, *"Signora . . . Signora . . . Scuza Scuza."* He made a quick reference to one of the officers, who exited only to return within minutes. In his hands he held two purses. They were empty of money but still contained their passports.

"Are these yours?" The one in charge asked in English.

"Yes," Mom said seethingly.

The two women filed their complaints, and the officers escorted them to their hotel. Mom and Ann were more than physically shook. They were deeply hurt that not one solitary citizen on the street or one bystander made any attempt to come to their aid. The illusion of a warm, friendly, sunny Italy was tarnished forever in the minds of the two women.

"Let's go home," Mom said to Ann.

"Yes, I've seen enough of Italy," Ann replied remorsefully.

There were other trips Mom would take, but never again would she leave the United States. She flew to Tulsa and spent time with Sam and Pat, becoming more familiar with their daughters Kristi and Keri.

Always on such trips, she would call Sam's first daughter, Toni. It was a chance to touch all the bases for her and renew ties with each granddaughter.

Some weekends, Mom and Terry would drive up to Pittsburgh to spend time with Joe and his family. Joe's and Angie's oldest daughter, Michelle, was now married and planned on making Joe and Angie grandparents. When their first grandchild was born, she was named Melissa Rose. Melissa was to have the same steel gray blue eyes as Grandma Rose, though she would never get to meet her.

When Mom just stayed at her home in Akron, she always invited one or two of Terry's daughters to stay the weekend. Terry's three girls, Toni, Vicki, and Lori, were very fond of their Nana Rosie.

It was Vicki who seemed most at odds with Terry, and so Mom often took her for a weekend. The two became great friends and spoke shared secrets to one another. Though Mom dearly loved all of her grandchildren, by virtue of time spent together Vicki had privileges the others never knew.

In the fall of 1978 Mom and Aunt Mary flew to Kansas City. They spent time with me and my family and saw their first live professional football game. The two ladies were enthralled by the magnificent structure of Arrowhead Stadium. I bought tickets for them to sit in one of the many boxes. It was a glassed-in area, carpeted and with leather seats. There was a small refreshment bar behind them and accessible restrooms nearby. I explained that I would report to the locker room, but if they went down the hall and turned to the right of the elaborate hospitality suites, the ladies would be served a special luncheon. The pre-game festivities for the hierarchy of pro football is second to no social outing. One could feel the electricity building. Lamar Hunt, the Kansas City Chief owner, had built within Arrowhead six lovely apartments. His own living suite was a huge living room with an equally large fireplace. It had refrigerators, long bar, leather couches, and a carpet that spelled out plushness. Adjacent to the large room were thirty or so rows of padded seats extended outward, facing the playing field. In another area, a spiral wooden staircase of mahogany led upwards to the grand living quarters.

I and the rest of Marv Levy's staff lived there for nearly six months when we first arrived. It had been a wonderful but lonely experience. The plush rooms with gold fixtures were constant reminders to all that we were guests in the quarters of the man for whom we worked.

In the hubbub of milling crowds, the sightseers, and the newly curious, Mom and Mary took a wrong turn in the hallway. There were so many paintings, statues, and artifacts to view, one could easily have been in a sports museum. Lamar Hunt was a collector of such items, and this edifice proved a remarkable display case for such a unique collection. When the two little ladies entered the area they thought was the suite for the luncheon, a very attractive, tall slender woman greeted them warmly.

"Hello, ladies," she smiled affectionately, "Isn't it a gorgeous day? Welcome, welcome. Come on in."

Mom sensed something was wrong and that the elaborately set tables with crystal and shiny silverware could not be the buffet for which her son Tom had provided tickets.

The hostess read the look on Mom's face and said, "Is there something the matter?"

"I don't think we're in the right place. My son said . . ." and as she paused, the hostess asked.

"Who's your son?"

"He's one of the coaches . . . Tom Pagna."

"Well, Mrs. Pagna," the hostess exuded warmth and charm, "I'm Mrs. Lamar Hunt, and you'll be my guests today and you certainly are in the right place."

The two ladies had never received such attention, nor did they ever view a game from such a comfortable vantage point.

When the game ended, both Mary and Mom thanked their hostess for her kindness. Mrs. Hunt assured them, "The pleasure was ours, ladies."

Returning to my home, Mom told us what had happened. I only asked if they got a bite to eat.

"Did we ever," my Aunt Mary replied, and then they filled us in on their afternoon.

We laughed about their good fortune and more than ever admired Mrs. Hunt for her caring and sharing ways. Great amounts of money did not seem a curse to those who never lost humility or thoughtfulness. For Mom and Aunt Mary, it became one more trophy in their memories containing special moments.

Mom loved to kid when she got home to Akron. She told Terry, "Oh, yes, Mr. and Mrs. Hunt. We had lunch together."

In the twenty or so years Terry had been married, she never really was too far removed from Mom. They talked, they argued, they shared laughter and tears. Because they were so close and Terry so much like Mom, Terry was often removed from the spotlight of attention. When we "boys" returned to Akron as individuals or as a group, it seemed we were treated as princes. Everyone catered to us with food, attention, and respect. It would have been very easy for Terry to become embittered at being taken for granted by aunts and sometimes even Mom. But that didn't happen, though she often wondered to herself how long her mother, her brothers, her sisters-in-law and her aunts would think of her as "the little sister." She had raised her own daughters, run errands for Mom and her aunts, cooked meals for them on holidays, and often held a full-time job. In the tradition of her mother, she was a doer. She did not look for praise or thanks. She had a mind of her own and used it to configure her life. She too had made the "sell this house and move upwards" kinds of actions. All of it she did with a quiet reserve. She had been a businesswoman, mother, daughter, nurse, driver, teacher, and "little sister" for a long time, and she had done it all with love in her heart.

It surely seems that life repeats its precious patterns. Anytime children grow up and move a distance from their parents, their valued friendship and worth becomes exaggerated. It was not completely true for Mom and Terry. In Mom's mellowing years, she pondered about Terry's life often. The two had argued and screamed at one another, laughed and cried with one another, loaned each other money. Surely Terry was my mother's best friend. Many mothers know this in their relationships with their daughters, but somehow being the mother becomes a barrier in letting the "dear friend" know of their status. Mom was no exception here.

She made her visits to her sons. She spent time with her sisters. She made her daily talks with Terry by phone or in person, and she molded her drapery-business employees into a group of friends. In all, she was very pleased with her life, and the shopping events in Italy dwindled in memory and stature.

Mom would make one more visit to Kansas City as another granddaughter was being married. Sandy met a young man in Kansas City. They were engaged and would be married the summer of 1979.

All of the family came for the wedding and Sam brought along five of his band members to donate their services.

I stayed just one more year in Kansas City. Though I had three more years on a contract, our circumstances changed. I loved being back in coaching, and I held Marv Levy in great respect. I never really thought I'd ever quit coaching because being in the NFL was a special thrill.

One evening, shortly after Sandy's wedding, I received a phone call from one of the city fathers in South Bend. It seemed there was a great position to be filled, and it called for the caliber of person I was thought to be. The job had a decent salary, provided a country club membership, a good financial retirement plan and bonus of a summer cottage on a lakefront. In the meantime, Shirley had just undergone her second thyroid removal. It was, as the first one ten years prior, found to be malignant.

When I saw her there in the hospital bed, with her eyes closed and her delicate body still from the tranquilizers and the operation, I felt deep guilt. I had moved to Kansas City to coach. I had taken her and her widowed mother a long way from our friends and home. I had pursued what I wanted. I never really spent enough quality time with her. Down deep I knew how coaching could consume your life. There was nothing that existed outside of it. "What price glory?" I asked myself.

In addition, my own mother was aging. I hated being so far from that friendly cup of coffee and our chats. I thought of all the anniversaries, the Christmases, the weddings, and birthdays I had missed because of football season. It was a tough decision to return to South Bend, but it seemed the right one.

In the few short months after Sandy married, our youngest daughter, Susan, also announced her desire to wed. She wanted just a small ceremony in our home. She wanted no fanfare. When it was announced that I would return to South Bend, she and her new husband made that same decision.

Susan and her husband made the move before the others. Shortly, Shirley and I, plus Shirley's mother, made the trip. We moved into a home in January of 1981. On February 9, ten days after we entered our new place, Shirley received a phone call from Kansas City. It was from Sandy's husband. Sandy had been struck by a drunken driver while she was walking across a pedestrian crossing. The driver was doing near fifty in a thirty-mile zone. When he struck her with his Volkswagen, the impact broke her lower right leg and vaulted her into the air. When she landed, it jarred her head upon the curbing. She was in a coma and fighting for her life.

Shirley, Susan, and I flew to Kansas City and the emergency room of the down town K.C. hospital. We spoke to the neurosurgeon who was attending Sandy. The doctor pulled the three of us into an alcove. He glanced at Susan as he began to speak. "You are her sister?"

"Yes," Susan replied.

"Good, we may need blood for transfusions."

He addressed Shirley and me then. "What I have to say is not going to be very comforting, but I feel that if I were in your shoes, I would want to know everything."

"Of course," we agreed.

"She's received a major blow to the side of her head, and there has been major bleeding. The swelling is pressuring against her skull and brain, and we're trying to relieve either the swelling or the pressure. She is now comatized, and we don't know for how long."

"What is a normal prognosis on this kind of injury?" I asked.

The doctor sighed, and it was obvious he was measuring his words. "We got her to oxygen only minutes after the accident, but I'm almost certain there is brain damage, and truthfully, I don't think she'll make it through the night."

Shirley gasped at this.

"I think there is a good chance she will not last long, and if she does, could very well wind up as a vegetable."

"We want to see her," I said, choking back my emotion.

The doctor allowed us entrance to the intensive care unit. It was 2 in the morning.

"I'll arrange for you to stay overnight in a nearby room."

Shirley, Susan, and I viewed our most horrible nightmare. Here was our eldest daughter, a bright beautiful lady, college educated, six months married . . . in a coma. Tubes were in her mouth and nose, a respirator hissed out its despicable sounds, and the metric beep of an electrocardiograph monitor punctuated every second. All of us stared in disbelief. None of it seemed real.

We spent the night in the next room down the hall from intensive care. We had not packed clothes or overnight bags. We slept fully clothed, sharing the room with another woman who was patiently suffering the same pangs for her husband. Downtown Kansas City and the various hospitals had been robbed often. The hoodlums of the area would walk in late at night and burglarize or rob any and all. There seemed little security, so the doctor advised of this.

"Keep your door locked. If there is news, I'll bring it to you."

For nearly three days, there seemed no change. The good doctor, whose name was Syzmanski, told us to get out, get some rest and a shower. There was nothing we could do here, and we would need all our strength as the duration of such things was unknown.

Lamar Hunt offered me and my family the use of the stadium bedroom apartments through the club's vice president. The three of us – fatigued, tired and grieving – made our entrance to Arrowhead.

At the very first chance I had, I called Mom in Akron.

"She's dying, Mom, and the doctor told us that if she does not, there is a good chance she'll wind up a vegetable."

Mom was stunned at the news. As we spoke, she recalled her Colorado days.

"Tom," she spoke with authority, "do you remember when we prayed together for one thing?"

"Yes," I knew in a moment what she meant.

"Well, we all will pray here, and you and your family pray there, and we'll be united in Christ's name. Do it!"

When I hung up, and Shirley and Susan had showered, we got ready for sleep. I asked them to join me. I felt very self-conscious about it all. It may even have appeared corny to my daughter or my wife, but I was determined.

Daughter Sandy.

"Look," I explained intensely, "Christ said that whenever two or more are gathered in his name that He'd be there. In other words, He will listen to a unified prayer. We've all got to pray for exactly the same things. I'll mouth the words, but you guys think them through with me, so we're asking for exactly the same thing."

With this, all kneeled down and joined hands.

"Lord Jesus Christ," I began. "I'm not sure how to say this, but reminded of your promise that whenever two or more are gathered together in your name, you'll be there . . . we're asking for the recovery, the full recovery of Sandy! Please God, let her live and be well. Please God, hear our united prayers and the prayers of all those that pray for her. We ask this in the name of Jesus Christ."

"Amen," the three of us said this and, without another spoken word, went to bed and slept an exhausted sleep. We placed Sandy's fate in the pure hands of God.

The following day, there was a report that perhaps the cranial pressure and swelling were subsiding. The doctors could not determine much else. X-rays had shown her right leg to be broken. It was now in a cast, but she remained in the coma. On the tenth day they removed Sandy to another room, out of intensive care. She, on rare occasions, showed signs of her eyes opening. After the twenty-third day her eyes were open, but they registered nothing, only a blank stare that looked through the eyes and face of her family. There was no movement on her right side. She was paralyzed in her right arm and leg.

Both Susan and I had been away from our jobs now too long. Our clothes, with no changes, were shabby. Doctor Syzmanski told us to go home. All that could be done was being done. She could be in this state for a day, a year, or forever.

He said to us, "Go home, make provisions for a longer stay."

We returned to South Bend, where we stayed for nearly two weeks, although we got daily reports from the hospital and our son-in-law. I was upset with him for the flippant way the young man was acting. He seemed like "laughing boy," . . . that this wasn't really happening.

Shirley and I drove our motor home down to Kansas City to again be with Sandy. When we saw how thin she had become, still in a coma and still staring at nothing. We became despondent. Daily, I spoke with Mom, and daily, Shirley spoke with her mother. Never, did our praying cease.

Slowly, awareness crept into Sandy's eyes. Though Shirley and I spoke with her, sat with her, and attended rehabilitation classes with her, it was apparent that she didn't know who we were.

Two more weeks passed, and Sandy was released from the hospital on crutches in the custody of her husband. We returned to South Bend. The nearly two-month ordeal was far from over.

Every day, Shirley or I phoned Sandy and spoke with her. Each day she made slow but steady progress. When we spoke with our son-in-law, he minimized her injuries and seemed glib and disrespectful.

He hadn't been my cup of tea in a long time. Only a year and a half into their marriage, the smart-mouthed son-in-law sassed me. I slammed the phone down, enraged! His insolence and stupidity overwhelmed me. Now, when decisions had to be made for maintaining Sandy in intensive care, Shirley and I were told that her husband was the next of kin and all decisions were his. We objected strongly, since we felt sure she needed more time and close medical supervision. Our son-in-law, more concerned over the cost of this, saw it otherwise.

Sandy was moved to a semi-private room, and Shirley and I walked in early the next day and spotted blood on the floor. It had been poorly and rapidly wiped up, but the traces made things obvious. We later found that Sandy had fallen out of bed and had pulled out the intravenous and blood-transfusion connections. She was unattended for periods of time in this room.

Later, the son-in-law insisted that his lawyer knew best and did not want my input on the legal aspects. The Notre Dame legal counsel, who was a dear friend of mind, had volunteered his services to me, but, again, we had no say.

My great concern was that should something happen to me and my daughter be unable to support herself, this worthless husband might abandon her. Instinctively, I knew that Sandy's husband was avoiding anything I thought or said. On the phone, he told me, "Shut up." Had he been in my physical presence, I could be writing this book from behind bars.

Because of the son-in-law blocking my attempt to gain a just decision when the insurance case came to court, he took over every decision without confiding anything to or with me. This affected the plea bargain and settlement with the insurance company, which was so paltry that my daughter could never have lived off it. Thank God her recovery made that inconsequential.

I wrote a scathing letter to the judge, who allowed the plea bargain to go through. I asked whether he would have done the same had it been his daughter. He wrote me an apologetic letter and assured me that he would not. He never knew the extent of Sandy's injury, and the drunk driver skipped the country to live in his homeland of Germany.

The judge I forgive, but I sin daily in that I cannot forgive or absolve the ex-son-in-law. I am still working on it. I am keenly aware of my Sicilian capacity for violence, and I am shamed by it.

In the meantime, several months passed in this fashion for Sandy and us, with daily calls and conversations. Then she began to call us daily. And one day it came – she told me that her husband wanted a divorce.

"Give it to him," I said flat-out. "He's an immature egotistical ass. Who needs him?"

"She's coming home," I said to Shirley, after hanging up the phone. "He isn't man enough to see her through this."

"Good," Shirley agreed. "Even if she never gets any better at all, we'll at least care for her!"

In the summer of 1982, Sandy arrived at the Chicago airport with her puppy in a pet box, one piece of luggage, and $2 in her wallet. I hugged my daughter gently. Shirley cried openly.

"Whatever life brings her," Shirley spoke deeply and emotionally, "we'll try to bring her back!"

We had Sandy tested for academic level while she was in rehabilitation. From an honor student at Notre Dame, she had slipped to about a second-grade math level and fourth-grade verbal. In about six months, her divorce became final.

Within another six months, our other daughter, Susan, was divorced. The four Pagnas were all back together. We became teachers for Sandy. We had no way of knowing then what the next ten years would bring. We only knew she would always be subjected to seizures and, for the rest of her life, be on preventive medication.

Susan and I played word games with Sandy. Shirley sat at the piano and encouraged Sandy to try. Slowly through the weeks and months, movement came back to Sandy's arm and leg. She had played the piano for ten years prior to the accident. It was through music she fought her way back to reading, writing, spelling . . . along with endless conversation and endless prayer. Within eight years, she would progress to a point of 99-percent recovery, finish her master's degree, teach school, and eventually remarry a very special and remarkable man. Though Sandy would suffer with seizures periodically, Shirley, Susan, I, and especially my mother felt God had granted us all a very special miracle. It had not been easy or quick, but there was never a doubt that there had been a prayer answered.

Sandy's original accident had happened on February 9,

1981. February was a month set aside in fear for Shirley. It had not been a good one for either of us. Shirley's dad died in February 1964.

Chapter 14
A Rose in Winter

It was New Year's Eve 1982 and for the first time in many years, all four of Mom's children would be returning for the holiday. Her preparations were extravagant. She had prepared handmade noodles for her wedding soup, which was always a favorite appetizer for all.

She also prepared breaded veal, chicken, and pasta for the main dishes. There were mounds of salad, and for dessert, apple pie and fresh fruit. It was a feast served in her specially made "basement banquet hall," awaiting just such an occasion. There were three long tables that seated twenty people each. Throughout the evening another thirty to forty would stop by for a drink. The piano, bass, and drums were nearby for the festivities that would follow. All of the children and their spouses, plus most of the grandchildren, were present for this homecoming. Sandy was unable to travel and not in attendance, nor was Sam's oldest daughter, Toni.

The food was marvelous. There were guests and friends,

Here I am with Uncle Mike at the piano and Joe on the drums at one of our family gatherings.

some relatives, and what was left of Mom's own sisters and their children. Laughter and conversation were plentiful, warm, and magnetic. It was the best of life in the confines of Mom's home, and all of it transpiring within the six to eight hours of feast and entertainment time.

After the meal, with the television on to show football games, but the sound turned down, Sam sat at the piano, Joe at the drums, and I with a homemade bass fiddle. We played everything called out to us, the children danced, the older folks danced, Mom danced. When they tired, they sang old melodies bringing back nostalgic sentiments. "Let Me Call You Sweetheart," "Old Shanty in Shanty Town," "Mexicali Rose," "Heart of My Heart," and many, many others.

As the evening peaked, midnight brought cheers, hugs, kisses and toasts to the new year. The merriment slowly wound down. In small groups, people were gathering their offspring, putting on clothes, warming up their cars, and brushing a light and recent snow from their windshields.

Mom stood near the staircase that ascended out to her drive. Each person would hug and kiss her and thank her for a wonderful time, a memorable party, a beautiful entry for the new the new year.

We all helped to put away chairs and broke down the folding tables, while a tired Rose rested a moment in a nearby chair. Her apron was still on.

"Do you think they all enjoyed themselves?" She asked simply.

"Oh sure, Mom," Terry answered for all of us. "So many people remarked as they left that they had a wonderful time."

"Good," Mom replied, "and we'll do it again next year."

As we bid Mom goodnight, we hugged and kissed her and spoke a heartfelt, "Thanks, Mom, it was great."

Only Mom and Terry remained in the basement. They were putting away the good china and silverware and wrapping leftovers for the refrigerator. At a certain point, Mom said, "Leave it till morning."

She then ascended the fourteen steps of her basement. She was very tired, having worked all day and rarely sitting down. At the height of her climb, when she reached her family room, she collapsed on the family room carpet. Terry, who had been following her, immediately called an ambulance. Mom was hospitalized in Akron, but the examination by her doctor compelled him to transfer her to the Cleveland Clinic. The next morning Terry called all of us, who by now were back home in our respective cities. We returned immediately.

Next to me is Terry, then Sam and Joe.

When our family entered the small room for counseling, the Cleveland Clinic surgeon laid out the details. "Your mother," he stated slowly, "is in good health, since she has never been a drinker or a smoker. Her lung capacity is fantastic for a seventy-four-year-old woman. It is her lungs that have sustained her, as there is a small leak in the passage of one of her heart valves. It emits only a fine spray of blood. She has had this leak for years, but her great condition has compensated for this. We will operate in the morning and try to replace her valve with a bladder from a pig. This has normally been accepted by previous patients with fine results. It is a relatively simple operation, but because of age there is a 6 to 10 percent risk."

All of us felt sure Mom would be fine.

Shirley and I, Joe and Angie, Terry and Sam Scaduto, Sam and Pat, all waited in the Cleveland Clinic waiting room. Nearly five hours passed before the doctor descended telling us all seemed well and Mom was in recovery, resting well. We were unable to see her at the time, and, since all seemed well and it was late evening, all of us returned to Terry's home. That very night as we were chatting over coffee at nearly midnight, a call came through. Mom, it seemed, had a setback. They learned later that the electrode from her heart to the monitor had pulled out. The doctors were going to put her under again and go in for a repair. We returned to the Clinic only to find that when they corrected the electrode and closed her, they had missed a "bleeder." The medical team went in again for the third anesthesia and corrected the bleeder. Joe and I remained on the site.

She was being held in intensive care, and we were allowed only fifteen minutes with her within a four-hour period. When we viewed her after the long wait, we were struck by the enormous girth of her body and face. She was always a small, petite person and her distortion shocked and startled us. With three back-to-back anesthesias, her body rebelled at the insult, and her kidneys shut down. Her body fluids were logged within her body, and she was swollen nearly twice her normal size.

The doctor explained that they were afraid of using a dialysis machine for fear it may bring on a stroke. There was talk of a wrist dialysis attempt, but by now Mom was nearly in a coma. In retrospect it is evident that she had a minor stroke. Joe and I waited another four-hour stretch and entered as she was resting on her back, tubes hooked up to her everywhere. I was, for all my glibness, incapable of speaking much. Joe was in complete control as we each took a side of her bed. Each of us cupped a hand around our mother's, and Joe spoke to her as only he could.

"Mom," he said full of strength, "you're going to make it. You've got to fight, Mom, and you're going to pull through. We love you, Mom, and we need you to fight hard. You're gonna pull through, Mom."

With this last Joe asked her, "Mom, if you can hear me, squeeze our hands." A weak squeeze of both hands signaled she could hear. Joe repeated, "You're going to make it, Mom."

With this, her eyes still closed, she rocked her head slowly in the "no" sign. Our fifteen minutes was up, and the nurse said we had tired her.

We stayed several nights in the hotel awaiting a change.

Top and above: at Mom's seventieth birthday celebration.

When we couldn't see her, we spent time in the small chapel. "Life," Joe said, fighting tears, "isn't worth a damn without her." I was in total agreement.

The next word we heard was that Mom had undergone a major stroke, was in a deep coma, and probably had suffered severe brain damage. The doctor knew we had no change of clothes and were both from out of town.

"Go home," he advised. "She could be in this coma a long time. Get some rest and a shower. We'll call you if there is any change."

Terry wanted to visit Mom. We begged her not to because we knew Mom's appearance and state would deeply wound Terry. Though we tried to talk her out of visiting, Terry's insistence won out.

Four days later, on February 9, 1982, Mom parted the curtain between life and death. We planned her funeral as she had designated. It was to be a one-time showing from 6 to 9 PM, with burial the next morning. She would be put to rest next to Dad, Dixie, and Mike, in the very plots she had set aside years before. Eventually Aunt Mary would join her.

At the funeral, our family sat together in an alcove reserved for us. Literally hundreds of people passed through to pay their respects. Sam, living at a distance for thirty-plus years, could not realize the magnitude of people and friends that knew Rose Pagna in some capacity. In her seventy-four years, with only an eighth-grade education, she had traversed the gamut of life. She had known bankers and millionaires, made their draperies and babysat for their kids. As a seamstress, all of Akron knew of Rosalia's Draperies. She traveled the United States and parts of Europe, visited several of the great universities, and knew much about the world and its business. When we reflected on her life, and realized that with a minimum of formal education, the things she accomplished, we were staggered.

Her life was a veritable sacrifice for the lives of others. The amazing thing was that she never became embittered, never felt stymied or dead-ended with her own life.

To raise, yes, literally raise, her own brothers and sisters, keep a house for her father, and nurse her own mother was itself the springtime of her life. When she married, she raised her own plus some of her sister's children. Yet nothing was given up. Our home was always pin neat, attractive, modern.

In the buying, moving, and improving mode, she improved the family's finances a great deal. Each home improved our lot and our bank accounts to an extent that she willed herself and all of us into the home of her "somedays."

In the doing, she learned and retained more knowledge of banking and lending, mortgages, equity, collateral, land value and construction style than many specialists in those fields. She never backed off from a challenge, and her ingenuity, which verged on manipulation, was of such a design that Machiavelli would have blushed.

But, with all of this, her greatest skill and love was in the realm of a seamstress. It allowed for her creativity and raw energy to combine. It was here that she took a simple talent, honed it, refined it, and expanded it beyond being someone else's employee. Her eye for interior decoration was garnered from studying magazines, visiting other homes, and real-estate tours. Everything she saw she could duplicate and, after that, actually improve. Her gift, however great or little, made her dreams materialize.

Mom and me at Sandy's wedding, July 28, 1979.

After my father died, she saw no reason to remarry. Her needs were few: "Get out of debt, make a living, raise my kids." She asked no quarter and gave, all the while, of herself.

Her greatest satisfaction was the joy of work and of accomplishment. In all of this she had no time for false pride or vanity. It was the journey she thrived upon, never the destination.

Moved from easy laughter to an abrupt manner in only seconds, she could as easily converse with carpenters and bricklayers as well as the mistress owners of mansions. My mother was in the truest sense a giver and nurturer. Perhaps what business people would see as a flaw was her greatest quality: She was generous beyond what people can imagine. If you could not pay, she would not charge. She gave free meals, food, time, effort, clothing, materials, her craft, and, yes, money to anyone truly in need. I think she knew that God surely loves a giver because she gave more than her share. It brought her friends for a lifetime, love, respect and gave meaning to her life.

Many, many people paid their respects. At wake's end, Sam said, "She was a wonder, but I never realized how many people knew it!"

At the grave site in the morning, the solemnity was more than we could bear. Trying to lighten our hearts, Aunt Betty said quietly, "Rose was one of a kind, and her life was a beautiful thing. It's too bad the world can't know her story. They'd be inspired." When we parted, those words rang in our ears.

As the priest at the funeral Mass said before the trip to the cemetery: "'One pebble in a lake makes many waves, and no one can ever count how many.' Rose was like a boulder splashing and added so much to so many, many lives. . . . When Rose died, God took one of our best."

After Mom's death, Terry and Aunt Betty, now the lone survivor of the Crimaldi family, became much closer. Aunt Betty had confessed to Terry in many different ways that Mom had always been a wonder to herself and other family members. She could not figure how it was that Mom commanded the deep love, the almost obsessive loyalty and respect from each of her children. She treated none of the four as a favorite and yet none was jealous of the other's "special relationship" with our Mom. Each of us became a friend of Mom's, in the process of being her child. Even when we were adults, she was first and foremost in our minds. It was true that, as we grew up, she appeared not to show affection as people think of it. In reality she felt deep affection. Each of us in our own way had become her personal hero, and she ours. As Mom mellowed, her open display of affection became abundant. Aunt Betty was mystified.

Chapter 15
It Will Be All Right

I saw Mom one more time in my life. It was at a very low ebb of my personal fortunes. At 59, I had no choice but to undergo a complete knee replacement. Having been a bleeder all of my life, this was not a promising operation. My knee had been operated on previously, no less then four times. The ultimate replacement was a necessity because the daily pain reduced me to just the simplest of tasks and gave me little pain-free time.

It was about on the sixth week of recovery from the operation when I was still hobbling on a cane that apparently the knee started to bleed internally. The ensuing swelling and pain were almost unbelievable. I was lying on my couch, packed with ice, and thinking over my plight.

Just the day before, I had been informed that "they" no longer needed my services at my place of employment. A young, brash, insensitive, and unthinking executive, drunk with his own power and authority, had as much as fired me because I had not repaired as rapidly as predicted.

Not only did this do away with a steady income, it did away with company hospitalization. I was allowed to carry it with the same carrier for the next eighteen months, but at an astronomical fee. It was a low blow, and I had neither the strength, youth, or courage to fight it. Out of work, out of hospitalization, at an age where others are planning retirement, I was near despair for the first time in my life.

My wife was still nearby as I lay on the couch. She was monitoring me and keeping the ice packs fresh. I had my eyes closed but was very much awake and in tremendous pain. At that quiet interval, while my wife was reading and I almost sleep, there occurred a lightening-quick episode of extra-sensory perception.

This was no dream. I was awake, and this was as clear and vivid as seeing a colored picture. Mom's face loomed before my closed eyes. I saw her every detail, the warm, almost luminous, hazel eyes, and a smile within them. Her flawless complexion with a natural flush in her cheeks, her white teeth in a knowing smile and a youthfulness that is unexplainable for me. Her face was minutely detailed and young, and her hair pure white. It waved naturally and was fairly short. When she smiled, she said my name, "Tom," and then, "it'll be all right." Then she vanished. I know that I had distinctly heard her words and there was no mistaking the detail of her appearance.

As soon as her image had spoken, smiled, and disappeared, I broke out into uncontrollable sobs. Knowing I do not cry easily, my wife rushed to comfort me in any possible way.

"No, no," I managed to blurt out. "I'm not in pain." I then explained to her the message and the visit. I was convinced my mother had brought to me.

It was about a month later that I began truly healing. Within the span of that month, a local television and radio station called my home. The manager heard me speak on occasion and wondered if I thought I could handle hosting a daily talk show. I auditioned, and in short order they signed me to a contract. Unfortunately it was as a private contractor that I worked for them, so hospitalization was still a major concern.

With former president Gerald Ford in the press box at Notre Dame.

It was not a month after I was working as a radio host that another phone call summoned me. This time the connection was one I could never have pieced together.

Almost as a lark I taught an adult education class at Indiana University at South Bend. It was "Understanding Football," primarily aimed at women but open to all. The class went on for three years and was a smashing success. I enjoyed it and the fun was being in the classroom with the gals who were thirsty to learn of a game that mystified them.

One of the students was the wife of a well-known developer and real-estate firm. She apparently had enjoyed the class and sang praises of my ability. The developer sold a plot of ground to a Phoenix firm, which wished to build a first-of-its-kind hotel/time share building geared to Notre Dame Alumni. They needed someone that had an identity in the community, a sound reputation, and could offer credibility to the hotel enterprise.

They hired me to a salary with complete benefits. That made a total of three jobs I was holding: (1) Mutual Radio Network for all Notre Dame Football games, (2) WSBT Daily Talk Show, (3) Varsity Clubs of America Hotel and Timeshare.

I could fight it out till retirement pretty well now, as the three jobs combined allowed me a comfortable income that I, heretofore, was never able to generate. All of this unfolded without any solicitation or seeking of my own. Several months back when I was near despair, depressed, limp, crippled, but not quite beaten, I could see neither the light nor the tunnel. Suddenly it all had changed, and not because of anything I had done. It was obvious that a force was looking out for me, and, as I had surmised long ago, those things I planned or tried to force never happened. When I turned it over to God, I could not worry anymore.

It has been said that, when we worry, we offend God. I now understand that, you put it in His hands. He must have allowed Rose Pagna a quick visit to carry the message.

Yes, such things truly do happen. I am the living proof.

Chapter 16
Reflections

Someone once said that anyone's hindsight is better than all of Napoleon's foresight. In the dozen or so years since our mother's death, each of her children has internalized and pondered the influence and impact that she and our father had upon us. The discovery of such does not happen in a one-time explosion of lucidity; rather, it gradually disperses through us on a daily basis. That we had splendid parents, we all agree. That we were blessed through inherited tendencies and a ritualistic environment was to our good fortune.

The influence and impact on our lives enriches all members of our family down to my mother's dozen granddaughters. Where each child had separate love stories in choosing his or her mate, this remains one great love story for all of us . . . our family.

Had our father, Tony, lived a normal life span, life would have been much easier on our mother and each of us. It is doubtful, however, whether we would have become as strong or as resilient had an easier life been our lot.

The hindsight I refer to, embellished by the insight of experience, allows me now to see quite clearly that our familial love, our sense of loss, and a divine guidance directed our lives. We became somewhat driven people, but the drive was not necessarily for personal gain. It became each one's goal to "make it" for the family.

Coming from have-not backgrounds, our parents were resolved to embrace the new country with high hopes and great expectations. They reasoned simply that if work is the secret ingredient in progress and ultimate success, then they would ultimately succeed. We would be broke often but never poor. "Broke is of the pocket book, poor is of the spirit." As children, we absorbed this notion. It rubbed off. We were on fire to "make it."

"Making it" encompassed honest work, coupled with imagination and creativity. It was meant to bring a certain security of life in that we lived well and could offer our children a higher standard in every facet of life's experience.

Our family pride in our name and who we were, restrained

our otherwise tempting tendency to seek out less than honest livings. "Never shame the name," spoken by our father, echoed in our ears whenever easy and quick money beckoned.

Our religious training gave us a conscience that superseded even our family ties. We were honest, almost to a fault. People sensing our way of openness and generosity often used or abused us in dealings. That is all part of the living experience, but I am sure that we can easily say that all of us were givers not takers, lifters not leaners, and gave much more than we took. That is "making it!"

That we looked out for one another long after our childhood proved to be a mystery to most. Friends, neighbors, even relatives could not comprehend or fathom that we were loyal forever.

We never owed money to one another or borrowed from one another. We just gave, when we had it, to those who didn't. When I think about that, it becomes the most precious of magnificent obsessions. Again, in an anonymous conversation, someone once said at the death of an acquaintance, "How much did he leave?"

The reply is no surprise, "He left it all."

Doesn't everybody? Surely, "the pride of dying rich causes the loudest laugh in hell."

I suppose we learned to give with joy, because we saw our parents do it all their lives.

To give with no thought of self-reward is a rare and wonderful thing. It makes me reflect on a saying I once read, "The true measure of a man is what he does for someone who can do him absolutely no good."

Having been raised with the responsibility to do for oneself, we expected nothing for nothing from anyone. Very, very few people ever offered.

Hillary Clinton won an award in 1997 for her book entitled *It Takes a Village*, the implication being that the village is behind the raising and nurturing of a child.

For me, what it truly takes is a family, a parent or parents, who give love and loyalty. It takes a family to stick together through thick and thin. It takes people who love you, without judging you, accepting you with allegiance. It is mother, father, brother, sister that live a lifetime contract that can never be broken or destroyed.

No village came to our rescue, nor did we want it or expect it. We only wanted or expected what America had promised people like my Mom and Dad and millions of other immigrants. The promise of opportunity, freedom to work, to worship, to become educated, to share justice . . . to be free.

Under the guise of "village" – or its synonym, government – self-determination gets hazy. When lives are micro-managed, freedom is choked off, and one is ruled by the whim of those in power. Such "freedom" costs too much and is a misnomer at best.

Now that I am in the autumn of my life, I can easily reflect on those things we did not accomplish. It seems we never made the big bucks. None of us owned our own company or reached the pinnacle of the corporate ladder or struck it rich through a particular enterprise. We came close, but as they say, "no cigar."

We did, however, work countless different jobs, made decent livings, and excelled at those things we pursued. We excelled, also, in raising our own families. What we could not accomplish was the recognition and financial security we all sought. Fame, wealth, and power remained all about us; they just never filled our glasses.

In earlier years this knowledge caused me to feel a great sense of failure. Now, I see it more clearly. Our goals were wrong and misdirected, though our motives were pure, since we all wanted to "make it" for one another.

Fame, wealth, power, and recognition are all false gods and misguided goals. Such goals are a farce and a myth, which, through the eyes of ego and misunderstanding, choke the life and uniqueness from people.

Had any one of us attained them, perhaps we would have become like so many other elitist types and fooled ourselves into thinking it was all done through our own superior intellects and our own talents. The Jewish people have a saying: "Man plans and God laughs!" It is an arrogant thought to think we accomplish anything on our own. Humility rarely has full pockets and cannot reside where one is convinced that only the self achieves.

Great success accompanied by wealth often has this negative effect on people.

My reflection, over time, has changed any complaint I may have felt and allowed me to become grateful for missing the hazard of great wealth.

If one of our family had "made it" big, that very circumstance could have dissolved the cement that binds us. Having enough is truly having it all. Having reached the destination is not nearly as fulfilling as the journey it took.

People speak of starting from nothing. Actually we started over with less than nothing because of the medical debts incurred. Not only had we lost our home, our savings, and our father, we were $30,000 in debt. In the '40s and '50s, $30,000 was like $300,000 today.

Being a sole proprietor, Dad had no Social Security, no life insurance, no hospitalization insurance. Had he known our predicament, his grief would have overwhelmed him. Gratefully, he did not.

Through a span of fifteen or twenty years, we paid off the debts. My mother, my brothers, and I must have held a total of one hundred different jobs in those years. We took employment in factories, we labored for others, and we always produced results. Each of us was never too proud at what the job was, so long as it was honest.

Always, on the side, was the ability to perform music and supplement our wages. For my Mom, sewing became her second and third job, eventually to become her primary one.

Our children know very little of our struggle. Each of them have lived in nice homes, with good clothing, food, and spending money. Each had opportunities we provided to attend college and travel. In a phrase, "they lived well." We saw to it!

Given less adversity than we faced, Sam and Joe probably would have completed college. Fate, however, forced us brothers and our sister to play different cards.

Sam rose near the top in his profession of music but never really crested the hill. It never made him less a man. He became a remarkable entertainer and thrilled audiences and dancers for years. He never lost the simple essence of being himself. Though

Sam on stage.

the world of entertainment and music is not known to be the most wholesome lifestyle, Sam avoided the pot, drugs, and zany temptations of many musicians.

With integrity intact, he supported our family when he had to, his own family in their turn, and never sacrificed a principle. He always stayed a large part of our lives, even when he lived a thousand or so miles away.

Joe was perhaps possessed with more talent than both Sam and I combined. Our father's death caused such a depth of grief and anger in him that it was a matter of great concern for us for many years afterward. During those years, Joe's personality could best be described as hostile.

Eventually, time and necessity reined in Joe's unbridled anger, and through his place in the family and through training (not from any village), Joe did what had to be done. He gave up college after only one year, forced himself out of the gambling and carousing life, and made a serious commitment to climb the corporate ladder. After nearly forty years in the loan business, combining hard work and his own creative insight within the company's game plan, he emerged victorious and well respected.

Joe assumed the largest chunk of our family debt and shouldered responsibilities longer than any one of us. He cared for my mother and Terry through the toughest ten years of their lives. It cost him time and money in his own life, but he would never have had it any other way. In return, this heavy responsibility caused Joe to become highly competent to succeed in his own marriage and the raising of four beautiful young ladies. Joe, like Sam before him, copied no one. Each remain uniquely his own self, and that is of itself, marvelous.

Joe too missed the big money, the corner office, the brass ring, and the key to the executive bathroom. Though he is not a rich man, he has retired from the grind and is bright enough to know he did not miss anything.

Terry, never having moved too far from our mother, lived in the shadows of the three brothers. Since she was always there with Mom, and we were the invited guests, Terry's talent and energy often seemed overlooked. She never saw this as a slight but forged her own life through hard work and planning. Today, she is very much her mother's daughter. She has the same bubbly explosiveness, is highly imaginative and impulsive, and of course, gets things done.

Our sister, through a solid marriage and high energy, willed herself to a position in life where most people struggle to be. She too sacrificed no principle in doing it. Today, her three wonderful daughters, her husband, and her in-laws are relatively secure. Terry's home is a tribute to her wisdom and work ethic. Her home is the one we all return to for reunions. It is a majestic home in a gorgeous area and, lo and behold, has a "small lake" (well stocked with fish) in her backyard.

Perhaps more than any of the boys, Terry's faith in God had never wavered. I truly believe she has a guardian angel. Most certainly, she has a pipeline to the Holy Spirit because her life has been visibly guided into serenity, dignity, and class.

When I reflect at what became of each of the original "petals from a Rose," our lives, our children and spouses, our relationships, careers, our faith . . . I am never unhappy because we did not "make it big." What we did was big! We made it on our own, through family, through love of God, work and sacrifice.

The "village" may take credit if it wants, but I know that it had no part in overcoming our trials and tribulations, our debts and defeats. It certainly was not responsible for our victories. We bought and paid for everything in our own way. We paid all our dues. None of us tried to beat the system; we just didn't want to depend upon it. We were not joiners. Clubs, fraternities, and social gatherings beckon to many. Our circle was comprised of friends and family, God, ourselves, and our children.

Today, a pseudo-intellectualism has risen among the general public. Though there are many faithful people who believe in God, others deny His existence. This notion gains momentum, and faith becomes adulterated.

You hear about people who worship nature or the Sun or themselves. New Agers create a sort of mystical polytheism. They, like some environmentalist extremists, never seem able to keep separate the creations from the Creator. Strange beliefs, compounded by some scientific findings, lead people in strange directions.

Life has taught me that if God is true, then true is for all time, not just for an interval until a more convenient and relative truth arrives.

Truly, "the fool, in his heart, says there is no God."

If there is no God, all rules are manmade. The fool really believes this. How soon before he changes the rules?

Our family, far from saintly, strayed often, but the underlying core of our existence was the belief in God, and the attempt to follow His rules. We'll live these beliefs until we die. My mother and father believed with great faith. They spoke of it often. They could not, and would not, deny Christ; nor can we.

I am very grateful for this gift of purest wisdom in my life. I did not learn it and may not even deserve it; it came by being born to great parents, and by my Italian heritage, I carry it with me. Sometimes it is burdensome as Italians and Catholics combined are highly sensitive to guilt complexes. Those without a conscience are dangerous.

Let me hurry to say that we were far from perfect people. We got angry too easily, judged too quickly, held lifetime grudges on the one hand and forgave too easily on the other. We made many, many mistakes, burning bridges behind us at will because of real or imagined offenses.

Without a doubt, the three brothers used the full contingency of the sin quotient – not seven times but seventy times seven. We were passionate people and felt deeply about things we thought really important. We were not always gentle and refined as our natures are explosive and impulsive, yet we are innovators and think uniquely and creatively, never following the crowd.

Either events were very important and needed acting upon or they mattered not. There was little in between. None of us, in the true sense, are heroes, yet we led heroic lives and, from our children, have earned their love and respect. Unfortunately, our twelve daughters and their children can never appreciate who we really are. I do pray they'll understand what we did for one another and that God and our parents were everything to us.

I view life as a school that we all go through in order to seek out truths. What we seek out and hold for ourselves pretty much is the core of our existence. There are many do's and don'ts that surface throughout this lifetime. The don'ts say, for example, that suicide is wrong, and abortion violates God's will. And there are countless other don'ts of a lesser importance.

The do's include, "Honor thy Father and Mother." The do's of life's experience say loudly to me that if what I believe is true, if Christ is the Christ, He cannot or will not lie. I don't think we're coming back here in another body, for another swing around the life clock. I had, years ago, abandoned the idea of reincarnation. In my arrogant youth, I didn't realize what an antithetical belief it is to Christianity. Besides this, I am aware that it takes more than a broken nose and a bald head to be a Knute Rockne. Christ says simply, "It is given unto man, but once to die." If it were otherwise, why would He suffer a crucifixion and then conquer death by a resurrection? This is the heart and soul of the Christian faith.

I have observed the world's superstars in various fields of politics, entertainment, sports, business. The world celebrates such icons and makes them into idols. Some of the so-called icons try to endorse certain beliefs as though their stardom has made them privy to information unattainable to the rest of us. One resounding thought permeates my mind: The knowledge of here and hereafter is not endorsed or spread, or learned, or heightened by icons. It is learned by the Holy Spirit opening one's mind as we traverse this lifetime I term school. Each one must learn for himself.

This great, immense reason is why a village can never convey, teach, inculcate what loving parents of faith can. The village cannot agree on even the tiniest of things, let alone the largest.

Though I know we do not live forever in this life, the thought that we too shall die becomes somewhat unreal. When we exit the stage as those before us have, what exists is the classroom. What

"Down time" at a commercial shoot with Ara.

exists for those that have passed is hereafter.

If we only live this short span on earth, get old and sick, have heartbreak and tragedy along the way, and then pass on to nothingness, life is a lie and a cheat. Since none of us knows with certainty what transpires, we reject or accept on faith what has been passed on to us through generations. We judge, every day of our lives, whether or not that information is true or false. We add this daily through our intellect and experience. The conclusion we draw governs how we live our lives.

As we internalize our life's experience, we verify and confirm or reject and discard. It is not an easy thing to maintain faith in a world that has lost sight and faith in morality, justice, and belief. What truths we accept have been diluted by the world. We are told that faith consists of pipe dreams, superstition, and myth.

Observing this, I can readily understand the admonition of St. Paul, to be *in* the world, but not *of* it!

If I ask myself the simple questions of why, when, and where we are to seek answers, there is only one answer. We are born, live, and die. For centuries the wisest of men have asked, "Where did we come from? What shall we do? Where will we go?"

The time we exist is the searching ground; there is a number pinned on all of us. Unlike "the fool" who says there is no God, my life has taught me otherwise. It is a wisdom I cannot explain. It came to me over a lifetime. I trust in it. To deny it is to deny what Christ has told us. To deny Him is to be denied before his Father when our time ends here.

When that time comes for our first-generation Italian-heritage family, our accomplishments or lack thereof will matter little. History will not record that Sammy Pagna became a world-famous concert pianist. Joe Pagna never had a bank name him president. I will not be remembered as a player or coach, and Terry will not become another Mother Theresa. Still, we loved our lives. Never facing an easy glide, we expected adversity and were not thrown into panic when it came. And it came often! Knowing only work, we would have been lost without it. In retrospect, our parents, our work habits, our love of learning, and our ability to laugh easily were our gifts. They served us as armor against the temptation to give in to defeat or despair.

We – Sam, Joe, Terry and I – are concerned whether the mystery of our familial love will endure with our children in a different framework of time, a separate set of circumstances.

We feel a deep responsibility to perpetuate the legacy we inherited. When our collective last page is written by our children, let them say of us: We believed in God, we honored family and parents, we fought the good fight and ran the race with a full heart.

My mother Rose was the inspiration of this story. I asked Sam if he would write a song to commemorate her life. He in turn, asked me to write the lyrics. The result became words and melody representing a metaphor of Mom's life.

When I was a very young boy, I'd close my eyes without sleeping. Through a strange and wonderful intuitive gift, I see "pictures behind my eyelids." I'm far from being psychic, but I have learned to trust these "pictures" whether they be past scenes or future.

There is but one more behind-the-eyelids scene I must relate to you. I am not sure just when or where this all transpires, but it is so very vivid that I could easily paint a picture of the scene, had I the talent.

There was this very large and magnificent rectangular ballroom. When I entered, I could easily see that huge white marble pillars with gold bases align the perimeter of the room. Centered was a dance floor of purest glass. Along the sides of the glass floor were growing beautiful flowers. I recognized roses, orchids, and others I cannot name. An arched ceiling seemed to appear as a midnight blue but was lighted plentifully with chandelier-like stars.

At one end of this glorious ballroom, elevated by several feet, was a very large orchestra all dressed in white tuxedos. Nearly two dozen violinists are playing a beautiful melody when the remaining musicians chime in. There are throngs of people surrounding the floor and sitting at tables. An atmosphere of joy and gaiety runs through the vast audience. The people are dressed formally in tuxedos and long flowing formal dresses. An electricity of expectation that is, at the same time, a calm, fills the air.

The many dancers on the ballroom floor, after hearing the crescendo of the orchestra's ending, clear an open space in the center of the floor. My mother Rose appears. She is young, vibrant, radiant, and dressed in a white gown of elegant taste. From the opposite side of the floor, a young man enters the circle. He is short, stocky, smiling, his dark hair smoothed perfectly, his dark tuxedo, flawless. It is Tony, my father. He walks gracefully to Rose, and they begin to dance Sam's waltz.

As they glide their solo dance across the floor, effortlessly, all in attendance are focused only on them. Some of the faces are blurred for me, but some I recognize instantly. Uncle Mike stands tall without crutches, many of my aunts and uncles are close by. Very visible is Donna Theresa and, yes, Grandpa Joe Crimaldi. They are smiling, laughing with approval, loving from their hearts.

The orchestra ends the waltz with a deep and harmonious

chord. There is thunderous applause, warm, enthusiastic and sincere.

A magnificent voice, warm and approving, clearly distinctive, says with great clarity, "Well done, good and faithful servants. Well done!"

"Petals from a Rose"
A Waltz

1. A fragile Rose lies 'neath the snow
    Awaiting yet her time to grow,
    And when she meets with sun and rain,
    She'll know full well of love and pain.
    It makes one wonder,
    It makes one wonder.
2. Full blossomed now, Spring is her season.
    A gift of love, for just one reason,
    Her thorns belie, Her bloom so tender,
    A blaze of life, in all Her splendor.
    It makes for wonder,
    It makes for wonder.
3. Soft Summer winds caress this Rose,
    For just how long nobody knows,
    Her days are full of lilt and laughter,
    A sparkle rare, to last here after
4. Her time near past, she's not as tall,
    The blush is gone, an early fall,
    And Autumn brings a lonely tear,
    Her work undone, life so unclear.
    It makes her wonder,
    It makes her wonder.
5. Is that all to life and know not why,
    Just why we live or why we die,
    But tho she fades, she surely knows
    She'll leave behind the petals from a Rose . . .